THE MANAGEMENT FUNCTION:

A Positive Approach to Labor Relations

by LEONARD A. KELLER

BNA Incorporated   Washington, D. C.

1963

Printed in the United States of America
Library of Congress Catalog Card Number: 63-17562

To my wife,

Betsy

FOREWORD

This book is an outgrowth of workshops presented for management officials by the Employers' Association of Detroit in cooperation with the Institute of Labor and Industrial Relations, University of Michigan-Wayne State University. The writer acted as the discussion leader of these workshops.

The encouragement and assistance provided by the officials of the Association in the completion of the manuscript were of significant aid. In particular, I wish to thank Wayne Stettbacher, General Manager, Kenneth B. Porter, Research Director, and Robert R. Fortney, Assistant Research Director. The assistance given by the Institute of Labor and Industrial Relations, and particularly by E. J. Forsythe, Director, Management Division, in arranging the workshops, is also gratefully acknowledged.

The manuscript was read in its entirety by a number of management representatives and others experienced in the labor relations field. Malcolm L. Denise, Vice President-Labor Relations, of the Ford Motor Company, and his staff were extremely helpful. The same is true of the labor relations staff of General Motors Corporation, especially Fred H. Schwarze. My thanks are also due to R. Heath Larry, Administrative Vice President of United States Steel Corporation; H. C. Lumb, Vice President, Republic Steel Corporation; Millard E. Stone, Sinclair Oil Corporation; R. F. Tagg, Labor Relations and Personnel Division, Swift & Company; D. D. Reichow, Director of Union Relations, The B. F. Goodrich Company; Jerome O. Cross, Director of Industrial Relations, Huron Portland Cement Company; Stanley H. Brams, Publisher of Labor Trends; Irving Paster, Labor Relations Consultant; Justin T. Rogers, Jr., General Coordinator of Personnel Relations, Ohio Edison Company; Ralph C. Bretting, Union Relations Supervisor, Consumers Power Company; John L. Waddleton, Chief Counsel, Industrial and Community Relations Division, Allis-Chalmers Manufacturing Company; Fred D. Hunter, Director of Employee Relations, American Brake Shoe Company; and Eugene

A. Keeney, Assistant Manager-Labor Law, Chamber of Commerce of the United States.

Professor E. Robert Livernash, of the Harvard Graduate School of Business Administration, and one of the authors of "The Impact of Collective Bargaining on Management," the most penetrating and authoritative study of union-management relations available, deserves special thanks for his helpful comments. With his permission I have appropriated some of these. Discerning readers will see the influence of the book itself in my text. It is perhaps unnecessary to say that the opinions expressed in this book are those of the author alone and are not necessarily shared by those who have read it. This applies particularly to the views expressed in Chapter 14, which has not been read by Professor Livernash prior to publication, or by some of the others named above.

This book attempts to construct an affirmative approach to union relations for management. It is believed that most of the principles in the book are applicable to manufacturing generally, although many of the illustrations are drawn from the automobile industry with which I am most familiar. Many of the observations apply also, in my judgment, to non-manufacturing industries such as transportation and retail trade.

One caution is necessary. Every industrial plant is a living community with its own roots and history. Wide variances in attitudes and practices appear between these industrial communities, not only as between plants owned by different employers, but also as between the plants of a single employer located in various cities. Similarly, the approach to the problems discussed in this book varies greatly as between international unions and from one local union to the next. No one can prescribe effective remedies for improper industrial relations practices without studying the environment in which they are to be applied and the people who live and work in that environment.

Detroit, Michigan
April, 1963

Leonard A. Keller

CONTENTS

PART ONE

THE DYNAMICS OF THE LABOR AGREEMENT

Chapter 1

A GOOD LABOR POLICY—CONFLICT OR COOPERATION?

Explaining the success of the relationship between union and management in his plants, a director of industrial relations gave credit to the fact that each side recognized the other's sphere of authority, and told this story to illustrate the point:

> The captain and the chief engineer of a big ship argued one day as to who was more important to the vessel's operation. Finally they decided to have a showdown by swapping jobs. The engineer climbed to the bridge and the captain went to the engine room.
>
> After less than an hour, the begrimed skipper climbed back on deck. "You win," he called to the engineer. "I can't run her—can't even make her budge."
>
> "I reckon you can't," replied the weary, befuddled engineer. "She's been on this mud bank the last fifteen minutes."

For many years, idealists have endorsed labor-management cooperation as a panacea for labor strife. Clinton S. Golden, for many years an official of the Steelworkers, and then on the staff of Harvard University, thought that the road to progress is through "wide consultation on possible solution to problems of common concern. . . ." There are, he said, "relative degrees of industrial peace. These range from a precarious equilibrium of mutually hostile forces for a stated period of time—the life of an agreement—to an enduring, harmonious and cooperative relationship of a really creative character." [1] The second he thought of as the ideal.

The advocates of labor-management cooperation recommend what they call a problem-solving approach to disputes, actual or potential. By this they mean on-the-spot discussion and settlement of problems at the grass-roots level rather than reliance upon

---

[1] Golden, "Introduction", *Causes of Industrial Peace Under Collective Bargaining*, Edited by Golden and Parker (New York: Harper and Brothers, 1955), pp. 8, 9.

managerial "prerogatives" and the literal language of the agreement. This technique they would apply to the everyday administration of work: scheduling, assignments, production and quality standards, and employee conduct. Given a problem in these areas, they say, sit down and settle it then and there, realistically, not legalistically. Similarly, they see no reason for conflict on such matters as cost reduction, elimination of waste in time or materials, technological improvement, training, safety, and the employment of outside contractors. Granting that management must aim for economy and efficiency, they would give labor a voice in achieving these ends.

"Problem solving" sounds good. An aura of human benevolence surrounds such words as "harmonious" and "creative." Cooperation is a good word; conflict a bad one. All the same it is a pernicious notion unless it recognizes the fundamental difference between the functions and responsibilities of management and those of the unions. Confusion of these distinct functions and responsibilities leads, as the engineer and captain discovered, to the mud bank.[2]

Management's Job

A really viable approach to good labor relations starts with the acceptance of the inescapable truth that it is management's job to promote the success of the entire enterprise. Management is, of course, interested in the security and well-being of its employees. But no matter how deep the desire of the employer to improve the conditions of his employees, he cannot escape the proposition that wages and other benefits are costs of production and that it is his duty, in one way or another, to lower those costs. The employer must consider the interests of shareholders. If he does not, he finds capital only with difficulty and higher charges. He must consider the interests of the community; a high cost plant will ultimately have to be closed. And he is the guardian of the con-

---

[2] Another story, this one told by Justice Arthur J. Goldberg when he was counsel for the AFL-CIO, illustrates the point even better, although Justice Goldberg's point was not the same. It seems that the records and accounts in an army post were a mess. The colonel in charge reviewed the personnel records and found the card of a private who had filled in the space for recording his peacetime occupation with the letters "C.P.A." The colonel promptly promoted the private, putting him in charge. When a month later the colonel found that the records were in a worse mess than ever, the former private ruefully explained that in his case "C.P.A." stood for Cleaning, Pressing, and Alterations.

sumer. As Sumner Slichter said, "In bargaining, management represents the interests of consumers. The lower the costs of production, the lower competition forces prices or the higher it forces quality." [3] Our economic system relies on management to control costs. If management fails in this duty, if it does not keep costs at a level which enables the business to prosper and grow, then it fails utterly in its responsibility to all, to customers, to the public, to its shareholders, and to its employees.

Employee and union relations is only one, and perhaps not the most important, of the decisional situations which face management as it goes about its overall task of assuring the survival and growth of the business. It has been said that management must strike a bargain, not merely with labor, but with many other elements in the business which make claim upon it. The customer makes the most compelling demand. The government has its voice; regulations as to quality, labelling, advertising, and other aspects of business must be met. The people who supply capital are keeping a watchful eye on the profits and the dividends produced. Suppliers are quick to display their ability to furnish raw materials and semi-finished parts, or tools and machines at prices under the employer's own cost of manufacture. Each of these elements has its own representative in the management. Just as the demands of the union and the employees are brought into focus through the director of employee relations, the claims of the customers are reflected by the sales manager, the interests of suppliers by the purchasing department, and the shareholders and creditors have their representative in the person of the treasurer or the company controller. Competition between these departments is a well-known phenomenon in business. The board of directors and the chief executive must take the views of all into account and strike a balance or a "bargain" between them. It is their function to satisfy all of them as best they can.

Many of these decisions have to be made on the basis of factors which cannot be anticipated or controlled. A new process may be entering the market which will outmode existing machinery and methods, and perhaps the skills of workers acquired and practiced in the plant for many years. Yet survival dictates its adoption, whatever the cost. A competitor may develop a dramatic improve-

---

[3] Slichter, *The Challenge of Industrial Relations* (Ithaca: Cornell University, 1947), p. 30.

ment in product. Patent rights or tax complications may demand a course of action which is vital to the business, but which the workers can only view as damaging to their security. Frequently decision turns on information which cannot be disclosed or explained. Perhaps it must be kept secret, or is so technical that even if disclosed it cannot be readily understood. The decision may depend on an "educated guess," not easily justifiable but nevertheless a basis for expenditure of a large sum of money with the possibility that it may be lost. Sometimes these decisions must be made at the last moment and no time for explanation remains, yet delay would be fatal.

Since it is management alone which must account for these decisions in the market place, the responsibility for making them cannot be delegated or shared. To throw them into the area of joint determination is to abdicate the function of management. In a factory, problem-solving is no substitute for management's right of administrative initiative. It may be unfortunate, but it is the fact that the interests of the other groups which surround the business, the customers, the shareholders, and others sometimes are in conflict with the interests of labor. Good will cannot eliminate the need for the harder effort to define policies and draw lines which enable management to act quickly and decisively. It may only confuse the realistic appraisal called for by the needs of the business. Appeasement may be only an evasion of principle. As Harry Shulman, late Dean of the Yale Law School, and for many years impartial umpire for the UAW and Ford, said, " an industrial plant is not a debating society." [4] Management must act.

The Nature of Unions

What the advocates of "togetherness" overlook is that the unions in the United States are instruments of conflict. In Russia, unions are instruments of an omnipotent state. In the United States their business is to protect and enhance their power in the interests of their members. In the preamble to the Wagner Act, Congress declares one of its purposes to be the promotion of equality of bargaining power. The issue of power is the paramount one in every negotiation. All talk of "community of interest" must bow to the fundamental aim of labor—to get more for its members and

---

[4] *Ford Motor Co. & United Automobile Workers,* Shulman, 3 LA 779 (1944).

to make no concessions detrimental to them. A union leader who lost sight of this basic union need would soon be replaced. He does not represent the consumer; still less does he consider the shareholder, unless perhaps the company must have concessions to remain in business. Management represents many interests; labor unions only one.[5]

One may grant that labor has a stake at least equal to that of capital in the American industrial system. One may admit that some unions promote, or at least do not hamper, technological improvement. But anyone who thinks the Steelworkers Union is a "partner" of U.S. Steel or Bethlehem, or the Auto Workers a "partner" of General Motors is naïve. Nor are they counterparts of each other. A union represents not merely the employees of a particular company, but of many companies, not infrequently in wholly different industries. The Auto Workers must consider not merely those of its members who work for General Motors; it must also represent those at the other auto companies as well as those employed in the aircraft and farm equipment industries. In addition it includes members in a host of other companies which have little in common with autos, aircraft, or farm machinery. The union represents them all. It strives to maintain the same standards for all, the higher the better.

A company is organized from the top down; a union from the bottom up. No matter how autocratic the union leadership, it must always keep an eye on membership loyalty. Even though rank and file participation is kept to a minimum, the most arrogant union bosses see that the members get what they want. A dissident group will soon find a rival union in which they are welcome. Schism is common. In the democratic unions which encourage membership participation, all of the characteristics of ward politics appear. Log-rolling, the "rump" caucus, machines erected on the basis of skills (craft workers v. unskilled production people), local union leadership or strength, and geographic areas are as conspicuous in the labor union as they are in a political party. The company, greatly to the dislike of its officials since its own structure is monolithic, finds itself compelled to await the verdict of a heterogeneous assemblage which includes the body of employees in its own plant, their committees, the local union leadership, and finally

---

5 This chapter deals only with the union-management relationship, not with the numerous public and social activities of unions.

the international with its own broad patterns of acceptability. Each of these groups may vary in their interests and reactions to a given settlement. It is not only politically wise for the union leader to obtain a consensus of consent; it is his obligation of office. The 1959 Labor-Management Reporting and Disclosure Act stresses this duty, but it has been accepted by most union leaders for years.

The long term economic benefits which might follow for the economy as a whole, and labor as a class, from a policy of abstention in collective bargaining have little practical significance for unions. Most workers would quote economist Keynes who said, "In the long run we are all dead." No union leader can sell austerity in the here and now for the sake of generations of unionists yet unhired. Workers are not impressed with statistics designed to show that if costs are reduced the business will prosper and they with it. They want to alter the existing share in their favor. Their leaders must conform to this conviction in their ordinary dealings with employers, even if they do not wholly share it. Cost reduction programs are palatable only when a high cost plant is about ready to close. Then it is usually too late.

It follows, as I have suggested, that collective bargaining is an exercise in relative power between institutions which have little in common with each other except the fact that they are joined together like Siamese twins who cannot be separated except on penalty of death. This truth, which leads to the suggestion of cooperation, actually intensifies the struggle and keeps it alive (witness the railroads) through the years. It is unlikely that this will change for many years to come.

Conflict on the Floor of the Shop

The struggle over the wage bargain is beyond the scope of this chapter. Our concern is with the more subtle, more difficult, and perhaps more important, problem of the day-to-day relationship between management and its union employees. But the power struggle is not different in this area. Theoretically, conflict should come to an end when the contract is signed. Practically, it goes on in less dramatic form. The "armed truce" is a normal state of affairs. The temperature of this cold war varies, of course. In some plants accommodation is achieved. In others, war breaks out in the form of frequent wildcat strikes.

The conflict is grounded precisely in the cleavage already described between management goals and management structure, and the aims and methods adopted by unions. Management wants to run a taut ship, quick to take advantage of a shift in tide or wind. Labor wants stability, security, and protection of the human being against the vicissitudes of economic storm. Management calculates unit costs and strives to lower them by increasing productivity. "Productivity" to a laboring man smells suspiciously of "speed-up." Management approves of the efficient worker; the union seeks to eliminate competition between workers by the adoption of common rules. Management seeks to promote the individual it thinks most able; the union thinks length of service should be rewarded with advancement. The "lump of labor" theory—"there is only so much work; it should be husbanded and made to last as long as possible"—still has currency in spite of seniority rules, unemployment compensation, and other benefits. Restrictions upon output, upon the effective assignment of labor, upon letting work to outside contractors, and upon other management techniques to cut costs are common even in mass production plants. "Make work rules" are still a thorn in the side of management in many industries. At this point, we can pause to analyze some actual conflicts illustrating what difficulty attends the solution of some of these problems.

The most forceful illustration, perhaps, is the "local working conditions" issue in the 1959 steel strike.[6]

Speaking before the Virginia Manufacturers Association, R. Conrad Cooper, U.S. Steel vice-president and chief negotiator for the industry, explained how the now-famous work rules clause became the problem it was in the strike. After noting that many steelworkers were convinced they were fighting to protect rights won on the picket line, Mr. Cooper said:

> The truth is, of course, that this controversial clause ["2-B"], which deals with local working conditions, was written into the master agreement of United States Steel without any strike whatever, and nobody walked a picket line at all. I know that to be a fact because I confess with considerable chagrin that I was one of the six negotiators who put that language into the contract. And David McDonald—on the Union side—was another.

---

[6] In this and succeeding examples, I present only the management position as illustrative of the conflict. No attempt is made to present counter-arguments or to assess the merits. Persuasive arguments can be made for the retention of particular work rules in many cases.

The circumstances may interest you, and give you a better insight into the problem as we face it today.

In the master agreements there had been—and there still is—a clause stating clearly that management shall have the right to manage the business. At the same time there were—at the local plant level—numerous agreements, both written and oral, designed to protect the steelworkers against any unreasonable action by management, should some plant official attempt to take such action. It was argued by the Union that the rights of management, as spelled out in the master agreement, might be construed to conflict with the agreements and understandings which had been taken at the local level, and that this possible conflict should be cleared up by the insertion of a clause in the master agreement that would deal with local working conditions.

That clause was finally written and approved at four o'clock in the morning, by six brain-weary men who were racing to beat a strike deadline. That was in 1947, and in the years that have followed it has been interpreted in arbitration to mean many things that it was never intended to mean.

Thus, it has been a constant source of friction, and a deterrent to the cooperative effort necessary to achieve the greatest degree of efficiency in operations. And to a degree that was never contemplated by its authors, it has also impaired management's clearly stated right to manage. In this way it has served to perpetuate wasteful practices and to prevent economies—and all in the guise of protecting the rights and the job security of the steelworkers, whereas—as a matter of actual fact—the waste and inefficiency which has resulted from the misinterpretation of this provision stands as a far greater threat to the job security of every steelworker than could any possible action that management would contemplate were this restrictive language to be removed entirely.

And the truth is, of course, that all that the company negotiators were seeking when the storm blew up was that the Union negotiators should join them in drafting language that would say unmistakably exactly what the original language was intended to say—and would do what the original language was intended to do.[7]

The union refused the steel industry's offer to arbitrate the question of whether "2-B" should remain in the contract. A joint committee was appointed to study the problem and make recommendations. No recommendations have appeared yet.

Pittsburgh Plate Glass Company, after taking a 130-day strike, was more successful. A three-man arbitration commission with

---

[7] BNA, *Daily Labor Report,* No. 218 (1959): p. D-1 at D-4 (Nov. 6).

Paul N. Lehoczky as its chairman was appointed to decide a number of questions, including the establishment of a new set of seniority rules for the Creighton plant, whether changes should be made in the contract provisions governing the operation of the incentive system, what changes should be made in the agreement to restore the company's right to determine operation speeds, what the company could do to reduce crew sizes and eliminate the use of unnecessary employees, and others. The decisions, issued in 1959, won the approval of David G. Hill, Pittsburgh's president. They permit the company to install new incentive rates promptly, increase operation speeds without prior union consent, and eliminate waste and inefficiency. Mr. Hill was quoted as saying that if the company had to choose again, "we would follow the same course. . . . We are now on sounder ground." [8]

For our third example, we turn to the *South Bend Tribune* of August 8, 1954. In it was a full-page statement by The Studebaker Corporation, signed by Paul G. Hoffman, Chairman of the Board, and H. S. Vance, President. Sales had dropped more than two-thirds. Cars were being sold below cost. More than half of the employees were laid off. Here were some of the reasons why the company felt compelled, after the membership of the union had rejected the company's modest proposal for improvements, to terminate its union agreement:

1. Studebaker employee average earnings are $2.39 an hour for all hourly rated employees.

Average hourly earnings on a day-rate basis for our principal competitors are $2.03—thus Studebaker is paying 18% more.

2. Work standards at Studebaker (the amount of work required for eight hours of pay) are considerably below those prevailing in the rest of the industry—in some departments as much as 20% below.

3. Plant-wide 'bumping' and transfer privileges are resulting in wasteful costs which totaled $789,000 in the first four months of 1954 alone.

'Bumping' and transfers in the plants of major producers are accomplished without such wasteful costs.

---

[8] Hill, *Labor Trends*, No. 747 (Detroit, Michigan: Stanley Brams, Feb. 13, 1960), p. 3. The *Pittsburgh Plate Glass Co.* cases are reported at 32 LA 945, 957, 978 (1959); 33 LA 614 (1959); and 36 LA 21 (1960). For a fuller discussion, see Donald J. Sherbondy, "The Productivity Challenge and the Pittsburgh Plate Glass Strike," *Meeting the Productivity Challenge*, Report No. 40 (New York: American Management Association, 1960), p. 30.

4. Personal time—that is the time given workers for personal needs, rest, and wash-up periods—totals 40 to 43 minutes per working day for each worker at Studebaker.

The common practice in the industry is to allow 24 minutes per working day for each worker. With comparable work forces of 10,000 employees Studebaker's daily loss of productive work hours is almost 3,000 more than that of each of its major competitors.

5. Studebaker is paying a night shift premium of 10 percent.

The industry is paying 5 percent for the second shift and 7½ percent for the third shift.

6. Studebaker is paying employees time and a half for working on Saturday and double time for working on Sunday, as such, regardless of previous time off during the week for any reason.

Major competitors pay time and a half for Saturday and double time for Sunday—but only after an employee makes up any time lost for personal reasons in the preceding five days.

None of these three companies had followed a "tough" policy toward unions. None of them could be accused of deliberately maintaining an "armed truce." "Big Steel" had carefully adopted, under various leaders, the policy of acceptance of the union and the assumption that this would carry with it acceptance by the union of the needs of the company. It was quite willing to tackle plant problems realistically at the grass roots level. Studebaker, under Hoffman and Vance, had been widely praised as a forward-looking company which practiced union-management cooperation. Studebaker and its union, the United Auto Workers, have since corrected many of its problems. Presently, Studebaker is competitive in work practices, wages, and benefits. Its labor relations climate, as a result of and despite strikes, is excellent.

The American Oil Company withstood a 191-day strike at Texas City, Texas, to end the union's practice of barring workers classified at one job from handling other duties. Pittsburgh department stores chose to suffer through a 17-month strike in order to stop the Teamsters Union from limiting the number of daily deliveries and insisting on a helper on parcel delivery trucks. By standing firm, the stores were able to eliminate 324 unnecessary jobs and also to speed deliveries.

Good Contracts and Good Policies

It will be observed that restrictions upon the right to a flexible and efficient operation, which generally can be labelled "restrictive work rules," are created in two ways. They can come into being as the result of an unfortunate concession in the contract, as Mr. Cooper pointed out. If a company concedes contract language which limits its rights to schedule work, to transfer workers as needed for efficient operation without costly "bumping," or to require overtime work, or prevents it from buying from outside vendors or using contractors, it is stuck with it until it is changed. What U.S. Steel was willing to concede in 1947, other companies have refused. There are no clauses in the auto industry similar to the "local working conditions" clause in the steel industry contracts.

The second source of restrictions is bad administration. Loose practices, ineffective supervision, and weakness in enforcing proper standards and rules of conduct can blunt and defeat management functions just as surely as restrictive provisions in the agreement. This was a large part of Studebaker's problem in 1954 as can be seen by analyzing the nature of its six complaints against its union employees. Divergence between contract and plant practice is a common phenomenon. Sometimes this works to the benefit of one side, sometimes in favor of the other. Concessions in practice are sometimes justified as realistic solutions. This may be true if they are sound. If they create undesirable habits and precedents or they water down management's effective control and cancel out the express reservations in the agreement of management's right to operate efficiently, they are not realistic. They undermine the entire labor relations structure of the plant.

What is a sound contract? The chief purpose of the labor agreement is to protect the worker against unfair and arbitrary treatment. Collective bargaining has as one principal aspect the introduction of civil rights into industry, that is, of requiring that management be conducted by rule rather than arbitrary decision. The rule finds expression in the agreement. It is the law of the shop, or, as it is sometimes called, the constitution under which a system of shop law is built up.

Labor unions are entitled to great credit for having won these civil rights for their members. Protection against arbitrary discharge by the "just cause" restriction and against discriminatory layoff by the seniority principle are only two examples among many of the substantial advances in the security and dignity of the

American worker which unions have won. The substitution of shop law for the whim of the boss may in the end prove to be of more significance than any other activity carried on by organized labor. No employer today can deny this. Even those who operate non-union plants have introduced, more or less systematically, the principles of protection which appear in union contracts.

Unfortunately, this bright coin has its reverse and dull side. A contract which, under the guise of protection of the worker, stultifies management in its effort to use that worker's time efficiently, or, even worse, hampers the full use of the machinery and equipment which he operates, is not wholesome. Seniority rules primarily designed to secure the older man against layoff are often turned into a nightmarish web of forced transfers across departmental and job lines with little relationship to the skills required to perform the work. Restrictions on the right of the employer to establish production standards unilaterally almost inevitably mean less output. Limitations on the use of foremen and non-union employees in experimental and technical work are frequently nonsensical, but nevertheless they must be observed. The same is true of the right to require and select the employees for overtime work. The employer may be unable under the contract to loan employees to a department where they are urgently needed from another where their services can be spared. Crew sizes may be fixed regardless of the amount of work needed or available. Examples like these could be multiplied endlessly.

The elimination of unnecessary restrictions upon the effective use of labor, as we have seen, has been a major issue in recent years. It is not generally realized to what extent restrictive work practices have permeated American industry, not merely in the old line craft unions, such as the building construction workers, but in our factories. An extensive list of these practices has been gathered by the United States Chamber of Commerce showing that they exist in many operations.[9] Unions are beginning to recognize that the worker must be protected through unemployment compensation, severance pay, and relocation and training allowances, not through work rules. But little progress has been made toward this goal even in the older organizations such as the railway unions.

---

[9] *The Menace of Restrictive Work Practices* (Washington: Chamber of Commerce of the United States: Legal Department, 1963).

As things stand now, the problem, a matter of conflict, remains in the arena—an aspect of the struggle for power.

The test of a good contract for management is a negative one: the absence of restrictions which hamper management unreasonably in the effective discharge of its responsibility to manage. On the other hand, good administration is positive: it is the development and execution of sound policies and procedures to make the management function as fully effective as the contract permits. Many employers, large and small, have defaulted these responsibilities. In large measure, they have themselves to blame for the inevitable losses which have resulted. This observation has been thoroughly documented in the important study of union-management policies by Professors Sumner H. Slichter, James J. Healy, and E. R. Livernash of Harvard University, published by the Brookings Institution.[10] In a preliminary report on it, Professor Livernash said:

> Of all of the variables of significance in particular union-management relationships, management policy stands out as being of crucial importance. Companies which had achieved relative success in labor relations gave clear evidence of (1) management by policy, (2) effective administration at the worker level, and (3) management initiative in labor relations. Basic policies in such companies were not empty slogans but were made effective at the worker level by adequate implementing and procedural policies. Companies with well developed policies gave evidence that labor relations were of vital concern to top management. Both policy formulation and administration were dynamic and open and frank communication existed within management.[11]

A company which follows this formula will have good labor relations. The "fair but firm" employer, who has insisted on literal compliance with the contract and undertaken seriously his responsibility to install good policies and practices, has no apologies to make to the idealists who call him "legalistic" or castigate him for insisting upon "managerial prerogatives" in the manner of a medieval tyrant. They are wrong, not he. Union leaders acknowledge this privately and sometimes publicly. David Mc-

---

[10] Slichter, Healy, and Livernash, *The Impact of Collective Bargaining on Management* (Washington: Brookings Institution, 1960).

[11] E. R. Livernash, "Brookings Research Project on the Influence of Unions Upon Management: A Reappraisal of Union Policies and Industrial Management," *Proceedings of the Twelfth Annual Meeting of Industrial Relations Research Association* (Madison, Wisconsin, 1959), pp. 180, 188. The importance of management policy is stressed throughout the book; see especially pp. 10, 880, 951.

Donald, president of the Steelworkers, has said, "I want the company to enforce the contract fairly and honestly. . . . Nothing could be worse than to have management appease the union and nothing could be worse than to have the union appease management." [12]

Writing on the subject of wildcat strikes in the *Harvard Business Review,* Garth Mangum quotes the president of a large Auto Workers local union as saying, "God protect me from a soft management. If I have to deal with a tough management, I know how to go about getting what I need. But I don't know how to correct the abuses and problems that develop when there is a soft management that gives in to everything the employees demand." [13] The "tough" employer establishes an atmosphere of certainty and reliability which is invaluable to the union. The workers know the company will enforce its policies firmly and the temptation to license is checked by the fear of discipline.

Since a firm management has established its position, it can afford to consult with the union on matters which lie outside the contract or in the domain of "management rights," without fear that a precedent will be created leading to joint determination in the future of matters within its unilateral control. The employer who knows his rights and insists on retention of them is in a much better position to develop an atmosphere of mutual responsibility and good will than the soft employer who has let joint determination occupy areas which he should have reserved to himself. There is no harm in permitting the union to come saying, "We have a problem with our membership which you might help us lick," and replying, "Well, we'll be glad to hear about it and maybe we can do something." As long as the company and the union both understand that this is a matter of courtesy and good will, not of right, much can be accomplished.

But if the camel's nose, once in the tent, is followed by the rest of him, things become very uncomfortable for the owner of the tent. As a matter of practical everyday relations, this is why consultation with the union, even when the union recognizes that

---

[12] David J. McDonald, "Labor's Long-Range Objectives," *Key Problems in Human Relations,* General Management Series #181 (New York: American Management Association, 1956), pp. 32, 41.

[13] Mangum, "Taming Wildcat Strikes," *Harvard Business Review* (Vol. 38: No. 2, March-April, 1960), p. 95.

under the contract the company has the right to make the final determination, can be dangerous. "Consultation" is a favorite panacea in the minds of labor-management idealists. But it can slip quite easily into joint determination; indeed, the union is likely to advertise to its members that it is joint determination. In *Causes of Industrial Peace,* Professors Harbison and Coleman say "From the standpoint of the union, discussions of this nature can be tantamount to negotiations. Under such circumstances, the union leaders are in a position to claim that they are sharing control with management over vital issues affecting jobs." [14] This is true, and it may lead to disaster.

A word should also be said about the charge that a company which insists upon literal compliance with the agreement is "legalistic," an epithet of undeserved opprobrium in the writings of economists and psychologists. Actually, the agreement is the "law" of the shop. It is negotiated, annually or at longer intervals, with the full force and intelligence of both sides brought to bear upon its provisions. It is a bargain, a contract enforceable in arbitration and in the courts. It is an instrument of exchange, not merely of wages for hours of labor, but of a whole galaxy of provisions which are the result of argument and persuasion, of trading, and perhaps the use of economic force or threats of force. Is there any reason why, having expended so much effort in working out its provisions, the employer (or the union, for that matter) should say when a problem arises, "Forget the contract—it's only a piece of paper. Work out a realistic settlement and live with it." Such an attitude would lead not to industrial peace, but to complete confusion. In the employer's case, it hamstrings the management function.

The first essential of good labor-management relations is to know where one stands. A contract which retains the right to manage, and points out clearly in what respects the right is limited, is necessary and desirable. Clarity and certainty bring security to the union, the company, and the employees. As has been said of the public law, an agreement marries hostility to reason. The idea that an agreement should be a loose compendium of ambiguous phrases which can be disregarded on one occasion and on the next

---

[14] Harbison and Coleman, "Working Harmony: A Summary of the Collective Bargaining Relationships in 18 Companies," *Causes of Industrial Peace, op. cit.,* at p. 41.

filled in by an arbitrator's notion of what is good industrial relations or what will heighten shop morale is destructive.

Good contract administration, important as it is, does not eliminate the necessity for good contract language, because however well planned and executed management policy is, it cannot be carried into execution on the factory floor if the contract plainly forbids it. The importance of good language is demonstrated with striking force by the degree to which industrial management is reviewed by arbitrators. In thousands upon thousands of cases, management action has been reversed or modified not because the arbitrator thought it unwise or improper but because of his interpretation of the language of the agreement. The emphasis on the factory floor and even in the lower steps of the grievance procedure may be upon good relationships and good administration. In the higher levels, "reasonableness" tends to lose its influence—the parties have progressively exhausted their capacity to reach "sensible" as opposed to "legal" solutions. And at the final step, the arbitrator is usually expected to act as a judge of what the contract commands.

Creative Conflict

We can now approach the question in our chapter title—conflict or cooperation? "Conflict" is not always the horrid state it is made out to be. There can be creative conflict, perhaps the best way to characterize collective bargaining today. Conflict in economic life is natural. It may be that it produces adjustments which have more vitality and permanence than cooperation. After all, our society is built upon the theory that opposing interests will clash; the fundamental reason for government is to provide laws under which these conflicts may be resolved honorably. When the stakes are high, as they are in collective bargaining, objective thinking and hard work are required, not sloppy evasion of the issues. The labor agreement is referred to as the constitution of the enterprise, which means previously agreed rules and regulations and "due process." It does not necessarily embrace good will and compromise. Even in the "make-work" rules disputes, the unions will insist that specific rules are justified. Management and large sections of the public may be critical, but if it is labor's point of view, labor has the right to assert it, backing it up with a strike if labor thinks it worth the cost. Professor Bakke puts the whole thing very well when he says:

> Too much antagonism is self defeating. A hardening of antagonisms is crippling to adaptive effort. But I would also venture to say that too much cooperation, at least some kinds of cooperation, is self defeating. It is not to the benefit of the members of unions if management cooperates by rolling over and does not do its best to watch its costs, maintain systematic and orderly organization, the right to make necessary decisions, and to allocate the proceeds of production to the continued improvement of the instruments of production, including both men and machines. And it is not to the benefit of management if the union leaders become so much a cooperative arm of management that they lose their power to present forcefully and effectively the needs and demands of workers for an increasing standard of living and an increasing voice in making the rules and controlling the conditions under which they work and live. If each does that job well, he is cooperating with the other party, whether that party gives him credit for it or not.[15]

Management everywhere should heed the General Motors declaration: "Management's responsibility for managing the business must be recognized and maintained." This is no proclamation of legal rights, much less of kingly prerogatives. It is practical philosophy, worked out carefully by such men as Alfred Sloan and W. S. Knudsen, who accepted collective bargaining but also knew they were guardians not merely of one interest but of several. If this position is taken firmly and carried into practice intelligently and effectively, everyone, including labor, will benefit.

---

[15] E. W. Bakke, "Mutual Survival After Twelve Years," reprinted in part in Bakke & Kerr, *Unions, Management and the Public,* Second Edition (New York: Harcourt, Brace & Co., 1960), pp. 635, 644.

Chapter 2

MANAGEMENT RIGHTS

The term "management rights" has been abused. It has been equated with the concept of the kingly prerogative, with arbitrary and unreasonable management conduct, and with technical legalism. Such tinges of definition are unfortunate and quite unfair. Because of them, some management spokesmen prefer to use the phrase "management functions" and "management responsibilities." They reflect more accurately the truth that management has the duty, as well as the right, to manage. But the term "management rights" should be restored to an honorable place in the nomenclature. It is both practically and historically accurate. Collective bargaining is by law and historically a procedure by which unions have sought to limit the virtually unlimited common law rights of employers. At the bargaining table, the unions demand concessions which bring management's unilateral power wholly or partly into the sphere of joint agreement. What is left are "management rights" not brought under joint control.

What Do We Mean By "Management Rights?"

Here we must pause to define our terms. Management rights can be divided into two categories. The first embraces the operation of the business itself; the second relates to decisions affecting the employees. One could imagine a completely automatic plant, with the raw materials being supplied at one end by the vendor and the finished product being carried away by the customer at the other. Decisions in the first category would remain: the company's officials would still have to settle on the nature of the product, the location of the plant, and the kind of equipment needed, layout and techniques, engineering, accounting and sales policies, production schedules, and the methods and processes of manufacturing. But since there were no employees, problems in the second category could not arise. Management's rights would be truly exclusive.

The second category includes decisions which call for exercise of the "right to direct the working forces." Here new working arrangements may be called for, such as new schedules, changes in classifications, alteration of work assignments, and the resetting of wages. Employees, rightly or wrongly, may believe their rights are violated. At this point, labor is likely to resist any assertion that the employer has an "exclusive right" to take action and to call for acceptance, instead of labor's "equal rights."

The distinction between these two categories cannot be adopted without reservation or pressed too far. The so-called "exclusive" right interlocks closely with the effect of its exercise upon the employees. It may cause reverberations of protest from the employees, leading to demands in the next contract negotiations for limitations upon the management right in question, particularly if it has been abused or exercised with arbitrary and perhaps callous indifference to its consequences. Or it may affect the rights of the employees under the agreement, express or implied, with the result that grievances are successfully prosecuted and management finds to its discomfiture that it did not have the right to act as it had thought it did.

Another way of looking at the two categories, functions which are exclusively those of management versus those which affect employees, is to draw the line between what is arbitrable under the typical contract and what is nonarbitrable. In the famous Supreme Court decisions on arbitrability, chiefly Warrior and Gulf Navigation Company,[1] the court has made it clear that the phrase "strictly a function of management" must be interpreted as referring only to that over which the contract "gives management complete control and unfettered discretion." This means, of course, that other management functions not thus clearly taken outside the ambit of arbitration are challengeable, although the arbitrator, construing the agreement, may well find that a particular management function is not limited by the agreement and hence may be exercised unilaterally and exclusively by the employer.

Secondly, we must, in each case, determine the extent to which a particular management right has been limited by the contract.

---

[1] *United Steelworkers* v. *Warrior & Gulf Navigation Co.,* 46 LRRM 2416, 34 LA 561, 363 U.S. 574 (1960); see also *United Steelworkers* v. *Enterprise Wheel & Car Corp.,* 46 LRRM 2423, 34 LA 569, 363 U.S. 593 (1960), and *United Steelworkers* v. *American Manufacturing Co.,* 46 LRRM 2414, 34 LA 559, 363 U.S. 564 (1960).

Management rights are not necessarily those which completely exclude the employees and the union from a voice in their implementation. They may be partially limited, or limited by a general phrase, which still leaves much room for management decision-making. For example, if a contract provided that discharges should remain "within the sole and unfettered discretion" of the employer, the right to discharge would be completely exclusive. The typical "just cause" limitation leaves the employer a great deal of latitude to establish what constitutes just cause by his policy and practices. A contract could go further; it could provide that an employee could be discharged only with the consent of the union. Here the employer has shared the control equally with the union. Finally, the contract might provide that the employee could not be discharged except with his own consent. In this case, there is no real control by the employer since if the employee would consent to discharge, he would merely quit, a right which he can exercise at any time.

Other examples could be given. If the contract provides that the employer must pay a minimum wage, as is common in craft union contracts, his right to pay more than the minimum is not limited, and merit increases may be given. The right to promote may be so severely limited by the seniority clause that the employer has, practically speaking, lost the right to recognize ability, or he may have retained under the common "ability being equal" clause, a substantial area of choice. To this extent, he has preserved the right to decide who shall be promoted.

Another distinction must be drawn between management rights and management's right to act, even though its action is in violation of the agreement. Except in the few cases in which management must obtain the consent of the union before it acts (the so-called "mutual consent" clause), the labor agreement contemplates the possibility of violation and provides its own machinery, the grievance procedure and arbitration, to remedy the violation. When we speak of "unilateral rights" and "unilateral action" as contrasted with "joint control," this distinction must be kept in mind. Management places the agreement in motion by exercising its right to run the plant and to direct the working forces, that is, it has the right of administrative initiative. If this action is within management's exclusive rights, the matter ends there; it is not subject to challenge in any way. But if the employees or the union think it violates the agreement, they may test the action in the grievance procedure. The term "joint control" is employed in this sense; it does not ordinarily mean that the consent of the union must be secured before the action is taken.

Actually, we find little conflict in respect to union or employee rights which are plainly expressed or the exercise of management functions which nobody disputes. The problems lie in the exercise of functions which are not expressed at all, or are curbed (at least in the opinion of the union) by some other provision of the agreement. Many arbitration cases must turn on a management right which is "residual," that is, unexpressed, and an asserted limitation on that right, also unexpressed, based on plant practice, or on an ambiguous provision designed primarily to accomplish some other purpose.

The Importance of the Management Function

Whatever the terminology employed, the social and economic importance of the operating factors which underlie the exercise of management's functions has to a considerable extent been neglected in the literature of industrial relations. The nature of the management function and the considerations which make it effective need stress particularly in collective bargaining and in arbitration. Few union people have any realistic grasp of the problems which management must overcome to keep an enterprise sound and growing. This is even true of arbitrators, most of whom are lawyers or economists with little direct experience in plant operation. The management function has an intrinsic value, not because of some abstract legal theory of "rights," but because the knowledge and judgment of plant management is the prime factor in keeping a plant running safely, economically, and efficiently. Only when the fundamental importance of the management function is recognized, and only when it is made fully effective, do employees enjoy real security. Closings and relocations of high-cost factories are a common occurrence in these days of narrow profit margins. If the exercise of management rights is thwarted, there will be fewer and fewer employees left to enjoy their rights under the agreement. No opportunity should be lost to assert this underlying fact of industrial life and to impress it upon the thinking of employees, union representatives, and mediators and arbitrators.

What the worker and the layman who is unfamiliar with plant management may fail to appreciate is that the operation of a plant requires a daily balancing of numerous factors, tangible and intangible, which vary from day to day and hour to hour. The plant manager must bring into focus a great many variables in order to secure production. Before a man can be assigned to perform a given task, management must supply him with a plant, machinery, equipment, and tools, the raw or semi-fabricated materials on which he works, engineering and scheduling services, and provide means for delivering the product to carrier and customer. No matter how good the planning, accidents happen, unforeseen delays are common, materials fail to arrive, or when they arrive are found to be of poor quality. Mistakes are made in blueprints and in the preparation of specifications. Machines break down, power failures occur, and weather conditions interfere with traffic in and out of the plant. New products, new equipment, new processes, and new methods are developed and incorporated into production schedules. Inspection must be provided, and defective products reworked. In this complex interchange of men and materials, judgment is required of all levels of supervision, not once, but a hundred times a day. A plant will not run automatically.

In scheduling and assigning work, decisions are required as to (1) the priority of one product, or one operation, or one job, as against another, frequently a matter controlled by the customer or other departments in the plant; (2) the availability of materials, machines, tools and equipment; (3) the composition of the work force on hand at the moment; (4) the coordination of the work of one group or individual with that of others; and (5) safety and respect for human beings. Over all and through all of these elements, time is a prime consideration. Delays and interruptions must be avoided, wherever possible.

In assigning work, supervisors must take account of the variance in the requirements of jobs. Some are simple, some intricate. Some are heavy, some light. Some are fast and some slow. They require varying degrees of skill, education, training, initiative, strength, dexterity, and coordination. And in just the same way, individuals vary in the characteristics needed for a particular task.

Finally, there is the attitude of the employee to be taken into account. Employees will work more effectively on jobs they like.

It is the duty of management to adjust men to machines and materials in the most efficient manner possible. Production management, if it is to survive, must keep costs in line. If operations lose money, they must eventually be discontinued. The market place is a hard and relentless taskmaster, hence the importance of the management function. When we speak of "management rights," we are talking of an indispensable attribute of a healthy economy.

A Labor View of Management Rights

It is worthwhile to study the discussion of management rights by Justice Arthur Goldberg, when he was general counsel for the United Steelworkers of America and special counsel for the AFL-CIO. The concept of management's reserved rights, he said, "overlooks the degree to which collective bargaining modifies workers' rights—the right to cease work, the right to press a point without regard to any set of rules or guides, the right to improvise concepts of fairness on the basis of the necessities of the moment without commitment to the future."

Justice Goldberg then went on to describe the point at which management's rights interlock with labor's "equal rights."

> The right to direct, where it involves wages, hours or working conditions, is a procedural right. It does not imply some right over and above labor's right. It is a recognition of the fact that somebody must be boss; somebody has to run the plant. People can't be wandering around at loose ends, each deciding what to do next. Management decides what the employee is to do. However, this right to direct or to initiate action does not imply a second-class role for the union. The union has the right to pursue its role of representing the interest of the employee with the same stature accorded it as is accorded management. To assure order, there is a clear procedural line drawn: the company directs and the union grieves when it objects. To make this desirable division of function workable, it is essential that arbitrators not give greater weight to the directing force than the objecting force.
>
> * * * *
>
> Management determines the product, the machine to be used, the manufacturing method, the price, the plant layout, the plant organization, and innumerable other questions. These are re-

served rights, inherent rights, exclusive rights which are not diminished or modified by collective bargaining as it exists in industries such as steel. It is of great importance that this be generally understood and accepted by all parties. Mature, cooperative bargaining relationships require reliance on acceptance of the rights of each party by the other. A company has the right to know it can develop a product and have that improvement made effective; establish prices, build plants, create supervisory forces and not thereby become embroiled in a labor dispute.

Our ability to have this accepted without question depends on equally clear acceptance by management of the view that the exercise of these rights cannot diminish the rights of the worker and the union. For instance, a new method of manufacture may raise several issues of working arrangement, crews, spell periods, schedules, rates, etc. These are usually susceptible to determination by application of contract clauses, practices, precedents, etc. An effort to claim that the exclusive right of management to establish a new method of manufacture keeps the worker from objecting effectively to the resulting working conditions not only confuses the labor-management issues, but it makes more difficult unequivocal acceptance of the rights of management. We are entirely in agreement that the company can establish the manufacturing methods, but, if management attempts to use this right as the basis for diminishing labor's rights, then there must inevitably develop hostility to the whole concept of exclusive management rights. This oft-used technique of argument—and even propaganda—represents a disservice to management's best interests and should be avoided if we hope to develop an increasingly mature basis for stable relationships.

In addition to these exclusive rights to do things without any union say, the exclusive rights to manage and direct should be very clearly understood by all parties. The union cannot direct its members to their work stations or work assignments. The union does not tell people to go home because there is no work. The union does not notify people who are discharged to stay put. The union does not tell employees to report for work after a layoff (except perhaps as an agent for transmitting information in behalf of management). The union does not start or stop operations unless perhaps some urgent safety matter is involved and there is some contractual or other basis for such action.

This is not an easy concept. Very often union men are disturbed by decisions they consider entirely wrong. Nevertheless, a company's right to make its own judgments is clear.

But the union has rights too; the worker has rights. In fact, the union has the duty and as a union man the employee has the duty as well as the right to challenge the company's acts when they violate the workers' rights. That challenge is made through the grievance procedure, not through rebellion. But the grievant should lose nothing by carrying out the company's direction. If arbitrators act on any other basis, they help to drive labor toward demands which would curb the right of management to manage. It is high time that management and counsel for management understand this. When arbitrators are asked to attach extra weight to a management judgment because of the right to direct and manage, then management is playing a dangerous game. To make an argument, to win a point, the whole balance of management's directing right and labor's grieving rights is being jeopardized.[2]

Some of Justice Goldberg's statements deserve reflection. It will be noted first that he said nothing about a union voice in the initial decision-making which precedes management action. Instead, he stresses labor's grieving right. The role of the union is one of protest—for very good reasons—and its object is to see that the employees "lose nothing by carrying out the company's direction." Union men realize that "co-determination" in day-to-day shop affairs is an impracticable procedure. Second, he suggested that no "extra weight" can be attached to management's judgment. So stated, it is a fair sounding idea. But if Justice Goldberg meant that unions and arbitrators should be allowed to substitute their judgment, long after the fact, for that of management in decision-making, he is in error. Management should be allowed decisional areas in which its discretion, if soundly exercised, is not subject to second-guessing by others. We shall examine some of these areas as we go along.

Most importantly, Justice Goldberg adopted the view that managerial rights are limited not only by contract clauses, but by "practices, precedents, etc." It is here that management is likely to become bogged in interpretations of the contract which are gathered from various sources, such as "implied obligations," "good faith," and "the purpose of the contract as a whole." These obligations, we will find, constitute a large area of what is called "industrial common law," though one reading the contract word by word can find no suggestion of their existence.

---

[2] Goldberg, "Management's Reserved Rights—a Labor View," *Management Rights and the Arbitration Process* (Washington: BNA Incorporated, 1956), pp. 120-121, 123-125. For a recent review of the management rights issue in arbitration, see "Management Rights and Labor Arbitration: A Symposium," *Industrial and Labor Relations Review* (Ithaca, New York: Cornell University, New York State School of Industrial and Labor Relations), Vol. 16: No. 2, p. 183.

Management Rights and the Duty to Bargain

As we go into an examination of the management rights concept, we inevitably find at the threshold the statutory duty to bargain collectively. Modern collective bargaining is built upon the philosophy expressed in the federal law and could hardly exist without it. Moreover, there is confusion, even in the minds of experts, as to the requirements of the law.

Before 1930, there were few restrictions upon the employer's common law right to make individual contracts with his employees upon such terms as he chose. Then came the New Deal and a series of statutes restricting the employer in his relations with his employees. One familiar law is the Fair Labor Standards Act. Another is the National Labor Relations Act (1935) [3] which for the first time imposed the duty of collective bargaining upon industries engaged in activities affecting interstate commerce. In the Taft-Hartley Act (1947),[4] this obligation was continued. The employer is required to bargain with the chosen representative of his employees in an "appropriate unit." Collective bargaining is defined as:

> the performance of the mutual obligation . . . to meet at reasonable times and confer in good faith with respect to
>
> wages, hours and other terms and conditions of employment or
>
> the negotiation of an agreement or any question arising thereunder, and
>
> the execution of a written contract incorporating any agreement reached if requested by either party,
>
> But such obligation does not compel either party to agree to a proposal or require the making of a concession. . . (Section 8 (d), Taft-Hartley Act).

The Scope of the Duty to Bargain

Questions arise immediately under this language as to the scope of the phrase "wages, hours and other terms and conditions of employment." Are there subjects as to which an employer may refuse to bargain? Are internal management matters open to question and investigation by unions? May the employer refuse

[3] National Labor Relations Act, 49 Stat. 449 (1935), 29 U.S.C. § 141, 1 LRRM 803; as amended, 29 U.S.C. §§ 151-168 (1952); as amended, 29 U.S.C. §§ 153-187 (Supp. I, 1959).

[4] The Labor-Management Relations Act, 1947 (Taft-Hartley), 61 Stat. 136, 29 U.S.C. § 151, 21 LRRM 3025, as amended.

to bargain as to employees not covered by the "appropriate unit" represented by the union?

It has often been said that no fence can be built around any area of truly exclusive management rights, and the law has tended to sustain this view. The National Labor Relations Board and the courts have upheld the right of unions to bargain on all the numerous subjects commonly embraced in labor agreements, such as work loads, working schedules, plant rules, subcontracting, union security, incentive rates, and merit increases. The law also requires bargaining with respect to fringe benefits, such as pensions, insurance, profit-sharing plans, and stock purchase plans. The only subjects which have been definitely excluded from the bargaining area are those which are illegal from the standpoint of public policy, such as the closed shop.

However, this is not the whole story. A distinction has been drawn between subjects which must be bargained upon, and those which are voluntary. The subjects which are "permissive" in nature are those which the parties may, if they wish, settle in negotiations and incorporate in their contract. But since they are not in the "mandatory" area of "wages, hours, and other terms and conditions of employment," either party may refuse to discuss them, and insistence by the other party upon their inclusion is an unfair practice. This was the gist of the decision in the Borg-Warner case,[5] where the Supreme Court held that the employer could not insist upon two contract clauses, one making the uncertified local union the exclusive bargaining agent, even though the international union was the certified agent, and the second requiring a secret ballot vote by the employees before a strike could be called. The second was said to concern only relations between the employees and their union.

A number of cases have been decided on this subject since Borg-Warner. In a Carpenters Union case (Mill Floor Covering, Inc.),[6] the Board decided that the union violated the Act by insisting on the inclusion in the contract of a clause requiring an employer to contribute to an industry promotion fund, since participation in the latter is not a mandatory subject of bargaining. In *Sylvania*

---

[5] *NLRB* v. *Wooster Division of Borg-Warner Corporation,* 356 U.S. 342, 42 LRRM 2034 (1958).

[6] Carpenters Union (*Mill Floor Covering, Inc.*), 136 NLRB 769, 49 LRRM 1842 (1962).

Electric Products, Inc. v. *NLRB,*[7] the Court of Appeals held that an employer did not refuse to bargain collectively in violation of the Act when it refused to give the union information as to the cost to the employer of the premiums it paid to maintain a non-contributory group insurance program. Although the benefits could be said to constitute wages, the court said, the costs of the benefit plan did not.

The Borg-Warner decision has been criticized by legal writers who think it projects the NLRB into the specifics of the bargaining agenda and tends to make it the judge not only of the good faith of the parties but of the extent to which collective bargaining, an evolving and flexible process, should be confined by public policy. This view may ultimately result in a retreat to the position taken by Justice Frankfurter in his dissenting opinion that any proposal should be regarded as within the statutory ambit of "mandatory" bargaining unless it is "clearly outside the reasonable range of industrial bargaining." [8]

Are matters which are solely the concern of management within the area of "mandatory" bargaining? In Fibreboard Paper Products Corporation,[9] the "Eisenhower" Board, member Fanning dissenting, upheld an employer's refusal to discuss the merits of its decision at the expiration of its union contract to subcontract out all its maintenance work, admittedly a decision made for economic reasons. The Board said "we do not believe . . . Congress intended to compel bargaining concerning basic management decisions, such as whether and to what extent to risk capital and managerial effort." Court decisions contain similar views. In Rapid Bindery, Inc.,[10] the court said that a decision to move a plant was not a required subject of collective bargaining as it was clearly

---

[7] *Sylvania Electric Products, Inc.* v. *NLRB*, 291 F.2d 131 (C.A.1, 1961), 48 LRRM 2313. See also *North Carolina Furniture, Inc.*, 121 NLRB 41 (1958), 42 LRRM 1271; *NLRB* v. *Winchester Electronics, Inc.*, 259 F.2d 291 (C.A.2, 1961), 49 LRRM 2013; *Local 164, Painters* v. *NLRB*, 293 F.2d 2163 (C.A.D.C., 1961), 48 LRRM 2060; *Arlington Asphalt Co.*, 136 NLRB 742, 49 LRRM 1831 (1962); *Longshoremen's Assn.* v. *NLRB*, 227 F.2d 682 (C.A.D.C., 1960), 45 LRRM 2551; *NLRB* v. *Local 19, Longshoremen, AFL-CIO*, 286 F.2d 664 (C.A.7, 1960), 47 LRRM 2420; *NLRB* v. *IBEW*, 266 F.2d 350 (C.A.5, 1959), 43 LRRM 2875; *NLRB* v. *Cummer-Graham Co.*, 279 F.2d 759 (C.A.5, 1959), 46 LRRM 2374; *U.S. Pipe & Foundry Co.* v. *NLRB*, 298 F.2d 877 (C.A.5, 1962), 49 LRRM 2540.

[8] *NLRB* v. *Wooster Division of Borg-Warner Corporation*, 42 LRRM 2034 at 2037.

[9] *Fibreboard Paper Products Corp.*, 130 NLRB 1558, 47 LRRM 1547 (1961), reconsidered and reversed, 138 NLRB No. 67, 51 LRRM 1101.

[10] *NLRB* v. *Rapid Bindery, Inc.*, 293 F.2d 170 (C.A.2, 1961), 48 LRRM 2658.

"within the realm of managerial discretion." The court went on to say that having made that decision, the employer should have given notice of the move to the union so that collective bargaining could take place as to the employees whose conditions of employment would be affected by the move.

An employer, let me hasten to add, should not assume that he may brashly refuse to discuss a particular subject at the bargaining table because he thinks it a matter of concern only to management. He will do well to consult a competent lawyer before he takes this position. Following the appointment of two new members to the Board by President Kennedy, member Fanning's dissent in the Fibreboard decision was adopted as the Board's decision in Town and Country Mfg. Co.,[11] which also involved subcontracting. The Board has now reconsidered and reversed the earlier decision in Fibreboard Paper Products. All that is suggested is that this is a developing area of the law, the course of which must be carefully watched by employers in the future.

What Is Bargaining in "Good Faith"?

"Good faith" is an expression we meet often in labor relations. By and large, it means having honest and substantial reasons for one's actions and assertions. This is in effect what the Act requires at the bargaining table. The good faith doctrine has itself been limited in a few cases by the rulings that certain postures are unlawful *per se,* such as the refusal to reduce an agreement to writing, once its terms have been settled, and sign it. But for the most part, conduct at the bargaining table is subject, in case by case analysis, to the test of "good faith."

The statute, it should be observed, provides that neither party is compelled to "agree to a proposal" nor required to make "a concession." In the early and important Jones and Laughlin case,[12] the Supreme Court stated that the Wagner Act "does not

---

[11] *Town & Country Mfg. Co., Inc.,* 136 NLRB 1022, 49 LRRM 1918 (1962). Other cases of interest are: *Renton News Record,* 136 NLRB 1294, 49 LRRM 1972 (1962); *Phillips* v. *Burlington Industries, Inc.,* 199 F.Supp. 592 (N.D. Geo., 1961), 49 LRRM 2144; *NLRB* v. *New Madrid Mfg. Co.,* 215 F.2d 908 (C.A.8, 1954), 34 LRRM 2844; *NLRB* v. *Lassing,* 284 F.2d 781 (C.A.6, 1960), 47 LRRM 2277; *NLRB* v. *R.C. Mahon Co.,* 269 F.2d 44, 47 (C.A.6, 1959), 44 LRRM 2479; *NLRB* v. *Houston Chronicle Publishing Co.,* 211 F.2d 848, 851 (C.A.5, 1954), 33 LRRM 2847; *Jays Foods, Inc.* v. *NLRB,* 292 F.2d 317 (C.A.7, 1961), 48 LRRM 2715.

[12] *Jones & Laughlin Steel Corp.* v. *NLRB,* 301 U.S. 1, 45, 1 LRRM 703 (1937).

compel agreements between employers and employees. It does not compel any agreement whatever. It does not prevent the employer 'from refusing to make a collective contract and hiring individuals on whatever terms' the employer 'may by unilateral action determine.' "

Later decisions which met with the approval of the Supreme Court gave more content to the good faith concept by stating that the parties must deal with each other with fair and open minds and a sincere purpose to find a basis of agreement. The test has also been stated negatively. If a party enters negotiations with a fixed resolve to avoid agreement, he will be found to be acting in bad faith. The state of mind brought to the bargaining table by a party is of course difficult of proof and ordinarily must be shown by inference from external conduct, such as stalling, repudiating understandings already made, and introducing new demands at the last moment to prevent agreement.[13]

The Kennedy NLRB is engaged in a re-examination of the "good faith" concept, considering among aspects of the problem the so-called "Boulwareism" approach.[14] Boulwareism has been

---

[13] Cox, "The Duty to Bargain in Good Faith," 71 *Harvard Law Review* 1401 at 1414 (1958). This article is a trenchant analysis of the cross-currents of judicial and administrative opinion on the problem of regulation of the substance of collective bargaining by use of the good faith principle. See also Feinsinger, "The National Labor Relations Act and Collective Bargaining," 57 *Michigan Law Review* 807 (1959). Recent cases of interest: *Fitzgerald Mills Corp.*, 133 NLRB 877 (1961), 48 LRRM 1745; *McGregor & Werner, Inc.*, 136 NLRB 1306 (1962), 50 LRRM 1002; *Alberto Culver Co.*, 136 NLRB 1432 (1962), 50 LRRM 1026; *General Tire & Rubber Co.*, 135 NLRB 269 (1962), 49 LRRM 1469; *Fetzer Television, Inc.*, 136 NLRB 557 (1962), 49 LRRM 1826; *St. Clair Lime Co.*, 133 NLRB 1301 (1961), 49 LRRM 1023; *International Powder Metallurgy Co.*, 134 NLRB 1605 (1961), 49 LRRM 1388; *Raleigh Water Heater Mfg. Co.*, 136 NLRB 76 (1962), 49 LRRM 1708; *Bethlehem Steel Co.*, 133 NLRB 1400 (1961), 49 LRRM 1018; *Oates Bros., Inc.*, 136 NLRB 1295 (1962), 49 LRRM 1676; *Altex Mfg. Co.*, 134 NLRB 614 (1961), 49 LRRM 1212.

[14] In April 1963, Trial Examiner Arthur Leff issued an Intermediate Report in which he concludes that General Electric did not bargain in good faith in 1960. The Trial Examiner rejects use of the term "Boulwareism." Instead, he accepts G.E.'s own description of its approach as a "fair and firm offer." This approach, the Trial Examiner says, does not permit the flexibility of discussion and persuasion required by the Act. He held that the G.E. course amounted in effect to a unilateral determination of employment terms. BNA, *Daily Labor Report*, No. 64 (1963): p. AA-1 (April 2).

In *Philip Carey Manufacturing Co.*, 140 NLRB 90, 52 LRRM 1184 (1963), the Board held that an employer did not violate the Act by substantially adhering to his so-called final offer during the seven negotiating meetings that were held between the date the offer was made and the date on which the strike began. The offer was made at the seventh meeting between the parties and included a wage increase. The Board said "That the respondent regarded its offer as final is a

defined as the presentation of a prepared position in bargaining on a "take it or leave it" basis. Deeply involved is the question as to what extent concessions and counter-proposals are necessary to good faith bargaining.

In the American National Insurance Company case,[15] the Supreme Court approved the employer's insistence upon a management rights clause in the contract reserving unilateral control over promotions, discipline, and work schedules. The Court said the Board could not "sit in judgment upon the substantive terms" of the agreement, and that agreement upon management functions clauses was a common thing. Moreover, it said, adamancy by itself was not a violation; "fruitless marathon discussions" are not required by the law.

In *L. R. White* v. *NLRB*,[16] the Fifth Circuit Court of Appeals went even farther, holding that insistence upon a clause which in effect was a reservation of control over all standards of employment was lawful economic bargaining. And in the Lewin-Mathes case,[17] the Seventh Circuit said, "It is not an unfair labor practice for an employer to bargain in good faith for agreement assigning particular subjects of collective bargaining to management's exclusive control for the duration of the contract."

The Supreme Court, construing the Railway Labor Act in the famous work rules dispute, held that the procedures prescribed by that Act had been exhausted, subject only to the provisions for the creation of presidential emergency boards. The Court said: "So far as the Act itself is concerned, those conditions (working conditions) may be as bad as the employees will tolerate or be made as good as they can bargain for. The Act does not fix and does not authorize anyone to fix generally applicable standards for working conditions." [18]

---

matter of its own judgment. One need not listen to argument endlessly. There comes a point in any negotiation where the positions of the parties are set and beyond which they will not go. Where that point is obviously depends on all the facts of the case." This subject is discussed in an address delivered October 19, 1962, by NLRB member Fanning, before the Ninth Annual Institute on Labor Law, Southwestern Legal Foundation, Dallas, Texas, 51 LRR 200.

15 *American National Insurance Company*, 343 U.S. 395, 30 LRRM 2147 (1952).

16 *White* v. *NLRB*, 255 F.2d 564 (C.A.5, 1958), 42 LRRM 2001.

17 *NLRB* v. *Lewin-Mathes Co.*, 285 F.2d 329 (C.A.7, 1960), 47 LRRM 2288 at 2290, upheld the employer's right to insist upon retention of unilateral control over work assignments and a clause granting superseniority to employees who had replaced strikers.

18 *Locomotive Engineers* v. *B & O RR Co.*, 372 U.S. 284 (1963), 52 LRRM 2524.

Thus, absent bad faith, the employer's right to insist upon the reservation of those functions he considers essential to the successful management of the business is a matter of bargaining power. To quote the trial examiner in the White case, "Economic strength is still the underlying touchstone of success at the bargaining table." Perhaps the White case should not be taken too literally. The Board, in considering it, thought the employer was attempting to destroy the union. In future cases of the same sort, the evidence may support the Board in this finding, at least in cases including acts or statements evidencing bad faith over and beyond the mere insistence upon reservation of unilateral control over some, or even all, of the phases of the employment relationship.

It seems clearly established that the Act does not compel an employer who acts in good faith to surrender his rights at the bargaining table. He may lose them through economic weakness, through miscalculation of the effect of contract language, in the process of "horse-trading," or in the genuine belief that a measure of joint control is desirable. But he may insist upon the retention of those rights he thinks necessary to the successful operation of the plant and resist encroachments which he believes unduly burdensome. His decision is a matter of conviction and strength, not law.

Unilateral Action Under the Agreement and the Duty to Bargain

A third problem which management should keep in mind is the possibility that unilateral action during the term of an existing agreement may be regarded as a refusal to bargain and hence an unfair labor practice. The NLRB has exclusive jurisdiction to remedy unfair labor practices. An activity which violates the Act may also involve a violation of the agreement. How this is to be determined and by whom is a question not always easy to answer.

The Board seems increasingly inclined to leave the parties to their contract remedies, when the action taken is not repugnant to the provisions of the Act. In Crown-Zellerbach Corporation,[19] the Board dismissed a complaint charging a violation of the duty to bargain where the question of the propriety of the employer's unilateral action in reducing piece rates raised an issue of contract

---

[19] *Crown-Zellerbach Corp.*, 95 NLRB 753 (1951), 28 LRRM 1357.

interpretation which could have been settled in the arbitration procedure provided by the contract. In the United Telephone Company case,[20] the Board was of the same opinion where the issue of whether the employer's unilateral action violated the contract had been placed before a court in a suit for declaratory judgment and the possibility of arbitration had not been exhausted. The Board said in this case, "as the Board has held for many years, with the approval of the courts . . . 'it will not effectuate the statutory policy . . . for the Board to assume the role of policing collective bargaining between employers and labor organizations by attempting to decide whether disputes as to the meaning and administration of such contracts constitute unfair labor practices under the Act.' " A similar ruling can be found in the McDonnell Aircraft Corporation case [21] where the employer's unilateral action in changing work assignments was held to be a matter for determination under the contract procedures and not an unfair labor practice.

An interesting development in this field came with the decision of the Court of Appeals for the Fifth Circuit in *Sinclair Refining Co.* v. *NLRB*.[22] In this case the court refused enforcement to a Board decision that Sinclair had violated its duty to bargain collectively by refusing to furnish certain work scheduling data demanded by the union in connection with the processing of a grievance. Sinclair was willing to submit the issues in dispute, including the relevance and necessity of the data sought, to arbitration for decision in accordance with the contract. The court, in reversing the Board, rested its decision in large part upon the recent Supreme Court decisions [23] declaring that the protection

---

20 *United Telephone Company of the West,* 112 NLRB 779 (1955), 36 LRRM 1097 at 1098.

21 *McDonnell Aircraft Corporation,* 109 NLRB 930 (1954), 34 LRRM 1472; cf. *Hershey Chocolate Corporation,* 129 NLRB 1052 (1960), 47 LRRM 1130; see also Wollett, "The Interpretation of Collective Bargaining Agreements; Who Should Have Primary Jurisdiction?", 10 *Labor Law Journal* 477 (1955); Beatty, "Arbitration of Unfair Labor Practice Disputes," *The Arbitration Journal* (Vol. 14: No. 4, 1959), p. 180; Cummings, "NLRB Jurisdiction and Labor Arbitration: 'Uniformity' v. 'Industrial Peace,'" 12 *Labor Law Journal* 425 (1961); "Arbitration and/or the NLRB," an address delivered by NLRB Chairman Frank W. McCulloch, to the National Academy of Arbitrators, February 1, 1963, 52 LRR 107, reprinted in *Labor Arbitration and Industrial Change* (Washington: BNA Incorporated, 1963).

22 *Sinclair Refining Co.* v. *NLRB,* 306 F.2d 569 (C.A.5, 1962), 50 LRRM 2830. The decision contains an exhaustive analysis of the leading decisions on the question of the resolution of disputes which involve both possible violation of contracts and the Act.

23 *United Steelworkers* v. *American Manufacturing Co., op. cit.; United Steel-*

and enforcement of arbitration agreements in the federal courts was a matter of major federal policy. The Board was not the proper forum to determine whether or not the data should be produced, the court held, since the determination of this question necessarily required construction of the agreement itself. This, the court said, was a matter exclusively for arbitration.

In *Smith* v. *Evening News Association*,[24] the U.S. Supreme Court held that the fact that a claimed violation of a collective bargaining contract also may be an unfair labor practice under the Act, admittedly within the jurisdiction of the NLRB, does not deprive a state court of jurisdiction of a suit to enforce the contract.

Using the Evening News Association case as its basic precedent, the Second Circuit Court of Appeals upheld the right of the IUE to demand arbitration of several grievances which the General Electric Company claimed were within the exclusive jurisdiction of the NLRB. One of the cases involved the assignment of bargaining unit work to employees outside the bargaining unit. The second involved the assignment of work normally performed by IUE employees to other employees in a different unit represented by a different union. In a third case, the company had removed certain employees from the production and maintenance unit converting their jobs from hourly pay to salary jobs without changing their duties. In the fourth case, the lower court had refused arbitration of a seniority grievance. It was this court's view that a seniority provision which had a discriminatory effect gave rise to an unfair labor practice and held the matter to be within the exclusive jurisdiction of the NLRB. The appellate court ordered arbitration.[25]

The problem is complicated if the action taken by the employer is charged by the union to be a violation of the continuing duty to bargain. Section 8 (d) of the Labor-Management Relations Act provides that there is no duty to bargain about proposals to make changes in an existing agreement to take effect during its term. But in the Jacobs Manufacturing Company case,[26] the Board held that "those bargainable issues which have never been discussed by

workers v. *Warrior & Gulf Navigation Co., op. cit.; United Steelworkers* v. *Enterprise Wheel & Car Corp., op. cit.*
[24] *Smith* v. *Evening News Association,* 371 U.S. 195 (1962), 51 LRRM 2646.
[25] *Carey* v. *General Electric Co.,* 315 F.2d 499 (C.A.2, 1963), 52 LRRM 2662.
[26] *Jacobs Manufacturing Co.,* 94 NLRB 1214, 28 LRRM 1162 at 1165 (1951).

the parties, and which are in no way treated in the contract, remain matters which both the union and the employer are obliged to discuss at any time."

This doctrine calls for a determination (which the Board certainly has the right to make) whether the employer's unilateral action is in fact a matter not treated in any way in the contract and not discussed in negotiations. The employer may be able to point to a specific provision in the agreement, for example in the management rights clause, which in general terms authorizes the action taken. He may be able to cite the history of negotiations and show that the subject was discussed and the union acquiesced in his position that the right to take the action remained a management prerogative. Or, if the contract is silent, he may be able to rely on the "residual rights" theory, which is discussed in the next section. The Board will take into consideration the availability or the non-availability of procedures to resolve the question, thus the fact that the matter is arbitrable or that it can be settled in proceedings in the state or federal courts.

An express waiver of the right to demand collective bargaining on a subject not mentioned in the agreement will be respected by the Board. In the Jacobs Manufacturing case, the Board pointed to the General Motors clause [27] as an example of a waiver which would effectively block the assertion of new demands. A waiver must be "clear and unmistakable," the Board has said, to discharge the statutory duty to bargain.

Since the trend seems to be in the direction of leaving the parties to the remedies provided in the contract, it is important for the employer to determine what remedies the contract provides if the union contends his action involves a violation of his statutory duty to bargain. Various clauses in the agreement may bear upon his study. Among them are the management rights clause, the grievance procedure and arbitration provisions, the waiver clause, and the no-strike clause. The examination of these clauses and the determination of their effect upon the right to manage are important, of course, for other reasons. Clarity and understanding of the

---

[27] The General Motors waiver clause is reproduced at BNA, *Collective Bargaining Negotiations and Contracts*, p. 36:422 (Oct. 13, 1961) and also at p. 20:346 (Sept. 29, 1961). Other cases involving waivers are *Shell Oil Co.*, 93 NLRB 161, 27 LRRM 1330 (1951); *Phelps Dodge Corp.*, 96 NLRB 982, 29 LRRM 1613 (1951); and *NLRB v. Item Company*, 220 F.2d 956 (C.A.5, 1955), 35 LRRM 2709; and *Tide Water Associated Oil Co.*, 85 NLRB 1096 at 1098 (1949), 24 LRRM 1518.

scope of the contract will go far, however, to preclude the charge that unilateral action is a violation of the obligation to bargain.

Reserving the Right to Manage

No labor contract has yet been written which defines exactly and in detail the rights of management. Nevertheless, a line does exist between the area of management's rights and the area of union or employee rights under the agreement. The line may be fuzzy and difficult to find and fix. It may be drawn by express language, by the application of the residual rights theory, by arbitral interpretation, by unwritten agreement, or by plant practice. But in all cases it is there. The problem is to discover at what point management's functions are limited and to what extent they are limited by the agreement. Archibald Cox pointed this out in his leading article on the subject of arbitral jurisdiction, saying:

> Occasionally the sphere of joint government is expressly delineated with all the rest reserved as management prerogatives. More often the impossibility of making an explicit compromise, coupled with the impossibility of not reaching an agreement, results in a pregnant silence. The task of finding where the boundaries would have been drawn if the parties who signed the contract had drawn them explicitly is a problem of interpretation, for it is the agreement that draws the boundary line even though it does not draw it expressly. The interpreter must remember that the contract goes a distance but also that it stops, because it is a product of competing wills and its policy inheres as much in its limitations as in its affirmations. Nor is the interpreter left wholly without guidance. Even a vague management-functions clause suggests that the boundaries may be narrower than under a contract without one. An integrated-writing clause bespeaks narrow interpretation. Surely an open-end arbitration clause indicates a wider area of joint sovereignty than a clause limiting the arbitrator to the "interpretation and application" of the contract. . . . Whatever the indicia, however, they must be found in the relationship created by the particular contract, and no obligation which is outside the context of the contract may be imposed upon a company by an arbitrator. In this sense the management-rights theory seems sound. The imperative which requires a body of "industrial jurisprudence" within the general area marked off for joint government has no place in deciding what area has been marked off.[28]

---

[28] Cox, "Reflections Upon Labor Arbitration," 72 *Harvard Law Review* 1482 at 1505 (1959).

The "Residual Rights" Principle

One of the means by which the line is drawn, as Cox indicated, is the "residual rights" principle—what management has not bargained away it necessarily has retained. As I have said, it is unfortunate that the management function has been labeled with a legal title which obscures its vitality and importance. The same is true of the phrase "residual rights," which has an artificial sound to workers and union leaders. It means exactly what Arthur Goldberg described when he said, "somebody has to be boss; somebody has to run the plant. People can't be wandering around at loose ends, each deciding what to do next." [29] If, in the course of running the plant, the boss violates the agreement, a grievance will be filed and the worker awarded redress for the violation. But if there is no violation, the boss has acted within his "residual right" to direct the operation.

A good many arbitrators have adopted this as a rule of construction. C. M. Updegraff, professor of law at Iowa State University Law School, and a leading authority on labor arbitration, puts it this way:

> It is now a well-established generalization that every employer continues to have all powers previously had or exercised by employers unless such powers have been curtailed or eliminated by statute or by contract with a union. [30]

Another statement, by Professor Charles O. Gregory of Virginia Law School, an equally well-known authority on labor law, is worth quoting:

> What if an agreement is completely silent about a certain matter, such as whether or not separate operations may be coordinated and put on assemblyline production, and whether or not the various jobs in a certain department may be changed from an individual to a group-incentive basis? If these matters are not covered at all, does this mean that management has the right during the life of the contract unilaterally to make these changes as part of its function to manage? I have always supposed that it did mean just that. Naturally, the union may interpose bargaining demands concerning these changes with a view to modifying them in the next contract. But I should think management would have to have this unilateral right, as long as its acts are

---

[29] See note 2 in this chapter.
[30] This quotation by Updegraff is taken from Elkouri and Elkouri, *How Arbitration Works* (Washington: BNA Incorporated, 1960), p. 288.

not inconsistent with provisions of the current agreement. * * * Nowadays, this unilateral right is always subject to curtailment if the union insists upon bargaining over the subject matter involved. Whether or not management's unilateral innovations become modified depends entirely upon the course of the bargaining itself.[31]

Then there is the decision of the Sixth Circuit Court of Appeals in *United States Steel* v. *Nichols,* which adopts the same principle in construing the United States Steel Corporation contract with the Steelworkers. The court expressed the rule this way:

> . . . a collective bargaining agreement does not necessarily express the full coverage of employment rights. It covers such matters only as the parties may have been able to agree upon and leaves unresolved such issues as the parties may not have been able to agree upon and with respect to which the law does not require a concession by either party. . . . The Union was within its rights in refusing to agree to a compulsory retirement policy which the evidence shows was presented by the Company in collective bargaining sessions, without it being linked to an adequate and satisfactory pension plan. But such failure to reach an agreement did not deprive the Company of its common law right to hire and fire at will until such an agreement was reached. Accordingly, instead of searching for a provision in the contract authorizing termination of employment by reason of age, we think it is necessary to determine from a consideration of the terms of the contract whether termination of employment by reason of age was prohibited by the contract.[32]

The residual rights doctrine, in the word of Professor Updegraff, is a "generalization," a rule of construction. As we have observed, it is both historically and practically accurate to look at collective bargaining as a process by which organized labor wrests part of the control of industry away from management. The collective agreement expresses those parts which have been taken out of the exclusive domain of management and placed under joint agreement or control. An arbitrator or court, failing to find any language in the agreement which subjects a particular function to union control, or which shows that the act complained of was intended to be regulated or restricted by the parties, adopts the residual rights theory as the legal basis for his opinion that it

---

[31] This quotation by Gregory is taken from *How Arbitration Works, op. cit.,* pp. 293-294.

[32] *United States Steel* v. *Nichols,* 229 F.2d 396 (C.A.6, 1956), 37 **LRRM** 2420 at 2423.

remains within the control of management. It follows naturally that if there is language in the agreement which indicates an intention to withdraw the subject to some extent from the employer's control, the doctrine, to the same extent, does not apply.

Management Rights Clauses

Because of the residual rights theory some management representatives have taken the view that no management rights clause is necessary or desirable in an agreement. Since management has retained all the rights not limited or restricted by the agreement, they ask, why attempt to express them and run the risk of not expressing them properly or of missing some of them? It is thought that management's right to do a particular thing can be better established when the case arises, and should not be anticipated. This view has lost ground. It is now generally conceded that a well-drafted (though not necessarily detailed) management rights clause is desirable.

One of the reasons for including a management rights clause is that full advantage can be taken of the residual rights concept in the clause itself. The clause, usually as part of the introductory sentence, contains language such as this: "all rights which ordinarily vest in and are exercised by employers, except such as are clearly relinquished herein by the company, are reserved to and shall continue to vest in the company. This shall include, this enumeration being merely by way of illustration and not by way of limitation, the right to: (specified rights)." In this way the agreement itself makes clear that management rights are not created by it; they are retained except to the extent limited by the agreement.

Parenthetically, it may be observed, another way of incorporating the residual rights rule in the scheme of the contract is to provide in the arbitration clause that the arbitrator's power "shall be limited to deciding whether the company has violated the express terms of this agreement, and the arbitrator shall not imply obligations and conditions binding upon the company from this agreement, it being understood that any matter not specifically set forth herein remains within the reserved rights of the company under the management rights clause."

A second reason for a management clause is that it can cover, in broad language, the entire management function without pinpointing specific rights, and thus provide a kind of general charter against which the various limitations and restrictions on the management function can be tested. This is well illustrated by a consideration of the second paragraph of the General Motors management clause,[33] (Paragraph 8) which reads simply: "In addition, the products to be manufactured, the location of plants, the schedules of production, the methods, processes, and means of manufacturing are solely and exclusively the responsibility of the corporation."

The right to determine the "products to be manufactured, the location of plants, and the schedules of production. . . ." implies a good many things. The right of the corporation to determine what it shall manufacture and the location of its plants has never been effectively questioned. There are two provisions in the agreement dealing with the effect of the opening of new plants or the transfer of operations between plants upon employees with seniority. They may apply, with preference for a period of 18 months over new employees, for employment in a new plant, provided their previous experience with the corporation shows they can qualify. If they are accepted, they take the status of temporary employees. If as a result of the transfer of major operations between plants, employees with seniority are permanently laid off, the corporation and the union will review the matter, and, if employees are allowed to transfer to the new plant, they do so with full seniority (Para. 95-96). Paragraph 59 provides for plant-wide seniority for employees displaced by changes in "methods, products or policies."

Scheduling production is one of management's most important functions, and from it flow several ancillary responsibilities. Management must, in scheduling production, determine how much is to be produced, and hence how many employees will be needed and the daily and weekly hours they will work. Inevitably, this means changes in working hours and in establishing shift hours and lunch periods. In such a case, the union naturally considers the impact of such changes upon the personal lives of the employees. To take care of this situation, the corporation agrees, in Paragraph 88, to discuss the changes as far in advance as possible with the shop committee. This does not mean, however, that emergency changes may not be made without notice.

---

[33] The General Motors contract is reproduced in full at BNA, *Collective Bargaining Negotiations and Contracts*, p. 20:299 (Nov. 24, 1961).

Other provisions in the agreement are, to some extent, qualifications upon management's basic right to determine production schedules, the hours of work, and the assignment of employees. Thus the provision that the workweek may be reduced before layoffs take place is in itself a recognition of a management function, but there are certain limitations on its exercise (Paragraphs 65 and 66). And though the right to schedule includes the right to schedule overtime work, it must be "equalized . . . so far as practicable." (71)

Since the term "schedules of production" necessarily implies the number of man-hours needed to produce a given number of units, it follows that management must determine the rate of production or production standards. This is further recognized in Paragraphs 78 and 79, which provide that standards must be fair and equitable, and establish a procedure for re-examination of a standard in dispute.

The right to determine the "methods, processes, and means" of manufacturing likewise gives the corporation complete control over what work shall be done, how it shall be done, and what tools and equipment must be used. The right to establish job duties is a necessary consequence which, although unstated, has been completely recognized. In GM-UAW Decision F-18, the Umpire said: "In this case Management has done no more than exercise its recognized right to determine the means and method of manufacture, a basic component of which is the right to establish and reorganize the contents of an operation or job." In the same decision, the Umpire commented that this might result in changes in wages and in seniority groupings "when Management breaks up an existing cluster of duties and regroups them in another arrangement. . . ." In cases of change, a reclassification in the wage structure of the changed work may be necessary, and a procedure for this is provided in Paragraphs 102 and 102 (a).

One may also note, from an inspection of agreements, that management rights may be expressed throughout the agreement. The United States Steel agreement [34] states, for example, "When and if from time to time the company, at its discretion, establishes a new job or changes the job content of an existing job. . . ."

[34] The United States Steel agreement is reproduced in full at BNA, *Collective Bargaining Negotiations and Contracts*, p. 22:141 (May 11, 1962).

The value of this approach has been overlooked by many draftsmen. Such clauses, even more than the general statements of management rights, attach the employee rights conferred by a particular clause directly upon the exercise by management of its functions. In the example cited above, the element of managerial judgment is clearly indicated.

But the management rights clause itself has the same value, even though its statements are not tied directly to their consequential effects upon the employees. The management clause places the responsibility to manage where it belongs. It eliminates any vague notion of joint determination, of government by committee. It places administration of the agreement by the supervisor in the proper light—as his affirmative and positive task. It lays the groundwork for a system of policies and procedures by which the management function can be effectively implemented in the light of the provisions of the agreement. It eliminates the false notion that the agreement is wholly negative. Many a foreman has been misled by a union committeeman who asks, "Where does the agreement give you the right to do that?" If the foreman is properly schooled in the effect of the management clause, he can point to it, and say, "The company has the right to direct the working forces: you show me where the agreement says I can't do it." Even the employees themselves come in time to be educated on the nature and importance of the management function. Hence the management rights clause has great value as a practical operating man's text. It is not, as some people think, merely a technical legal reservation of value only to lawyers.

The Arbitration and No-strike Clauses

As Archibald Cox said, the line between the areas marked off for joint determination through the grievance procedure and the area reserved exclusively to management is drawn by the agreement, even though it is not explicitly drawn. The area of joint determination is the area in which interpretation of the agreement is required, by the parties themselves in the first instance, and if they disagree, by an arbitrator.

In drawing the line, we have already seen, a management rights clause may be important, and the residual rights rule of construction is also brought into play. Perhaps even more important is the scope of the arbitration clause. If a dispute between management and the union, or the employees, is arbitrable, it is subject to joint control in the sense that it is the arbitrator who decides whether the management right in question is limited, expressly or implicitly, by the agreement. Closely allied to this question is another: what is not arbitrable may (or may not) be strikeable. If it is strikeable, the union has reserved joint control over the matter in dispute to the extent it is willing to strike to win its point. Strictly speaking, to put the problem in reverse terms, a management right is only truly exclusive to the extent it rests within unilateral determination by the employer without union or employee appeal either to an arbitrator or to the use of economic pressure.

The problem has been given much emphasis by the decisions of the United States Supreme Court, especially those in the Enterprise Wheel and Car Corporation, American Manufacturing Company, and Warrior and Gulf Navigation Company cases.[35] These cases confer broad latitude upon the power of arbitrators, and equally curb the power of the courts, to interpret and apply labor agreements containing arbitration clauses.

In the view of the Court, the arbitrator "is not confined to the express provisions of the contract." Instead he is to look to "the practices of the industry and the shop" which are "equally a part of the . . . agreement although not expressed in it." He is, the Court says, selected because the parties have "confidence in his knowledge of the common law of the shop and their trust in his personal judgment to bring to bear considerations which are not expressed in the contract. . . ." He may consider "the productivity of a particular result, its consequence to the morale of the shop, his judgment whether tensions will be heightened or diminished."

If the arbitrators were to take this romantic description of their function seriously, no doubt changes in the language of the agreement would be necessary to confine them to their true function: interpretation and application of the terms of the agreement. A great many experts have taken this view, recommending drastic curbs on arbitration.

---

[35] *United Steelworkers* v. *American Manufacturing Co., op. cit.; United Steelworkers* v. *Warrior & Gulf Navigation Co., op. cit.; United Steelworkers* v. *Enterprise Wheel & Car Corp., op. cit.*

For example, the Labor Relations Committee of the Chamber of Commerce of the United States has published a pamphlet entitled "Model Arbitration Clauses To Protect Management Rights," [36] saying "Increasingly arbitration has been used as a device by which unions have broadened their authority within the business enterprise" and recommending that action be taken with respect to arbitration language in future union contracts to ameliorate the effect of the Supreme Court decisions.

Many others, however, are less fearful, believing that arbitrators will continue to act within the authority given them by the parties, resorting to the "common law" of the shop only when the agreement itself is ambiguous or obscure in stating the intentions of the parties. In a study of management opinion, based on correspondence with about 75 experts in labor relations law, Professor Russell A. Smith found that their reactions varied.[37] Many believe that attempts to write contract clauses which specifically state what is and what is not exclusively within the management area, or which specifically exclude management rights from arbitration, would be difficult both from a legal and a practical point of view.

John Waddleton, Chief Counsel for the Industrial and Community Relations Division of Allis Chalmers, commenting on the Supreme Court decisions, says:

> All of this simply highlights that we in the industrial relations end of our employer's business find ourselves in no different position than those engaged with us in other aspects of the enterprise—sales, manufacturing, engineering, finance or accounting.
>
> Each day brings to us as well as to them new difficulties, new problems and new challenges which must be successfully overcome.
>
> In this particular case one can only reemphasize the fundamentals we already know:
>
> 1. To negotiate each provision carefully, fully, and frankly, noting in the negotiations the extent of each concession being made.
>
> 2. To keep as detailed minutes of the negotiation discussion on each provision as possible.

---

[36] Reproduced as Appendix A, p. 255.

[37] Smith, "The Question of 'Arbitrability'—The Roles of the Arbitrator, the Court and the Parties," Address delivered at the Eighth Annual Institute on Labor Law, Southwest Legal Foundation, November 4, 1961, *Southwestern Law Journal* (Vol. XVI: No. 1, 1962), p. 1. Reprinted by the Institute of Labor and Industrial Relations, University of Michigan-Wayne State University, Reprint Series No. 22 (1962).

3. To see that the person drafting the contract provisions has the opportunity to be and is as meticulous as possible in drafting, testing the draft exhaustively with the operating people, and then, as will practically always be indicated, redrafting each provision.

Then, if we do these things and a certification to arbitration occurs, we will be in the best position to convince the arbitrator of the proper disposition of the issue.

This means concentrating even more than we have before on the 'tackle and block' fundamentals of our business. It does not call for, in my view, such 'statue of liberty' plays as attempting to list and label non-arbitrable in the labor contract each and every management function.[38]

I would add that concentration on the "tackle and block" fundamentals should include the assiduous pursuit of good administrative practices and the careful elimination of practices and working conditions which hamper effective exercise of the management function. The wise employer will himself attempt to furnish the "common law" of the shop which implements and furnishes the context of the agreement. If he keeps his house neat and clean, he need not worry about arbitrator-created disorder. If an arbitrator falls into the error of dispensing his own brand of justice, it is usually because the parties themselves have neglected to provide him with adequate decisional standards. This means in most cases that the employer has failed to assume and discharge his own management responsibilities, since he has the initiative.

It must always be remembered that arbitration is what the parties make it. Equally, arbitrators are what the parties allow them to be, no more. Harry Shulman, in the early days at Ford, acted as a friend and counselor to the parties, mediating between them and writing lengthy expositions of his own wise and intelligent views on labor relations for their guidance. Such a relationship would not be possible, even if all arbitrators were possessed of Dr. Shulman's wisdom, in most situations. Neither management nor the unions wish advice and guidance as to what they ought to do—the possibilities of compromise and accommodation have usually been exhausted. What they want is a decision.

The no-strike clause has taken on new importance in the light of the Supreme Court decisions in the Steelworker cases enforcing

---

[38] John Waddleton, "Speech to the Industrial Relations Club in Milwaukee, Wisconsin," at BNA, *Daily Labor Report*, No. 7 (1961): p. A-8 (January 11).

collective agreements under Section 301 of the Taft-Hartley Act and in the process developing a new body of federal substantive law applicable to them.

Perhaps the most important aspect of the subject is the notion which seems to have gained currency that the no-strike clause is necessarily coextensive with the arbitration clause, that is, what is not arbitrable is strikeable, and vice versa.

The popularity of the idea stems from certain expressions in the Lincoln Mills case,[39] and again in Warrior and Gulf that the arbitration agreement is the "quid pro quo" for the no-strike clause. Justice Douglas in the latter case says:

> Complete effectuation of the federal policy is achieved when the agreement contains both an arbitration provision for all unresolved grievances and an absolute prohibition of strikes, the arbitration agreement being the 'quid pro quo' for the agreement not to strike. Textile Workers v. Lincoln Mills, 353 U. S. 448, 455.[40]

More recently the Supreme Court has adopted, as a principle of federal law, the view that if a dispute is arbitrable under the collective agreement it is not, even in the absence of an express no-strike pledge by the union, strikeable.[41] A promise by the union not to strike over such an issue is implied. At least one writer, Frederick U. Reel, a Trial Examiner for the NLRB, has argued that effectuation of the national labor policy requires that a no-strike clause be accompanied by an arbitration clause, so that insistence by an employer upon a no-strike clause, coupled with insistence upon the retention of unilateral control over the terms and conditions of employment, would constitute a refusal on the part of the employer to bargain in good faith.[42]

If all this taken together were to mean that the employer may not by contract reserve the right to act unilaterally on matters not specifically or by necessary implication covered by the agreement—if he must either arbitrate or take a strike over every demand made upon him during the term of the agreement—then the whole theory of reserved rights will have been modified in

---

[39] *Textile Workers* v. *Lincoln Mills,* 353 U.S. 448 (1957), 40 LRRM 2113.
[40] 46 LRRM 2416 at 2418.
[41] *Local 174, Teamsters* v. *Lucas Flour Co.,* 365 U.S. 868 (1962), 49 LRRM 2717.
[42] Reel, "The Duty to Bargain and the Right to Strike," 29 *George Washington Law Review* 479 (Dec., 1960).

the sense that everything the employer does, or refuses to do on the union's demand, is arbitrable or strikeable.

Such a conclusion will be precluded if the courts follow the actual history of bargaining, and its reality as expressed in thousands of existing agreements, and the Supreme Court thesis, as expressed in an American National Insurance Company case,[43] that the employer is permitted to demand the retention of unilateral control over such matters as discipline and work schedules as the price of its agreement. In this case, the court noted that the argument put forth by the NLRB "would seem to prevent an employer from bargaining for a 'no-strike' clause commonly found in labor agreements. . . ."

American National was carried to its logical conclusion in the Cummer-Graham case, in which the Fifth Circuit held it was lawful for an employer to insist upon a no-strike clause and at the same time refuse to give an arbitration clause. The court said:

> We do not think that the Supreme Court held, or intended to hold, in Lincoln Mills, that a no-strike clause and an arbitration clause were so much one that a persistent demand for the one without acquiescing in the other is a refusal to bargain in good faith.[44]

The no-strike clause is not the exact-agreed exchange for the arbitration clause. In most negotiations, a host of proposals are made and compromises reached, without any weighing of the exact value of each as consideration for another granted by the other party. As Frank H. Stewart has said, "the promise not to strike is the *quid pro quo* for every promise running from the employer to the union, for it is the only binding commitment the union offers." [45] Stewart has also pointed out that there are many issues which the union may take up in the grievance procedure

---

[43] *American National Insurance Company*, 343 U.S. 395, 408 n. 22, 30 LRRM 2147 (1952).

[44] *NLRB* v. *Cummer-Graham Co.*, 279 F.2d 757, 759-760 (C.A.5, 1960), 46 LRRM 2347.

[45] Stewart, "The No-Strike Clause," 59 *Michigan Law Review* 673, 686. Many contracts contain provisions exonerating the union from liability for unauthorized strikes with the proviso usually that the union disavow the strike and direct the employees to return to work on penalty of discharge. Evasion of such clauses is easy to the practiced union representative and proof that the union was actually supporting, or at least countenancing the strike, is difficult to secure. In such cases, the company should at least reserve the right to terminate the agreement. Rescission of the contract was held to be justified by an unauthorized strike in breach of a no-strike clause in the *Marathon Electric case*, 223 F.2d 838 (C.A.D.C. 1955), 36 LRRM 2175. An action for damages will not ordinarily survive rescission.

for which it would not strike. Therefore, to insist that everything not strikeable must be arbitrable is not sound logic.

That the *quid pro quo* equation is not a matter of law, but of the parties' intention, seems clearly recognized in the Sinclair case [46] in which the Supreme Court held that Congress, in opening the door of federal jurisdiction to suits for enforcement of collective agreements, did not intend to repeal the Norris-La Guardia Act so as to permit injunctions sought as remedies for breach of a no-strike clause.[47] In the dissenting opinion, written by Justice Brennan, he states that such injunctions should issue upon request where both parties are bound to arbitrate, since the furtherance of arbitration is a leading policy of federal labor law. He concedes there is no threat to the sanctity of arbitration if such injunctions are refused because of Norris-La Guardia if the union or the employer cannot be compelled to arbitrate. "Therefore," he concludes, "unless both parties are so bound, limiting an employer's remedy to damages might well be appropriate."

More impressive than any legal doctrine, however, is the history of collective bargaining, which demonstrates clearly that arbitration clauses are not necessarily the corollary of no-strike clauses. Provisions in contracts run the gamut from contracts such as that exemplified by Cummer-Graham, in which the employer has reserved the final say, to those in which the union has reserved the right to strike at the step prior to arbitration or at its election take the matter in dispute to arbitration. In the Teamsters Central States Over-The-Road Agreement,[48] the parties can agree to take a particular case to arbitration. If they do not, either party is permitted "all legal or economic recourse." In the General Electric-IUE contract,[49] if one party or the other argues successfully that a particular dispute is beyond the scope of the arbitration clause, a strike is permitted. In the automobile agreements,[50] the umpires have a specified jurisdiction, and certain disputes, such

---

[46] *Sinclair Refining Co.* v. *Atkinson*, 370 U.S. 195, 50 LRRM, 2420, 2432.

[47] The Sinclair case, it perhaps should be added, indicated clearly that a union-authorized strike would result in union liability for damages.

[48] Teamsters Central States Over-The-Road Agreement, 1961-1964 Agreement, Article 8, Section 1(e), BNA, *Collective Bargaining Negotiations and Contracts*, p. 27:758 (May 12, 1961).

[49] General Electric-IUE Contract, BNA, *Collective Bargaining Negotiations and Contracts*, p. 20:815 (Feb. 3, 1961).

[50] General Motors Agreement, BNA, *Collective Bargaining Negotiations and Contracts*, p. 20:312, 327 (Sept. 29, 1961).

as production standards, new wage rates, or in the case of Ford, health and safety issues, may be the subject of grievances, but at the end, if unresolved, the union may authorize a strike.

The important thing, also demonstrated by the automobile agreements, is that there are other grievances entertainable through the grievance procedure, but neither arbitrable nor strikeable. Perhaps the best illustration is that in an early Ford case, decided at a time when the labor agreement contained a provision for merit increases. The question was what remedy was available to an employee when his supervisor refused to join in a recommendation of a merit increase for the employee. Shulman decided he had no jusisdiction of the question under the agreement, saying:

> Clearly the agreement contemplates that a committeeman may negotiate with the foreman and seek to persuade him. Similar effort may doubtless be made with those representatives of the Company whose approval of a recommendation is required before it can become effective. If both sides confer in good faith and with minds reasonably open to rational persuasion, mutual agreement should result in a great many cases. The issue remains, then, with respect to those cases which do not result in agreement. In such cases the employee can doubtless file a grievance in normal fashion requesting that he be recommended for an increase. The grievance can be processed through all the steps of the procedure short of the appeal to the Umpire. The next question, and the real one upon which the parties are in dispute here, is whether appeal to the Umpire is available to an individual employee who was not recommended for an increase or whose recommendation was not approved.
>
> The Umpire's jurisdiction is considerably more limited than that of the parties in the preceding stages of the grievance procedure. The grievance procedure is prescribed for 'all grievances' without limitation as to the nature of the grievance and without any restrictions upon the jurisdiction of any of the agencies prior to the Umpire. But a number of paragraphs limit the Umpire's jurisdiction, both by inclusion and exclusion. Apart from a number of special limitations, his jurisdiction is limited generally to 'alleged violations of the terms' of the parties' agreements. He is specifically forbidden to 'add to, or subtract from, or modify any of the terms of any agreement'; or to 'substitute his discretion for the Company's discretion in cases where the Company is given discretion' by any agreement; or to 'provide agreement for the parties in those cases where they have in their contract agreed that further negotiations shall or may provide for certain contingencies to cover certain subjects.'

With these limitations in mind and in view of the nature and provisions of the 'agreement concerning merit increases,' the conclusion is inevitable that the Umpire has no jurisdiction over the question whether a particular employee is or is not entitled by merit and ability to a merit increase.[51]

In all of these cases, the grievances in question were dismissed by the arbitrators. Another class of cases are those in which the courts may find that, to use the language of Justice Douglas in Warrior and Gulf, the order to arbitrate must be denied because it may be said "with positive assurance that the arbitration clause is not susceptible to an interpretation that covers the asserted dispute. . . ." [52]

The scope of arbitration and of the no-strike clause are for the parties to determine in the collective bargaining process. They are not necessarily coextensive, the no-strike clause may prohibit strikes over matters which are not arbitrable and are within the reserved rights of management, or the union may reserve the right to strike over any matter, or all matters, if it wishes, and the employer, willingly or not, agrees.

Conclusion

The subject of the effective exercise of the management function is so complicated that we must, at the risk of overemphasis, repeat that many observers of the industrial scene, including prominent government officials, arbitrators, and writers, have failed to see that the whole structure of employee rights, the common law of industry of which the unions are rightly proud, depends for its existence upon the health of industrial management. Whatever may have been the situation many years ago, today management is struggling to make the private enterprise system work, with full consciousness of its obligation to workers which it has neither the desire nor the power to avoid, but also recognizing that it has an even more compelling obligation to the

---

[51] *Ford Motor Company*, Opinion A-150, Shulman (1944), Shulman and Chamberlain, *Cases on Labor Relations* (New York: The Foundation Press, 1949), pp. 813, 814. See also *Chrysler Corporation*, Wolff, 6 LA 276 (1947), 28 LA 162 (1957). Similar decisions have been rendered in the steel industry: *United States Steel Corporation, National Tube Divison, 3 Basic Steel Arbitrations* 1467, 1470. See also *American Steel and Wire Division*, Crawford, 1 *Basic Steel Arbitrations* 135; *Tenn. C. I & R. Co.*, Crawford, 2 *Basic Steel Arbitrations* 699, and *Jones and Laughlin Steel Corp.*, Cahn, 2 *Basic Steel Arbitrations* 1339.
[52] 46 LRRM 2416 at 2419.

consuming public. It is not too much to say that the survival of our economic system depends upon effective management.

This means, among many other things, that management should not be unnecessarily hobbled in its day-to-day job. The removal of cumbersome restrictions upon the effective use of workers should be regarded as a duty of all directly concerned in industrial relations—union officials, government representatives, and arbitrators, as well as management people. It should not be necessary to take long strikes to force reform of labor contracts which are unduly restrictive, or to eliminate bad practices. There can be no true peace in industry until this is accepted.

The draftsman of the agreement and its interpreter have a special responsibility here. As Cox said, the contract goes a certain distance in sharing the management function with the union, but it also stops. The limitations it imposes should be explicit, even though general. Where the contract is silent, it should be assumed that the matter in dispute was left where it was—within the province of management decision. This presumption should also be adopted normally in cases of ambiguity. Unions have both the knowledge and strength to make a limitation clear. Arbitrators should not fill in the agreement with their own notions of good industrial relations unless the parties clearly have conferred this broad power upon them.

CHAPTER 3

HOW CONTRACTS LIMIT THE RIGHT
TO MANAGE

Up to this point, we have been discussing the rights of management in a positive sense. We have adopted this affirmative approach since we are interested in discovering how the management function may be made most effective. When we examine union and employee "rights," we are actually talking about restrictions or limitations on the management function. The "right" of employees to be laid off in order of seniority, for example, does not exist independently of the basic management right to lay them off. It governs the order of layoff. It is a mistake, we believe, to view the labor agreement from the standpoint of the restrictions it imposes without setting these restrictions in their basic context of management rights, whether "residual" or expressed.

In the previous chapter we stressed the idea that, however obscure, there was a line between the rights of management and those of the employees and the union. It is our task here to discover how contracts limit or impinge upon management's freedom to act. It is useful in order to make this determination to divide union and employee rights into three types: (1) specific restrictions, (2) those which are general in scope, leaving room for managerial policy and the exercise of judgment in their application, and (3) restrictions which are "implied" from the agreement even though not expressly set forth. These divisions, of course, are somewhat artificial and are not clearly delineated in any agreement. Sometimes, one clause will fit both of the first two types; thus, paragraph 63 (a) of the General Motors agreement,[1] which we will examine, is an express restriction on the manner in which promotions are effected, and also sets up a general standard which management in the first instance must observe, i.e. the factors

---

[1] BNA, *Collective Bargaining Negotiations and Contracts,* p. 20:318 (Sept. 29, 1961).

which permit the determination of equality of merit, ability, and capacity.

We are concerned with determining how far limitations or restrictions on management's freedom actually go, exploring to the fullest extent management's rights in a legal or contractual sense. Employee "gripes" over working conditions may not constitute grievances in the sense that the agreement uses that word, and management may have no obligation whatever to allay dissatisfaction since the agreement has not been violated. Management may nevertheless, as a matter of policy, decide to accord employees consideration in areas which the agreement does not cover. Employee wishes may be taken into account when, for example, choice of machines, work assignments within a classification, conditions of personal comfort, or other matters not regulated by the agreement, are brought up. But our question at this point is "what are the rights of the parties under the agreement?"

Specific Restrictions

Specific restrictions in the agreement are easily identified, and, if their scope and effect are clear, there is little likelihood of a dispute except in the rare cases where one party or the other is seeking to violate his obligations. An obvious example is the agreement to pay a certain wage for a specific job. As long as the job remains unchanged, its occupant's rate remains fixed for the life of the agreement, and violations, if they occur, are inadvertent.

The scope and effect of express limitations, however, are in many cases far from clear. All too often, management representatives fail to appreciate that what is not specifically limited may fall into the domain of management rights. Examples will make this clear. In a United States Rubber Company case,[2] the contract provided for seniority preferences in case of layoff, recall, transfer, and promotions within the bargaining unit. Another section stated that seniority was by department and required posting of vacancies "in a department," which the equally-qualified senior employee bidding "in the department" was entitled to fill. The company established a new department. A senior employee who was laid off in another department requested a transfer to it, but the company transferred a junior employee to the job instead.

---

2 *United States Rubber Company*, Livengood, 28 LA 704 (1957).

The arbitrator, Charles H. Livengood, Jr. held that the company had not by virtue of the above sections, which confine seniority rights within departments, lost its right to make interdepartmental transfers without regard to seniority. At the Charles Bruning plant,[3] it was held by James P. Gifford, arbitrator, that the employer had the right to ignore seniority altogether and promote the best qualified employee when the contract provided that promotions were on a departmental basis only and the bidders were all from other departments. These cases illustrate, whether the arbitrator says so or not, the application of the residual rights theory.

An excellent illustration of this principle can be found by a study of Paragraph 63 of the General Motors agreement:

> The transferring of employees is the sole responsibility of Management subject to the following:

Paragraph 63 (a)

> In the advancement of employees to higher paid jobs when ability, merit and capacity are equal, employees with the longest seniority will be given preference.

Paragraph 63 (b)

> It is the policy of management to cooperate in every practical way with employees who desire transfers to new positions or vacancies in their department. Accordingly, such employees who make application to their foremen or the Personnel Department stating their desires, qualifications and experience, will be given preference for openings in their department provided they are capable of doing the job. However, employees who have made application as provided for above and who are capable of doing the job available shall be given preference for the openings in their department over new hires. In case the opening is in an equal or lower-rated classification and there is more than one applicant capable of doing the job, the applicant with the longest seniority will be given preference. Any secondary job openings resulting from filling jobs pursuant to this provision may be filled through promotion; or through transfer without regard to seniority standing, or by new hire.[4]

Paragraph 63(a) applies only to promotions if one is to be made. Management has no obligation under it to fill a vacancy by promotion. It does not give seniority employees preference over newly hired employees. It does not require posting or canvassing

---

[3] *Charles Bruning Co., Inc.*, Gifford, 25 LA 826 (1955).
[4] BNA, *Collective Bargaining Negotiations and Contracts*, p. 20:318 (Sept 29, 1961).

of applicants to see who wants the job, and applications are not a prerequisite. In short, this paragraph comes into operation only as a matter of unilateral action by the supervisor when he decides to advance an employee. It applies only to management transfers to higher-rated jobs. When such transfers are made, the question of "equal ability" in the group from which the employee is selected must be decided properly. That is all that is required.

Section 63 (b) applies only to openings in equal or lower-rated jobs. Comparative ability is not a factor as between applicants. An employee who has applied is given preference over new hires and those who have not applied, provided he is capable of doing the work. Seniority is a factor only between applicants. It does not apply to job assignments within a given classification, which are not "transfers," nor to transfers to another department, nor to transfers not involving applications. It does not apply to demotions which would ordinarily be handled within the framework of the disciplinary system.

As these examples show, language should not be construed to cover situations not expressly set forth.

General Restrictions

Here we enter one of the most neglected areas of the labor agreement from the standpoint of effective exercise of the management function. Most agreements do not and could not, with any regard for simplicity and brevity, spell out what will happen in each and every situation which occurs. It is impossible to provide specific criteria for each case which will automatically govern supervisory and union action. Consequently the agreement provides only a more or less general standard which requires reason and judgment in its application, and which the parties themselves must fill out in case-by-case situations.

In most of these cases, the unions can challenge management action through the grievance procedure. This, above all others, is the area in which the agreement is a constitution, which must be filled in by "industrial common law." The general standard is a restriction upon management's right to uncontrolled action. Its content must be filled in by specific applications, and if an arbitrator thinks management has failed to observe the standard properly and in good faith, he has the right to decide that the agreement has been violated.

The conspicuous example of this kind of clause is the company's power to discipline, which is exercisable only for "just cause." The union's interest here is in the opportunity to challenge each instance of discipline through the grievance procedure. Although in some plants rules are negotiated, unions do not, for the most part, challenge management's authority to make and change rules, except of course that in a specific case they will challenge not only the application of the rule, but the rule itself on the ground that it is unreasonable, inconsistent, or that the employees were not apprised of it, etc. Except for this, the company is allowed to take over the entire area of plant rules and discipline and to make it as effective as circumstances will permit. As long as its rules, and their applications to specific cases are just, management's power to maintain order and efficiency will be upheld.

Other examples of areas in which many contracts provide only a general standard, which must be implemented in initial applications by management, are:

(a) standards for production and quality;

(b) subcontracting;

(c) assignments between classifications;

(d) rules for the guidance of supervisors as to the assignment of work between union employees and those excluded from the agreement, and for the performance of work by supervisors themselves;

(e) the procedures to be used in handling promotions under the "equal ability" clauses, and the standards for selection;

(f) temporary transfers and other intraplant movements not regulated in full by the agreement;

(g) rules governing the scheduling of relief periods, and lunch and rest period practices;

(h) job content, initially and when changes occur;

(i) procedures providing for the division of overtime work as equitably "as practicable," under clauses for the assignment of overtime work;

(j) union activities in the plant;

(k) physical examinations and health requirements not detailed in contracts; and

(l) what is a "reasonable excuse" for failure to report for work (under seniority and holiday pay clauses).

The point here is that management has the right at least to initiate its policies and procedures, and to apply them in the first instance. Many employers let this opportunity go by default, through failure to think through the applications of the agreement in these policy areas, and to instruct their supervisors how to handle specific cases. The result is a vacuum which is filled without much thought by pressure from plant committeemen or stewards, by the making of obscure little "side agreements" in one or more departments, or by the growth of "practice" which the union insists is enforceable. Moreover, many companies, instead of anticipating and providing for future situations, settle specific cases in the grievance procedure, not heeding the fact that undesirable precedents are frequently established under pressure in partial situations which do not disclose the impact of the settlement in other situations or other departments of the business. We will discuss the practical implementation of the management function by the provision of standards, and what criteria can be employed to evaluate standards as effective and reasonable means to accomplish the purposes for which they are intended. If the employer acts intelligently, the chances that his actions will be respected by the union and upheld in arbitration will be greatly enhanced. But management should attempt to fill the areas not specifically controlled by the agreement, even though its decisions are later found to be improper. Granting that it is nice always to be right, the fact that management's policies may be later challenged, even successfully, in the grievance procedure, is of little consequence. The important thing is for management to undertake and discharge its own responsibilities.

Implied Restrictions

Obviously, there is no room for implied restrictions where the agreement speaks plainly on a given subject. For example, to use the expression of the United States Supreme Court, where the contract gives the employer "complete control and unfettered discretion" over subcontracting, there can be no implication in the agreement that this right is limited. Likewise, if the contract provides, as some do, that subcontracting is restricted in one way or another, one must look to the nature and extent of the restriction to determine what, in a particular case, the employer may or may not do.

The implied condition appears when the union alleges that despite the lack of precise language, the agreement prohibits management from certain actions deemed detrimental to the union or its members. The problem comes into prominence usually when the employer, for reasons of economy or efficiency or perhaps to adapt to a change in technology, changes the allocation and distribution of work. There are two main areas of work affected. One is the entire work of the bargaining unit, and the second the work of one classification or one seniority group, as against others. In the first category are union assertions that the work of the bargaining unit must be reserved to members of the union. These demands can be further subdivided. Unions insist that work cannot be assigned to clerical, technical, and supervisory employees, or taken outside the bargaining unit entirely, if the work is the kind performed historically by union members. They also resist subcontracting of maintenance and tool and die work, and special services such as window cleaning and janitor work, if they think their members are thereby likely to be deprived of work.

In the second category are union assertions that work performed by the members of one classification cannot, even in the interests of efficiency or economy, be assigned to the members of another classification. Similar demands are made with respect to the inviolability of the work performed by one seniority group as against another. Unions, for the same reasons, resist the alteration, by unilateral action of the employer without union consent, of the job content of classifications and of seniority groups.

The unions rely, in these instances, not on any express prohibition of employer action (since, if such clearly existed, the action would not be taken), but on implications derived from (a) the recognition clause, (b) the wage classifications and job descriptions (if these exist), (c) the seniority provisions, and (d) the intent of the agreement as a whole.

A number of arbitration decisions deal with these matters, some of which we shall explore as we discuss particular topics, such as the employer's unilateral right to revise the job content of classifications, to assign work to exempt employees, or to subcontract. Here I wish only to emphasize a few principles which should be taken into account, not only by arbitrators, but by employers when drafting agreements.

(a) The "Covenant of Good Faith"

It has been said many times in arbitration, and by the courts as well, that all contracts contain an unexpressed condition, the implied covenant of fair dealing and good faith. In considering this doctrine as it is applied in arbitration, the first thing to remember is that there is no general power in arbitrators to imply conditions as a matter of law. They are not judges; they are creatures of the parties and possess only such powers as the parties have chosen to give them in the agreement or perhaps by submission. The late Dean Shulman pointed this out when he said:

> . . . the judges' authority for imposing the implication is not the party's will; it is the superior authority of law, which transcends the party's will. The arbitrator does not have such superior . . . authority to impose implied conditions. The implications which he may find are only those which may reasonably be inferred from some term of the agreement.[5]

It follows that implied covenants must be implied "in fact," that is, to use the words of an authority on contract law, the late Samuel Williston, they depend upon "the manifested intention of the parties." Williston's description will make this clearer:

> Clearer cases of promises implied in fact are the promises implied in every bilateral contract not only not to prevent performance by the other party by which he will become entitled to receive counter-performance, but also to cooperate in such performance if cooperation is necessary from the nature of the case.
>
> A promise to develop diligently a mining, oil, or gas lease may be implied from a provision therein that the substantial part of the consideration moving to the lessor shall be from royalties. The underlying principle is that there is an implied convenant that neither party shall do anything which will have the effect of destroying or injuring the right of the other party to receive the fruits of the contract; in other words, in every contract there exists an implied covenant of good faith and fair dealing. Promises to pay when able, on the other hand, are not usually held to imply a promise to become able, and the retainer of a lawyer coupled with a promise to pay him a further sum if his services are required implies no promise to require them.[6]

When this is applied to labor agreements, one immediately senses basic distinctions between the situations described by

---

[5] Shulman, "Reason, Contract, and Law in Labor Relations," 68 *Harvard Law Review* 999 at 1012 (1955). Reprinted in *Management Rights and the Arbitration Process* (Washington: BNA Incorporated, 1956), p. 169 at 184.

[6] 3 *Williston on Contracts*, Rev. ed. (1936), § 670.

Williston in which promises not to prevent performance are implied and that encountered in plant operation under a collective agreement. At common law, in the absence of a special stipulation to that effect, the contract of employment is not for a definite term—a week, a month, or a year—but is one at will. The collective agreement does not usually alter this; if it did, we would not have this problem. The employer may go out of business, or discontinue the manufacture of an unprofitable item. If he terminates his business completely, he may discharge his employees. If he discontinues a department or moves his plant, the employees in that department may lose their jobs entirely, may go into other departments, or to the new plant location, depending on their seniority rights under the agreement. The right of management to make these basic decisions, so long as it does not violate the Labor Management Relations Act or a specific provision in the agreement, has been upheld uniformly by courts and the National Labor Relations Board. These possibilities demonstrate that no promise to provide work can be implied for the term of the ordinary collective agreement. Employment, like the lawyer's retainer described by Williston, is on an "as required" basis.

How then can a promise not to subcontract work or to assign it exclusively to the members of the bargaining unit as against other excluded employees be implied? Those who hold that such an implication exists do it by a curious exercise in logic which assumes the point in dispute. Again, we can use a statement in the Warrior case as our starting point for discussion. Supporting the decision that the existence of an implied restriction on subcontracting is a matter for the arbitrator to determine, Justice Brennan says, "On the basis of inconclusive evidence, (the courts below) found that Warrior was in no way limited by any implied covenants of good faith and fair dealing from contracting out as it pleased—which would necessarily mean that Warrior was free completely to destroy the collective bargaining agreement by contracting out all the work." [7]

From this it is reasoned that arbitrators may have the power, without departing from their role as interpreters of the intention of the parties as manifested in the agreement, to pass on the right

---

[7] 34 LA 561 at 572.

of the employer to let out a particular job. Dean Shulman put the question this way:

> . . . good faith, which must be an obligation of all agreements, requires that the employer do refrain from deliberately impairing [the bargaining unit] without sufficient justification. In this view the recognition clause is violated only if the letting of the work to the outside contractor is without sufficient business justification.
>
> But if this is the view found to be required by the agreement then it launches an inquiry for which the agreement provides no guides at all; what is sufficient business justification? To what extent is the employer's own assertion of business judgment significant? How much or what kind of evidence is necessary to bolster his judgment? How much or how little economy is necessary to justify the assumed impairment of the bargaining unit? [8]

The answer to his question is, I think, simple. The union, if it relies on the implied covenant of good faith, should be required to show that the employer is actually attempting to injure it—to destroy the fruits of the contract. To reason that because the employer *might* attempt this, he is by implication required to prove "sufficient justification" for his action is to erect as the precedent premise the proposition that the agreement by implication guarantees work for its term. From this premise, it would follow equally that the board of directors could not close a plant without the risk of having an arbitrator determine that there was an implied condition that he judge whether or not there was sufficient business justification for the closing. The relocation of a plant in another labor market area would be subject to similar scrutiny. It would no longer be the exclusive province of management to determine whether its products would be made of leather, rubber, or plastic, if the result might be a loss of job privileges. If the employer can be required to show sufficient justification for subcontracting, he can equally be required to prove it for all of these actions. The employer normally takes these actions in the exercise of his responsibility to manage the business in a sound and efficient manner. To flirt with such questions as the availability of equipment, which can usually be rented, or the possession of the necessary skills (the bargaining unit employees

---

8 Shulman, *op. cit.* at 1015.

may take a little longer to do the work), and similar "justifications" for subcontracting, is simply to invade the management function.

It might be different if the employer attempted to throw a cloak of legality over a deliberate evasion. If the union could show that the employer had mounted a deliberate attack upon the integrity of the bargaining unit and the union's representative status, such an action might well be a violation of the Labor-Management Relations Act, as in the "run-away" shop cases. It might also be a violation of the agreement, conferring a right of action in the federal courts, possibly cognizable in arbitration, and possibly justifying the union in treating its no-strike obligation as terminated under the familiar principle of contract law that a material breach by one party excuses the other from performance. In the New Park Mining case,[9] for example, the Tenth Circuit Court of Appeals held that the lower court should have inquired into the question of whether the employer actually quit business, thereby terminating the labor agreement, or merely entered into leasing agreements with some of its employees "as mere subterfuges for invading the bargaining contract." But this principle is not that adopted by the lengthy arbitration opinions which examine and weigh, with great care and in minute detail, the employer's reasons for subcontracting work or assigning it to other employees not in the bargaining unit. They assume that the implied covenant of good faith gives the arbitrator a veto power over management. This is wrong; they should restrict themselves to deciding at most whether the employer has embarked on a deliberate attempt to destroy the collective bargaining relationship and the contract with it.

The recognition clause has not, except in scattered instances, been given the interpretation sometimes sought by unions: that the clause embraces not merely members of the bargaining unit, but the work they do and that this work must be done by members of the union. The recognition clause is merely a statement confirming the employer's statutory obligation to bargain collectively with the union as the exclusive representative of the employees in the stated unit who have chosen the union as their representative. It clearly embraces people; in fact, they have the right to vote at intervals upon the right of the union to represent them. It

---

[9] *Steelworkers* v. *New Park Mining Co.,* 273 F.2d 355 (C.A.10, 1959), 45 LRRM 2158.

does not ordinarily attempt to reserve jurisdiction over work as such. Such provisions can be included. The standard contract form used by the Bridge, Structural and Ornamental Iron Workers Association, AFL-CIO, contains this provision:

> The Company hereby recognizes and confirms the right of its production and maintenance employees covered by this agreement to perform all work done by the Company in or about said plant or plants in connection with the fabricating of iron, steel and other metal products and in connection with such maintenance work, and for the duration of this agreement hereby assigns such work to said production and maintenance employees solely and to the exclusion of all other unions, crafts, employee groups, and to the exclusion of all other employees of the Company not covered by this agreement.[10]

When such clauses appear, and they are not uncommon in craft union contracts, they must ordinarily be honored. But there is no warrant from any standpoint—the history of collective bargaining, the records of the usual negotiations on the content and meaning of the recognition clause, or the language itself—for assuming that such an obligation should be implied from the recognition language usually employed in the industrial union contracts.

Another favorite phrase of those who would find implied restrictions in the agreement upon the right to manage is "the intent and purpose of the agreement as a whole." From this statement is fashioned, in a deceptively innocent and simple manner, the concept that the employees engaged in work under the agreement have the right to perform that work to the exclusion of others. The seniority clauses, for example, which in terms only regulate the order in which bargaining unit work is assigned to those within the unit, are pointed to as some evidence of intention to prohibit assigning work to employees outside the unit, or subcontracting. Similarly, the wage classification provisions simply provide a means of agreement upon rates for particular classes of work. Nothing is said as to jurisdiction over the performance of the work. It seems clear that no purpose to freeze work can be found, either in such separate sections of the agreement, or in the underlying purpose. It is instructive to read the statement of the

---

[10] This contract is not readily available, and I have not been able to find a similar clause in contracts reproduced in BNA's *Collective Bargaining Negotiations and Contracts*.

purposes of the agreement in many contracts. There is no implication in any of them that work once placed under the contract or assigned to a certain group must remain so placed and so assigned.

There being no tenable hypothesis for implying obligations of this sort, what is the basis for such decisions? In cold candor, what the use of the implied obligation concept has actually meant is the adoption of the "lump of labor" theory. American unionists are, as Selig Perlman put it, job conscious. They are interested in controlling job territory and establishing rights of occupancy and tenure in it. This has tended to Balkanize American industry; thousands of independent little satrapies have been established. It may be entirely natural if the workers in a given plant insist that their work not be farmed out to the employees of independent contractors, whatever the reason. Equally, their opposition to its assignment to other employees not within the bargaining unit, such as clerical or technical groups, is understandable. This in some cases means a diminution of the employment opportunities available to them. But what is not understandable is the use of the "good faith" doctrine to fasten their desires upon the employer. Arbitrators should not extend a protection to them which in the long run may be detrimental to the entire enterprise, including the workers themselves. We have had enough experience with restrictive work rules now to know that they enhance costs, and in time lead to the reduction of employment in the plant or industry affected by the restrictions. If the parties themselves create the restrictions, it is their own doing and they must live with them. But when arbitrators erect such restrictions out of whole cloth and justify them on the flimsy rationalization of implied conditions, they abuse the arbitral function. As Archibald Cox has suggested, quoting Judge Learned Hand, the arbitrator would do well to follow the quiet role which a judge is abjured to follow in interpreting a statute:

> If he is in doubt, he must stop for he cannot tell that the conflicting interests in the society for which he speaks would have come to a just result, even though he is sure that he knows what the just result should be. He is not to substitute even his juster will for theirs; otherwise it would not be the common will which prevails and to that extent the people would not govern.[11]

---

[11] Hand, quoted in Cox, "Reflections Upon Labor Arbitration," 72 *Harvard Law Review* 1482 at 1506. In an interesting paper presented to the National Academy

(b) Restrictions on Work Assignments

Turning to the second main area of implied obligations, we can consider the transfer of work within the bargaining unit from one group to another. The employer frequently finds it necessary, in the interests of efficiency, savings in man hours, expedition of the job, or other reasons, to assign work normally performed by members of one classification to members of another, or perhaps the transfer is effected between seniority groups or departments. Sometimes it is necessary to change the structure of a job, a department, or seniority group. In many cases, the agreement contains some provisions bearing upon the employer's right to make these decisions, perhaps by inference in a clause which protects the employee's rate of seniority when such assignments or changes are made. Some agreements, however, are silent. In such cases, can restrictions upon the employer be implied? As we shall see, some arbitrators have held that they can.

The subject of implied restrictions on work assignments was dealt with rather extensively by Dean Shulman when he was impartial umpire at Ford. In his principal decision, after analyzing the agreement to show there was nothing in it to prevent the assignment of a production employee to work out of his classification, he comes to a different conclusion as to the craft classifications:

> The situation with respect to the skilled trades is different. It is true that here, too, there are only classification titles, without job descriptions; and the Agreement does not in so many words prohibit the crossing of trade lines and working a tradesman on a job not in his trade. But other guides point in that direction. The classification titles are identifications of skills, trades or crafts of long tradition outside as well as within the automobile industry. Many of the trades are apprenticeable and the nature of their work is indicated by their apprenticeship standards. Generally, each trade is a different seniority group; seniority is reck-

of Arbitrators, John Perry Horlacher of the University of Pennsylvania, discusses the growth of the sense of job entitlement, which, in the eyes of the union man, protects him against dilution of his seniority rights through job structure changes or assignments to others not sharing his tenure. The notion seems to be growing that an employee has a kind of property right to his job. He discusses many decisions in which arbitrators have, under one theory of contract interpretation or another, implied restrictions upon management's normal and necessary responsibility to control operations efficiently and flexibly. John Perry Horlacher, "Employee Job Rights v. Employer Job Control: The Arbitrator's Choice," *Collective Bargaining and the Arbitrator's Role* (Washington: BNA Incorporated, 1962), p. 165.

oned from the date of entry into the particular classification, rather than from the date of hire by the Company; the classifications are not interchangeable for seniority purposes; seniority may not be carried over from one group to another; on a reduction of force in his trade, an employee may choose a layoff instead of a transfer to work outside his trade. A tradesman is hired not so much for a job as for his trade; he is a journeyman when he is placed on the classification. When it was necessary to use non-journeymen, the parties provided for upgraders or trainees by special agreement which safeguarded the claims and the status of the journeymen. There have thus been recognized, albeit without precision and with some variations, the complementary principles that the work of a trade should be done by employees in that trade and that a tradesman should not be required to do work in a trade other than his own.[12]

Whether or not Dr. Shulman was correct in finding the "guides" he did in the agreement (a matter of debate, since the same provisions exist in the General Motors agreement and the opposite conclusion was reached in arbitration under it), the case serves as an excellent example of restriction by implication on the employer's right to assign work within the bargaining unit. It also serves as an excellent example of the adoption by an arbitrator of the union view of job territory as described by Perlman. It has resulted in the filing of thousands of "lines of demarcation" grievances.

(c) The "Reasonable" Exercise of Management Rights

We come now to a vague doctrine arbitrators have inserted in their opinions without attempting to explain either what it means or where it originates. In various phrasings, they say an employer must act reasonably, that his actions must be based on reasons of substance. In some cases, of course, reasonableness is quite legitimately derived from an expression in the agreement: the "just cause" limitation on the employer's right to discharge certainly requires him to act reasonably. Lacking such a basis in the contract, and assuming that management has the right to do the thing in question, why must he be "reasonable"? In a discussion of this rule of "industrial common law," James C. Phelps, then of Bethle-

---

[12] *Ford Motor Company*, Shulman, 19 LA 237 at 240 (1952).

hem Steel, argued cogently that this mysterious concept should be left to the parties, saying:

> What are the net results of such an approach? First line management is told that, so long as it does not violate the agreement, its actions will be sustained in arbitration. At the same time, it is told that a managerial action will not be sustained if it should be regarded as an abuse of managerial discretion by standards which may not be determined until the arbitrator who will review the particular decision shall subsequently have been identified. It is not unlikely that the arbitrator who would eventually rule on whether or not the managerial authority was abused would be a stranger to the industry. He might be totally unfamiliar with the manufacturing processes and with operating customs and procedures which had long been unquestioned but which, to the uninitiated, might seem unreasonable. A management judgment might well be made by a supervisor who, with his background and experience, would have no reason to suspect that his action might be considered an abuse of his authority.
>
> The purpose of the arbitration process in industrial relations is not only to decide issues in dispute but to lay a foundation for the disposition of disputes by the representatives of the parties themselves without the need for an arbitrator's services. Arbitration awards which are based upon standards different from those which the parties have adopted in their agreement tend to defeat that purpose. That is particularly true when the arbitrator shows a predisposition to act as a reviewer of managerial actions which are not restricted by the contract.
>
> Not only must there be acceptance of the principle that managerial rights which are not curtailed or surrendered in the collective bargaining agreement are reserved to the management, but that acceptance must be complete. If the parties have not seen fit to write into their agreement a proviso that management may be free to exercise its reserved rights only so long as it does so reasonably and without abuse, it is not for the arbitrator to correct that deficiency unless the parties jointly request him to do so. The temptation to straighten out what may appear to them as the confused thinking of the parties and to do justice as they see it without paying too precise attention to what the parties have agreed to must, at least in certain cases, be difficult for arbitrators to resist. However, arbitrators who succumb to that temptation do a disservice to the parties.
>
> I have heard arbitrators say that they felt that they can make enduring contributions to the relationship between management and labor and that the role of an arbitrator offers too few satisfactions unless there is a chance for service beyond the mere calling of balls and strikes. Under appropriate circumstances, an arbitrator may find occasional opportunities to mediate disputes and at

such times he may indulge his yearning to help the parties to solve some of their inarbitrable problems. But the arbitrator who decides a grievance according to what he thinks the parties ought to have agreed to instead of what they did agree to may never learn that he has steered the collective bargaining ship into shoal waters without a compass and in a fog. When the pilot, who was hired only for the occasion, leaves the ship, the captain and crew may find themselves in a pretty predicament.

The responsibility for drafting their agreement and determining what goes in and what stays out rests with the negotiators. If their relationship is mature and they are reasonably experienced in the performance of their functions, they should be presumed to know what they want to write into their agreement and what they want to leave out. It cannot be questioned that their knowledge of each other and of the course of conduct which each can expect the other to pursue during the term of the contract is generally greater than is possessed by the most experienced arbitrator who might be requested to decide a dispute between them. Even if the relationship is not a mature one and if the negotiators are not experienced and one or the other makes a mistake in negotiating an agreement, their relationship cannot be improved as much by the assumption of their responsibilities by an arbitrator as it can by holding them to the contract to which they have agreed. The prospect of the next negotiation is a more effective sanction than an arbitrator's decision where either party abuses its rights under a collective bargaining agreement.[13]

Answering Mr. Phelps in the same discussion, Sidney A. Wolff, a leading arbitrator, undertook to defend the principle:

> Let us take a case I had some time ago. There the contract provided: The management reserves the right in its discretion to grant a leave of absence to any employee presenting a good reason for same.
>
> The company involved did light manufacturing, employing married women. For years, and without question, the company had granted maternity leave without any loss of seniority. Suddenly it announced a new policy—no more maternity leaves, that those who left to give birth would readily be re-employed, but only as new employees with, of course, loss of seniority on vacations, sick leave, furlough, etc.
>
> At the hearing, the employer offered no reason whatsoever for the change in policy. It stood fast on management's reserved right to grant or deny a leave of absence.

---

[13] Phelps, "Management's Reserved Rights: An Industry View," *Management Rights and the Arbitration Process* (Washington: BNA Incorporated, 1956), pp. 110-113.

It was my determination that, while the company had the right to grant or deny a leave of absence, still that right had to be exercised in good faith and not arbitrarily or capriciously. I said: It is my judgment that the Company, upon receipt of a request for a leave of absence, must weigh each request and exercise its discretion fairly and equitably to the end that justice is done not only so far as its own interests are concerned, but also with due regard to the interests of the employee involved. Concededly that was not done here.[14]

The fallacy in Mr. Wolff's statement is apparent in reading it. "Discretion" means, according to the dictionary, the "power of free decision; individual judgment; undirected choice." Obviously, the employer discontinued maternity leaves because "in its discretion" it had determined they interfered (as they often do) with efficiency in scheduling and assigning the work force. Maternity leave rights are common in contracts covering women workers. Mr. Wolff, who believes that to discourage the normal function of womanhood is contrary to public policy, read the quoted phrase as meaning "in the discretion of an arbitrator." In doing so, he changed the language of the contract in order to achieve what he believed a humane result.

Judgment and discretion must be used in almost all administrative decisions and since management has the responsibility to initiate action, it must be accorded the authority to make decisions. As many arbitrators have seen, it is not the arbitrator's function to review these decisions on the basis of his own judgment as to what is reasonable or unreasonable.[15]

(d) Past Practice

Finally, there is the matter of plant practice as, by implication, a part of the agreement the same as if it were expressly incorporated in it. Before going to this subject, it may be well to look at the conspicuous case in the steel industry of the express adoption of prior practices. As R. Conrad Cooper's speech, quoted in Chapter I,[16] demonstrated, this has been a major problem in the

---

[14] Wolff, "Discussion," *Management Rights and the Arbitration Process, op. cit.* at pp. 132-133. The case referred to is *Gem Electric Mfg. Co., Inc.*, Wolff, 11 LA 684 (1948).
[15] See "Managerial Discretion," Chapter 5, p. 102.
[16] See pp. 9-10.

industry. Pertinent to our discussion here, the contract reads as follows:

B. *Local Working Conditions*

3.[12] Should there be any local working conditions in effect which provide benefits that are in excess of or in addition to the benefits established by this Agreement, they shall remain in effect for the term of this Agreement, except as they are changed or eliminated by mutual agreement or in accordance with Paragraph 4 below.

4.[13] The Company shall have the right to change or eliminate any local working condition if, as the result of action taken by Management under Section 3—Management, the basis for the existence of the local working condition is changed or eliminated, thereby making it unnecessary to continue such local working conditions; provided, however, that when such a change or elimination is made by the Company any affected employee shall have recourse to the grievance procedure and arbitration, if necessary, to have the Company justify its action.[17]

The United States Steel Corporation filed a brief in 1952 with the Wage Stabilization Board in which it was said that these provisions have been:

. . . the main taproot through which is fed a large growth of misunderstanding and confusion. They encourage the restrictive, technical attitudes which both the Company and the Union deplore. The grievance and arbitration procedures are clogged up and bogged down largely because of the misunderstanding and confusion created by these provisions.

. . . This lack of mutual understanding is especially glaring as to cases where (a) Union representatives allege "local working conditions" which it is clear no one ever intended to "establish," and (b) Union representatives allege the existence of "local working conditions" which, if recognized, would nullify or substantially impair the understandings specified in provisions of other sections of the Agreement when the latter provisions constitute the policy mutually intended to govern. The volume of grievances and the difficulties encountered in arbitration makes self-evident the fact that the parties do not have a meeting of the minds. . . .

. . . bitter and sterile controversy has been caused in those areas by the "local working conditions" provisions. . . .

. . . There just is no sense to negotiating 17 other sections of an Agreement if one of the parties persists in trying to nullify such

---

[17] United States Steel contract, II, B, BNA, *Collective Bargaining Negotiations and Contracts,* p. 22:144 (June 22, 1962).

understandings by contentions made under a general provision called "local working conditions.". . .

The "local working conditions" provisions have been used in attempts to establish conditions of employment which there never was any mutual intent, nationally or locally, to establish.

. . . the great many grievances collectively constitute a massive attack, based on the "local working conditions" provisions, upon the right and responsibility of Management to organize the work and direct its performance by employees.[18]

These remarks demonstrate how difficulties are created by the growth of practices if the union can insist successfully that the employer is bound by them. They provide a perfect illustration of the necessity for management to avoid the incorporation of plant practice in the agreement by implication.

Some writers have talked of plant practice in the language of implied terms or conditions.[19] Others, and this includes Justice Douglas in the Warrior case, have referred to it simply as part of the agreement. The role of plant practice in the interpretation of the agreement and in filling in areas as to which the agreement contains only general language is important and will be examined in the next chapter. Here we deal only with the question of whether plant practice is binding upon the parties the same as if expressed in the agreement. The idea that it is was given some early support by Cox and Dunlop when they wrote:

. . . a collective bargaining agreement should be deemed, unless a contrary intention is manifest, to carry forward for its term the major terms and conditions of employment, not covered by the agreement, which prevailed when the agreement was executed.[20]

Archibald Cox has more recently suggested that the " 'amorphous methods, attitudes, fears and problems;' 'the mass of unstated assumptions and practices as to which the understanding of the parties may actually differ:' are not only the background of the agreement, but the flesh and blood which give it meaning." [21]

---

[18] National Wage Stabilization Board Brief (1952), quoted in Herbert Leibenson, "Research Memorandum, National Small Business Men's Association," BNA, *Daily Labor Report*, No. 210 (1957): p. BB-1 (Oct. 27).

[19] See Wallen, "The Silent Contract vs. Express Provisions: The Arbitration of Local Working Conditions," *Collective Bargaining and the Arbitrator's Role* (Washington: BNA Incorporated, 1962), p. 117.

[20] Cox and Dunlop, "The Duty to Bargain Collectively During the Term of an Existing Agreement," 63 *Harvard Law Review* 1097 at 1116 (1950).

[21] Cox quoting Harry Shulman in "Reflections Upon Labor Arbitration," 72 *Harvard Law Review* 1482 at 1492.

I do not mean to misquote Mr. Cox. The early statement as to the carrying for-

Now if a method is amorphous, it is by definition shapeless and without form. Contracts are not made of such stuff, nor of attitudes, fears, problems, nor unstated assumption on which the understanding of the parties differ. What lies in the back of every newly unionized plant is an unorganized community, subject to no law except the day-to-day determinations of the management. The arrangements between the worker and the employer are obscure; their contract simply is one under which the worker agrees to do the job and the employer agrees to pay him for doing it. Most of the job characteristics are left undefined. There is no understanding or assumption that they will not change. Consequently, no practice survives the execution of the agreement as a binding promise; what survives is the employer's right to deal with his employees as he sees fit except as the agreement limits that right.

Of course, when the contract is executed, practice may ripen into agreement by mutual consent, oral or written. Dr. Shulman pointed out the distinction between such oral agreements and the common run of plant practices in the best discussion of plant practice yet written:

> A practice, whether or not fully stated in writing, may be the result of an agreement or mutual understanding. And in some industries there are contractual provisions requiring the continuance of unnamed practices in existence at the execution of the collective agreement. (There are no such provisions in the Ford Agreement or in those of the automobile industry generally.) A practice thus based on mutual agreement may be subject to change only by mutual agreement. Its binding quality is due, however, not to the fact that it is past practice but rather to the agreement in which it is based.

> But there are other practices which are not the result of joint determination at all. They may be mere happenstance, that is, methods that developed without design or deliberation. Or they may be choices by Management in the exercise of managerial discretion as to the convenient methods at the time. In such cases there is no thought of obligation or commitment for the future. Such practices are merely present ways, not prescribed ways, of doing things. The relevant item of significance is not the nature

---

ward of the "major terms and conditions of employment" was made in a different context and applied primarily to wages, pensions, and similar benefits established by the employer before collective bargaining. The second quotation applies only to matters of joint concern under the contract. As I have already pointed out, Cox agrees that the parties are free to draw the line as they choose between matters of joint concern and those reserved to the exclusive determination of the employer.

of the particular method but the managerial freedom with respect to it. Being the product of managerial determination in its permitted discretion, such practices are, in the absence of contractual provision to the contrary, subject to change in the same discretion. The law and the policy of collective bargaining may well require that the employer inform the Union and that he be ready to discuss the matter with it on request. But there is no requirement of mutual agreement as a condition precedent to a change of a practice of this character.

A contrary holding would place past practice on a par with written agreement and create the anomaly that, while the parties expend great energy and time in negotiating the details of the Agreement, they unknowingly and unintentionally commit themselves to unstated and perhaps more important matters which in the future may be found to have been past practice. The contrary holding would also raise other questions very difficult to answer. For example, what is properly a subject of practice? Would the long time use of a wheel barrow become a practice not to be changed by the substitution of four-wheeled buggies drawn by a tow tractor? Or would the long time use of single drill presses be a practice prohibiting the introduction of multiple drill presses? Such restraints on technological change are alien to the automobile industry. Yet such might be the restraints, if past practice were enshrined without carefully thought out and articulated limitations. Again, when is a practice? How frequently and over how long a period must something be done before it is to be called a practice with the consequences claimed? And how is the existence of the past practice to be determined in the light of the very conflicting testimony that is common in such cases? The union's witnesses remember only the occasions on which the work was done in the manner they urge. Supervision remembers the occasions on which the work was done otherwise. Each remembers details the other does not; each is surprised at the other's perversity; and both forget or omit important circumstances. Rarely is alleged past practice clear, detailed and undisputed; commonly, inquiry into past practice of the type that is not the result of joint determination or agreement produces immersion in a bog of contradictions, fragments, doubts, and one-sided views. All this is not to say that past practice may not be important and even decisive in applying provisions of the Agreement. The discussion is addressed to the different claim that, apart from any basis in the Agreement, a method of operation or assignment employed in the past may not be changed except by mutual agreement.[22]

If, for example, the contract is silent as to the division of overtime, and the union and the foreman in a department agree in

---

[22] *Ford Motor Company*, Shulman, 19 LA 237 at 241 (1952). See also *Wyandotte Chemicals Corp.*, Mittenthal, 39 LA 65 (1962).

writing that "overtime shall be divided in X department as equally as possible by classification in the skilled trades and on a departmental basis as to production employees," an agreement has been made. If the same arrangement is clearly made by oral agreement, it is binding. And under certain circumstances, the agreement may be established by proof of facts sufficient to justify the inference that the agreement exists.

Clearly this is not a matter of implied obligations, nor does it lie in the realm of "industrial common law." It is a matter of the intent of the parties, established by proof sufficient to convince the trier of the facts (normally an arbitrator). Where a practice lies in the area of managerial discretion, where it represents nothing more than the exercise of management's right to act unilaterally, it is not a binding and enforceable obligation. It can be changed by management in the exercise of the same right.

Approaching the question somewhat differently, the Elkouris, in their study of the subject, support the principle that plant practice must bow to the right of management to act within its legitimate sphere of responsibility. Drawing a distinction between employee benefits customarily granted to employees even though the contract contains no mention of them and working conditions involving methods of operation and the direction of the working forces, they state:

> We have noted that where custom has been enforced the element of "mutuality" has usually been supplied by implication—that is, there has been "implied mutual agreement." In this regard, existing employee benefits usually affect all or at least sizeable groups of employees, and thus are likely to be in the thoughts of union and company negotiators. It may reasonably be assumed that the parties in shaping bargaining demands as to wages and other employee benefits do so with silent recognition of existing unwritten benefits and favorable working conditions. This accepted, such matters may well be called "major" (for those who would apply a "major-minor" test).
>
> It may be less plausible to assume that such bargaining demands are shaped with any comparable silent thought as to existing practices regarding methods of operation and direction of the working force—matters legitimately falling within the fundamental areas of basic management responsibility.
>
> In the final analysis, management in most cases is not really oppressed when it is required to continue customary benefits for the remainder of the contract term. Management itself, either

unilaterally or by mutual decision, initially agreed to grant the benefits in most cases. In negotiating the collective bargaining agreement management, because of existing benefits, may very well have been faced with tempered wage demands by the employees. On the other hand, in most instances, it does not oppress the employees to deny continuance of established methods of operation or established practice regarding direction of the working force. Management freedom of action in the latter matters, though sometimes considered unjustified by the frequently few workers directly affected, is essential for efficient and progressive operation of the enterprise, and this serves the long-run interests of all the employees as well as management.

The above discussion suggests a test of "employee benefits" vs. "basic management functions," with which test many reported arbitration awards are compatible. Moreover, some of the awards which appear at first glance to be contrary to this test may conform to it upon closer analysis, the award being based in fact upon some clause of the written contract. The test gives the employees the benefit of the doubt as to certain matters and management is given the benefit of the doubt as to others. From this standpoint, too, the test may be deemed "fair" or "just." [23]

Management should realize nevertheless that its rights can be limited by repeated actions and discussions on a subject, even though the right in question is not limited in the agreement. The employer should avoid tying his hands unnecessarily and instead reserve his power to exercise unilateral control over management functions and his right to exercise judgment and discretion in their application. Union invasion of management rights actually results more from management's neglect of its own responsibilities than from conscious intention by the unions to control management action. Joint determination by plant practice is in many cases the end result of management's own failure to assert its own affirmative right to act, to exercise its power of administrative initiative.

This means a careful schooling of plant management at all levels, down to the least of the foremen, to avoid commitments which can be construed as binding obligations. This, we may add parenthetically, is equally as applicable to practices under ambiguous or general language in the agreement as it is to areas in which the agreement is silent. Supervisors should be instructed not to make "deals" as to the distribution and assignment of work, as to crew sizes and individual output, as to rest periods and coffee breaks,

---

[23] Elkouri and Elkouri, *How Arbitration Works* (Washington: BNA Incorporated, 1960), p. 274. See also *Union Asbestos & Rubber Co.*, Volz, 39 LA 72 (1962).

and other ordinary shop practices. Unless the contract restricts them, they should make it clear that these matters are theirs to decide. In settling grievances, and especially in written replies, the supervisor's statement should be applicable only to the facts of that grievance, not generally or applicable to the future. Every settlement of a general nature, such as one giving all the overtime work on a particular job to a certain group of employees, or a statement that certain operations fall within one classification rather than another, should provide a means for termination and contain clearly qualifying phrases, thus: ". . . as the job is being performed today . . .;" ". . . under the present method . . .;" ". . . until this situation is cleared up . . .;" ". . . as long as it is practical . . .;" or ". . . if the employee is capable of doing the job. . . ."

Lest I be thought, in recommending this cautious and reserved approach, to encourage a technical and legalistic attitude, I hasten to point out that in 1952, in its brief filed with the Wage Stabilization Board, the United States Steel Corporation made this statement:

> Faced with a constant abuse by the Union of the "local working conditions" provision in contentions which would destroy managerial discretion, apparently a Company representative can safely protect managerial discretion only by carrying a large sign with him every day as he goes about his work, reading:
> "This is notice to all employees, Union representatives, and whomsoever else it may concern, that in any action I take today or any action I do not take, I am exercising the discretion which my Management status requires. I am not reflecting any intention to establish a local working condition, a local agreement, a local custom or practice, or a pattern of action which can hereafter be pointed to as evidence of the establishment of a condition of employment by which my discretion would be destroyed, and I specifically reserve my authority to hereafter exercise managerial discretion in some way other than that I may follow today." [24]

Assuming a binding practice exists, can it be changed? Perhaps the best answer to this question is: "You will never know until you try." But another answer is possible. Even under the "local

---

[24] United States Steel Corporation, National Wage Stabilization Board Brief (1952), quoted in Herbert Leibenson, "Research Memorandum, National Small Business Men's Association," BNA, *Daily Labor Report,* No. 210 (1957): p. BB-1 (Oct. 27).

working conditions" clauses in the steel industry, management has the right to abandon a practice when the circumstances underlying the practice have changed. In other words, practices are subject to the right of industry to make changes and improvements in technology and in methods. Implied restrictions upon management's right to alter job assignments, to combine, split and create new classifications, and otherwise to change the distribution and scheduling of work should not be favored when they fall in the wake of a genuine change in the underlying physical conditions of the operation.

This, I think, is implied when the practice is created. The parties, by long acquiescence, agree that it shall continue, but its consensual basis includes the circumstances which underlay it at the time of its birth. When these change, and management's right to change them is admitted in most cases, the practice should give way also, not stand as a barrier to full realization of the benefits of the change.

In some cases, a practice which hampers efficient operation may have to be changed in the course of bargaining, perhaps at grievance meetings in which settlements and concessions are made in return for the consent of the union to the elimination, perhaps gradually, of the cumbersome practice. A change in contract language when the agreement is open for negotiation may accomplish the same result, but, as we all know, in the pressure which surrounds economic negotiations, changes in contract language are apt to lose their importance and be dropped in the last minute rush to avoid a strike.

It should be obvious that the importation of implied conditions into an agreement is a procedure fraught with danger for the employer. In all the ways open to him, whether in negotiation, in grievance meetings and grievance settlements, or otherwise, he should make every attempt to eliminate restrictions which arise merely through practice or by implication upon his right to operate effectively. He must make every effort to effectively preserve his right to exercise managerial discretion.

Chapter 4

PLANT PRACTICE AND THE INTERPRETATION OF THE AGREEMENT

In Chapter 3 we looked at plant practice as modifying or supplementing the written agreement, concluding that if it was to be given such effect its source must be found in the intentions of the parties. As an aid to discovering the meaning of contract language which is ambiguous or obscure, or as the means by which the implementation of general language is accomplished, the role of practice (though not necessarily the proof required to establish it) is quite different.

Here we must take into account that the labor agreement is regarded as a constitution, the view which has now been adopted, in the Warrior case, by the United States Supreme Court. We are dealing with matters brought wholly or partially, even if obscurely, within the area of joint control, the ultimate decision resting in most cases with an arbitrator. As the previous chapter demonstrates, limitations on the management function, that is, the rights of the union and of the employees, can be specific, or they can be more or less general, erecting a standard which management is free to fill in by policy and practice, so long as the command of the general standard is observed. These are the areas in which management has reluctantly or otherwise in the process of bargaining consented to share its authority with the union and the employees. It is here, and in cases in which the language of the agreement is ambiguous or conflicting, that the "industrial common law" operates. These are the areas in which interpretation is required.

For our purpose, the construction of intelligent management policy, the important thing to remember is that practice is frequently the determining element in interpretation. The use of practice as a criterion to determine the propriety of the actions of both parties under the agreement is so universal that it has gone largely unchallenged. Both unions and employers, acting only with one situation or one set of facts before them, have used plant practice whenever it appeared to support their position with little heed to the effect of its adoption as a rule of thumb upon other situations or other relationships under the agreement.

Not infrequently, such uncritical acceptance of plant practice has been unfortunate; it tends to diminish the area of managerial discretion. If management permits its rights to go unexercised through mere default, practice is the chief medium by which the gaps will be filled. If management, for example, fails to provide a set of sound criteria and principles for the making of promotions, practices will evolve, perhaps bad ones, and varying from one department to the next, as promotions are made in individual cases by supervisors until an accumulated body of precedent is established. If no reliable procedure is established for the determination of production standards and for their revision when needed, the supervisor may, with the consent of the union steward, permit habits and customs to become embedded which resist improvement. Whenever it is necessary to determine job content, practice is the main criterion, unless written job descriptions exist—and even then practice usually determines what comes within the "edges" of the classifications. This may occur if the question arises of reclassifying employees because they are doing the work of another classification. Practice is most important in determining whether work has been properly assigned under clauses stating that work which is "normal" or "peculiar" to a classification shall be performed only by its members.

Revocations or modifications of penalties imposed in disciplinary cases because they are not in accord with past practice are legion. In fact, in almost every case where the agreement covers a particular subject but does not speak so clearly and definitely that no room is left for construction, past practice assumes a critical and frequently decisive role in determining how the provisions in question shall be applied.

We can now approach the problem of what proof is required to establish practice as a criterion for implementation of the agreement. As we have already indicated, in discussing the role of plant practice as the equal of the written agreement, practice must be more than "amorphous methods" and "unstated assumptions." This is equally true if practice is relied on as the test of interpretation in an area where the agreement speaks, but only generally or with a lack of clarity. The practice which is casual or fortuitous, as to which the parties disagree, and as to which convincing proof is lacking, is not a reliable guide to interpretation. Richard Mittenthal puts the matter in these terms:

> To allege the existence of a practice is one thing; to prove it is quite another. The allegation is a common one. But my experience indicates that where practice is disputed, the party relying upon the practice is often unable to establish it. This is not surprising. For the arbitrator in such a dispute is likely to find himself confronted by irreconcilable claims, sharply conflicting testimony, and incomplete information.

> * * * *

> The arbitrator, abandoned in this kind of maze, is almost certain to decide the grievance on some basis other than past practice. The only means of resolving the confusion, short of credibility findings, is through written records of the disputed events. Such records may be the best possible evidence of what took place in the past. Unfortunately, records of scheduling, work assignments, etc. are seldom maintained for any length of time. And even when available, they may be incomplete or it may be difficult and costly to reduce them to some meaningful form. Considering these problems, it is understandable that practices are most often held to exist where the parties are in substantial agreement as to what the established course of conduct has been.[1]

In short, to be truly authoritative, practice must be based on common understanding though it is shown by the negative fact of acquiescence. Knowledge and acceptance are essential elements, as they are in all contractual relationships, even though they are established by inference from the facts.

Practices which are, in Shulman's language, "choices by management in the exercise of managerial discretion" may be changed in the same discretion. Management is not bound to apply a practice in one plant or department however clearly established in another. Likewise, it is not bound to carry over a practice from one contractual relationship to another. A practice of awarding certain work to one classification for overtime purposes would not necessarily bind the company to so award it during the regular workweek. Under a loosely-worded seniority and ability clause, a practice for the determination of the requisite ability in cases of

---

[1] Mittenthal, "Past Practice and the Administration of Collective Bargaining Agreements," *Arbitration and Public Policy* (Washington: BNA Incorporated, 1961), p. 35.

layoffs and recall would not necessarily apply to choices for promotion.

It is worth repeating here that management should realize that its rights can be diluted and lost by repeated discussions with union representatives, by the issuance of notices, memoranda and written or oral instructions, and by grievance settlements. As I have said, the answer to a grievance may constitute a binding agreement. It may also establish a controlling interpretation, if it commits management to a continuing course of action. The foreman should be trained in methods of answering grievances so as to settle only the problem before him, and to indicate that fact by stating that the disposition may not apply under other conditions in the future. Management should avoid tying its hands wherever it can, and instead reserve its power to exercise unilateral functions and discretion in the application in all cases in which the agreement does not expressly confine the scope of managerial authority and discretion. It must be constantly alert to the growth of practices under the agreement. It must endeavor to establish good ones, to prevent the growth of bad ones, and when these are discovered, to change them if possible. There are sound criteria for the exercise of the management function in these areas in which the agreement itself does not speak decisively, which will be described in the next chapter. They should be actively and continually employed to improve labor administration.

Practice is perhaps the chief instrument of interpretation, but not the only one. Next in importance are precontract negotiations. The meaning of an ambiguous phrase will be given the intent displayed by the parties at the time the phrase was considered and adopted by them. Hence the importance of good records of meetings, and their preservation in the form of written offers, compromises, discussions, and written minutes.

There are other rules of construction, taken largely from those followed by our courts in construing contracts. Thus any doubt as to the meaning of words and phrases may be explained by reference to other words and phrases. All clauses of an agreement are to be interpreted with each other, giving each the sense that results from the entire agreement. The agreement will be construed in such a way as to avoid nullifying any of its provisions. An agreement will be given such an interpretation as is consonant with law; if an interpretation would result in violating the provisions of a statute, the contrary interpretation will be preferred. Ordinary words will be given their ordinary meanings, and trade or technical expressions their meanings in the trade, unless a different meaning is established. Specific language will prevail over general statements, as will provisos or exceptions to the general rule under the legal maxim *expressio unius est exclusio alterius* ("to express one thing is to exclude others").

These canons of interpretation, developed over the years in litigation, are not very helpful, except perhaps in arbitration. Practically, the accretions built up by the parties themselves in the form of plant practices, grievance settlements, and proposals in negotiations have the greatest weight in ascertaining their intent. Again, it is necessary to stress that management should look upon its actions and statements with care, since they are the best evidence of its construction of its rights and duties under the agreement.

When we turn to the meaning of the terms and phrases commonly employed in agreements, we find that there has been a great neglect of definition. Hence a great deal of controversy arises over the meaning of words and clauses, which the union has taken to mean one thing and the employer another. Such terms as "schedule," "assign," "transfer," "promote," "demote," "layoff," "temporary" and "permanent," "vacancy," "new job," "emergency," "reasons beyond the control of," "possible," "practicable," "legitimate," "justifiable," and "termination" are used loosely, and sometimes contradictorily, in many agreements. It would be well if their use in everyday operations could be analyzed and meanings established as to what action they permit or do not permit. If definitions can be agreed upon with the union, so much the better. But even unilateral definition for the benefit of supervision can be helpful in avoiding disputes and preserving essential management rights.

To illustrate, what does the word "transfer" cover, and how is it distinguished from "assignment" and from "promotion" and "demotion"? First, it must be realized that there is a difference between transfers made because of a reduction of force, and those dictated by operating considerations or as a result of employee choice. A layoff connotes release of an employee following a reduction in force because he is not needed where he is, and a transfer or "bump" following a layoff should be carefully distinguished from one dictated by the fact that the employee is needed in the unit to which he is sent, or a transfer made to satisfy his own wishes. A transfer of the first kind may be mandatory under the seniority provisions whereas the second type may be within the province of management, with due regard for the rights of the employee. A transfer of the second type may require a change in rate, if it is temporary; if it is permanent, it may involve the question of whether it is a promotion or a demotion with the result that the employer's right to make the transfer is limited by the agreement. The word "transfer" might be reserved for changes which involve record-keeping, and the word "assign" used to cover temporary and incidental work assignments, within or between classifications and departments, which do not involve changes in rates, seniority rights, or other "recorded" changes. Similarly, the distinction between temporary transfers, which are usually for short or pre-determined periods, and permanent transfers which are for indefinite duration, should be noted and preserved, and the effect of each on rates and seniority status made clear. "New jobs" are created by changes in techniques, new production items, or other situations in which employees have not been previously engaged, whereas "vacancies" are due to quit, discharge, or permanent transfers out of classification, and the like.

All the above terms concern intraplant (or interplant) movements of employees and of work. A constructive program of administration under the agreement requires their definition, a diagram of each type of movement, and a list of the criteria, whether required by the agreement or by good plant policy and procedure, which govern and the results which follow each one. The supervisor should not be left to guess whether the particular situation calls for application of seniority preference, is one falling within his discretion, or whether the employee's wishes in the matter are controlling. An appropriate system of records should be devised and installed so that the position each employee occupies at any given time and its results on his status and pay are clear.

Such phrases as "conditions beyond the control of the employer," "emergency," and "practicable," likewise require careful definition. "Emergency" has been defined as "an unforeseen combination of circumstances which call for immediate action." This might not apply, for example, to a failure of material to arrive, when the supervisor should have known that it had not been shipped or could have provided material to take its place. A machine breakdown, which could have been avoided by preventive maintenance, will not be regarded by the union as a "condition beyond the control of the employer." "Practicable" has been said not to include considerations of overtime cost or mere convenience, but does include scheduling difficulties, skill requirements, and similar operating conditions.

Another area in which confusion should be avoided is that of the status of inactive employees. Delineation of the right of the employer to terminate seniority should be marked out carefully and the effect of leave of absence and layoff status reconciled with it, so that at any given time the seniority and "fringe benefit" rights of each employee are readily ascertainable. Frequently, an employee is marked "quit" when he thinks he is on layoff or leave of absence status. The consequences of depriving an employee of his insurance benefits improperly can be serious. On the other side, insurance is sometimes continued through inattention when it should be cancelled.

The point of all this is not that rules of interpretation or definition of terms are important but rather that reliable guides to administration should be devised and promulgated for the benefit of all concerned. Supervision needs, among other things, to know the practical meanings and application of the terms of the agreement. To a supervisor in a public utility, "emergency" means a customer without service; the union says it means a sleet storm when the lines are down. "Available employee" to the supervisor means one at hand; to the union, it means one sitting in his home, ten miles away, who would be willing to come in if called. "Fair day's work" to a supervisor means eight hours of work; to the union it means whatever the employees have been doing, including informal "breaks" for coffee, smoking, wash-up, etc. Words are a frequent source of uncertainty and dispute on the factory floor.

CHAPTER 5

DEVELOPING MANAGEMENT POLICY

Top management develops basic labor policy, whatever it is and however unconscious and unstudied it may be. It can range from the fiercest hostility to unionism to the placid accommodation of deals made over luncheon tables between corporation and union vice-presidents. It can embrace acceptance of the union as the exclusive spokesman for the workers under contract, or it can be a two-sided policy which also courts the good will of the employees. The General Electric Company, for example, has for years made its views on labor-management problems known to its union employees, and other corporations in recent years have followed its example.

Policies may differ between divisions of the company and between plants. A plant which has been organized for years by a sober and responsible union may require quite different policies than one newly organized by a militant union. A company may adopt a policy of keeping plants well separated, even taking strikes to prevent the imposition of a master contract on its operations. Many companies deal, quietly and satisfactorily, with a union in one plant, fight the union tooth and nail in another, and, in a third, exert every lawful effort to keep the employees non-union. Policy need not be uniform between plants and must never be static, since its validity and applicability cannot be separated from the conditions actually in existence in the plant.

Management Initiative and the Grievance Procedure

The construction of policies in a union plant requires the recognition and use of two concepts. One is the legal relationship we have already discussed at length: the premise that the management function and management rights are the reservoir from which union and employee rights are taken. It would be possible, especially in a larger company with many arbitration decisions, to construct a diagram showing how the reserved right of management to operate its plants and to direct the working forces interlocks with the express and implied restrictions upon that right established by the union agreement. The second concept is the procedural system established by the labor agreement.

As an instrument of government, the agreement provides its own means of interpretation and enforcement through the grievance procedure and arbitration. In practically all cases, this machinery is put in motion by employer action, that is, by the exercise of administrative initiative. Management initiative is the force which activates the substantive rights of the parties. Its exercise calls, in cases in which the union or the employees think the agreement has been violated, for the filing and processing of a grievance. These two procedural forces, management's initial action and the union's reaction through the grievance procedure, are the machinery through which the enterprise is governed and rights are determined. They make the agreement work.

One exception to this is the occasional provision that before management can act, the consent of the union must be obtained. Another partial exception is a provision that before the employer acts, he must "consult" with the union or give it notice of his intention to act.

"Mutual consent" clauses can be found in some agreements. They, for example, permit a change in the regular working schedules only with the consent of the union or, sometimes, the employees affected. It is perhaps provided that ability, as a criterion in layoffs or transfers, is to be determined by the employer and the shop committee. The reduction of the workweek, perhaps to 32 hours instead of 40, can be accomplished sometimes only by agreement. Management advisers view these clauses with disapproval, since they give the union a veto power over action vital to management. A pamphlet published by the National Association of Manufacturers [1] cites two cases as examples. In one of them, union consent was required before discipline could be imposed, and the result was flagrant disregard of the company's rules of conduct. In the second, changes in existing jobs were prevented until the union agreed on the new rate to be paid.

---

[1] *Should Labor Be Given a Direct Share in the Management of Industry?* (New York: National Asociation of Manufacturers, 1946), pp. 11-12.

Discussion of the new rate, it was claimed, would go on for weeks, and the employee earned average rates but stopped work during that period.

It may be asked: "Do mutual consent clauses actually block unilateral management action?" May management act, leaving the question of whether the union should have consented to resolution through the grievance procedure? A decision by Harry Platt in a case involving the L. A. Young Spring and Wire Company [2] has indicated that a "mutual consent" clause will not be enforced when the union's consent is "unreasonably withheld." The contract in that case provided that work could be let outside if the plant lacked the equipment to do the work, "with the consent of the Chief Steward." The Chief Steward withheld his consent; the company sent the work out regardless, and its action was sustained. This view would seem to be supported by the fact that, in most cases, the employees would be made whole through the grievance procedure. In a troublesome case, the union might take the position that it had the right to strike. But the very purpose of the grievance procedure is to permit production to go on despite violations of the agreement. And "no-strike" clauses do not ordinarily exempt "mutual consent" clauses from their operation. However, failure to obtain the union's consent to a proposed action may mean an award of back pay.

A mutual consent clause which gives management more latitude than it would otherwise have is harmless. If, for example, the company may lay off employees without regard to seniority for short periods, such as five or ten working days, it does not restrict the company to include a provision that the period may be extended with the consent of the union. Other clauses which require mutual consent are not important restrictions upon management rights, such as those providing for the granting of leaves of absence with the consent of both the company and the union. In such a case, no management action is held up pending the union's consent.

As I indicated in the first chapter, there are advocates of advance consultation with unions, especially on changes which may affect

---

[2] *L. A. Young Spring and Wire Corp.*, Platt, 23 LA 400 (1954). In the typical case, employer will be held in violation of the agreement if he fails to secure the union's consent to a proposed action and back pay may be awarded, *Kennecott Copper Corp.*, Ross, Chairman, 32 LA 300.

the workers to their detriment. Some contracts require consultation on such matters as revisions of the working schedules, reductions of the workweek, and the displacement of workers through organizational or technological changes. Others require advance notice merely without a requirement of discussion. An arbitrary disregard of these provisions would of course create resentment, and possibly result in reversal of the management action taken on the ground that a necessary condition precedent to action was full discussion, even though "agreement" was not required. "Consultation" implies more than a gesture toward the union; it calls for sincere discussion with all the pertinent facts revealed, just as does collective bargaining "in good faith." Thus, if consultation is to be more than a mere matter of form it requires time. An action which may be more or less urgent may be delayed. From this, it is but a step to "stalling" on the part of the union with resultant frustration of the management objective. As I said in the first chapter, repeated "consultation" may soon lead, especially in view of the strong force of "established plant practice," to a situation in which agreement is in fact required. Full and free discussion of a subject may develop a tacit understanding that union objections to proposed management action are sufficient to block its execution.

On the other hand, there is a good case to be made for advance notice and consultation, especially in cases in which union cooperation is necessary to full accomplishment of the management objective, and where the union officials are responsible and interested in measures to promote good management and company success. Its supporters call it a "mature" technique. This is especially true where the more sophisticated international representative can be relied upon to "sell" improved technology or methods to rank and file members who might otherwise be antagonistic to change.

The "Human Relations Research Committee," established in 1959 in the steel industry, undertook to study, through subcommittees, such subjects as grievance procedure improvements, seniority difficulties, revision of the job classification systems, medical care and insurance, and others. These subcommittees, working at the local level and out of the spotlight, made a real contribution to the 1962 settlement, working out many problems in a manner acceptable to the companies and with cognizance of the concerns of the employees.

It must be remembered, as we have observed, that the short-run interests of the membership are apt to loom overwhelmingly in the minds of even the most far-sighted union officials, who are primarily politicians and not administrators of the economic system. Management planning, which in the long run is beneficial to the entire enterprise and the employees as a group, may be immediately detrimental to specific groups with their special classification and seniority rights under the agreement. A man faced with dilution of his own employment advantages is apt to care little about improvement of others, perhaps persons who have yet to be hired, and even less about long-term benefits to the company and the economy. The same is true of action which affects the "institutional" interests of the union and its representatives.

A few arbitrators have taken the view in scattered cases that discussion is required before certain unilateral changes can be made, even though agreement is not necessary. It is difficult to see how an arbitrator, acting under the ordinary clause which gives him only the power to interpret and apply the agreement, could imply such a requirement in a contract which made no mention of it. Moreover, such a requirement if commonly adopted by arbitrators might hamper the effective discharge of management responsibilities through delay. It could provoke discontent and difficulty instead of avoiding it, since the discussions would sometimes produce resentment and the belief among workers that management was acting in an arbitrary and callous fashion. If the discussions reached a stalemate and management attempted to carry its decision into effect, the employees, instead of cooperating, might do their best to nullify the change and the improvement sought by the company.

But mutual consent clauses and those requiring prior consultation are exceptional. In most cases, management simply acts unilaterally with notice to the union only when the action is actually under way or shortly before it is taken. This, as I have suggested, is the basic procedural step which results in the filing and processing of grievances.

Observance of this procedure by the union and the employees is of paramount importance in the administration of labor agreements. If the employees can disobey the orders of supervisors, or take direct action to resist managerial decisions, the procedural system established by the contract becomes meaningless, and the contract actually has no real force or effect. In one of his Ford opinions, Harry Shulman summed up the matter this way:

> Some men apparently think that when a violation of contract seems clear, the employee may refuse to obey and thus resort to self-help rather than the grievance procedure. That is an erroneous point of view. In the first place, what appears to one party to be a clear violation may not seem so at all to the other party. Neither party can be the final judge as to whether the Contract has been violated. The determination of that issue rests in collective negotiation through the grievance procedure. But in the second place, and more important the grievance procedure is prescribed in the Contract precisely because the parties anticipated that there would be claims of violations which would require adjustment. That procedure is prescribed for all grievances, not merely for doubtful ones. Nothing in the Contract even suggests the idea that only doubtful violations need be processed through the grievance procedure and that clear violations can be resisted through individual self-help. The only difference between a "clear" violation and a "doubtful" one is that the former makes a clear grievance and the latter a doubtful one. But both must be handled in the regular prescribed manner.

> Some men apparently think also that the problems here involved are evils incident to private profit enterprise. That, too, is a totally mistaken view, as a moment's reflection will show. The problems of adjustment with which we are concerned under the Contract are problems which arise and require adjustment in the management of an enterprise under any form of economic or social organization. Any enterprise—whether it be a privately owned plant, a governmentally operated unit, a consumer's co-operative, a social club, or a trade union—any enterprise in a capitalist or socialist economy, requires persons with authority and responsibility to keep the enterprise running. In any such enterprise there is need for equality of treatment, regularity of procedure, and adjustment of conflicting claims of individuals. In any industrial plant, whatever may be the form of the political or economic organization in which it exists, problems are bound to arise as to the method of making promotions, the assignment of tasks to individuals, the choice of shifts, the maintenance of discipline, the rates of production and remuneration, and the various other matters which are handled through the grievance procedure.

> These are not incidents peculiar to private enterprise. They are incidents of human organization in any form of society. On a lesser scale, similar problems exist in every family: who shall do the dishes, who shall mow the lawn, where to go on a Sunday, what movie to see, what is a reasonable spending allowance for husband or daughter, how much to pay for a new hat, and so on.

The operation of the Union itself presents problems requiring adjustment quite similar to those involved in the operation of the Company—problems not only in the relations of the Union to its own employees but also in the relations between the members of the Union. Anyone familiar with seniority problems knows that the conflict of desires within the Union are quite comparable to those between the Union and the Company. And any active member of Local 600 knows that the frictions and conflicts within a large Union may be as numerous and difficult as those between the Union and the Company. Such "disputes" are not necessarily evils. They are the normal characteristics of human society which both arise from, and create the occasion for, the exercise of human intelligence. And the grievance procedure is the orderly, effective and democratic way of adjusting such disputes within the framework of the collective labor agreement. It is the substitute of civilized collective bargaining for jungle warfare.

But an industrial plant is not a debating society. Its object is production. When a controversy arises, production cannot wait for exhaustion of the grievance procedure. While that procedure is being pursued, production must go on. And some one must have the authority to direct the manner in which it is to go on until the controversy is settled. That authority is vested in Supervision. It must be vested there because the responsibility for production is also vested there; and responsibility must be accompanied by authority. It is fairly vested there because the grievance procedure is capable of adequately recompensing employees for abuse of authority by Supervision.

It should be definitely understood, then, that a committeeman has no authority to direct or advise an employee to disobey Supervision's instructions; that his authority is expressed in the duty to take the matter up with Supervision and seek an adjustment through negotiations and the grievance procedure; that an employee must obey Supervision's instructions pending the negotiations or the processing of his grievance, except only in the rare case where obedience would involve an unusual health hazard or similar sacrifice; and that disobedience by the employee, or counsel of disobedience by a committeeman, is proper cause for disciplinary penalty.[3]

Are there cases in which the union or the employees may refuse to carry on production, either as individuals or in mass, without themselves violating the agreement? The unions would answer this, perhaps, by saying that the right to rebel is inherent in any case in which the grievance procedure is inadequate to do complete justice. This seems acceptable enough in *bona fide* health and

---

[3] *Ford Motor Company*, Opinion A-116, Shulman (1944), Shulman and Chamberlain, *Cases on Labor Relations* (New York: The Foundation Press, 1949), p. 44.

safety cases, but what else, if anything, should it cover? The right of a skilled employee to refuse an assignment wholly outside his trade has been upheld at Ford, and elsewhere, but only in plain cases, not those in which a reasonable doubt exists as to whether the assignment is proper. Arbitrators have made other suggestions: that an employee may refuse an assignment which is "indisputably" beyond the authority of supervision, or one which will cause "irreparable" damage.

It should be noted that acts of insubordination, including mass protests and wildcat strikes, are themselves handled through the grievance procedure and arbitration. The employees involved are given a penalty, perhaps a layoff, for participation. They in turn have the right to file grievances claiming justification and if they succeed, they may claim back pay.

The important point to remember is that the purpose of the grievance procedure is not only to preserve and enforce employee rights, but to accommodate management's right to act—to exercise initiative. There may be a few extraordinary situations in which the right to supervise without contradiction is blunted because the employees can refuse to obey instructions. But in all cases, the right to initiate and act exists, regardless of the outcome of a grievance protesting the action.

Top Management and Basic Policy

Perhaps the first element in the formulation of basic policy is the recognition of the importance of labor relations. If the corporation board of directors and its chief executive regard production and its costs as secondary in importance to engineering or customer relations and sales, it is unlikely that the company will be prepared or willing to stand up to the union. In any contract negotiation or plant disturbance, the immediate cost of giving in to the union is likely to be relatively small. The obvious and calculable increase in the costs of production is less important than continued production. If the company is busy and making money, a strike will impair the year's profits. If business is down, a strike will make a poor profit and loss sheet even worse. This has caused many a company, including some very large ones, to keep postponing the day of reckoning with the union. The result in many cases has been the growth of wasteful practices and increases in cost, sometimes to the point of abandonment of the plant. Many such employers have taken long and expensive strikes over such practices only to find that they were so deeply imbedded in the habits of the workers as to be ineradicable by agreement. Other companies have decided at the outset they would tolerate no nonsense and would take strikes if necessary to protect the efficiency of their plants.

A weak employer means a strong union. This means in turn high costs, except in those few industries in which unions have seen that survival of the small and weak employer is necessary to their own survival. Most small employers find union restrictions on the effective utilization of the work force more onerous and burdensome than do large companies. They are unable to offset these costs with more equipment and managerial techniques available to the larger employer. The union may water down its pattern demands, especially in the fringe benefit areas, but the cost of production restrictions is likely to be higher. "Equality of bargaining power"—one of the stated aims of the Wagner Act— is a myth. There are, it is true, many cases where power is sub-stantially in balance. In many more, it is unbalanced on one side or the other.

Some employers are unable to take a strike. It is common to hear suppliers say that their large customers, whose own produc-tion depends on the supplier, will displace them permanently with other suppliers, or will substitute their own parts or materials, if the supplier is struck. But in my experience, many employers could, if they were willing to endure losses for the strike period, take strikes successfully, and perhaps even find that in the end the strike was a wholesome business decision. Strikes should not merely occur in a fit of desperation. An employer should plan for a strike in the same way he surveys his product development costs and his market. Customers want protection, of course. They should be notified if a tie-up appears imminent or can be predicted. But many of them will, if treated with understanding, order their requirements in advance or stand by, making do with secondary suppliers, until the strike is over. In short, the cost of strikes is sometimes greatly exaggerated. Wherever he can, the employer should root his labor policy in his willingness to take a strike if necessary to maintain an efficient and economical operation and thus to match his competition.

The second keystone of a good labor policy is to give the subject the importance it deserves in the management structure.

Unions are interested only in their own advantage and those of their members. Being single-minded, their officials can focus their continuing time and attention (except the time they spend squabbling with each other) to these ends. This means not only sustained pressure, but a high degree of shrewd expertise. Management has failed, in many companies, to bring the same intense and intelligent effort to bear on labor problems. Though there has been a notable increase in the number of full-time labor representatives who possess ingenuity, strength, and professional know-how, many companies still skimp their employee relations departments. Only the most enlightened top executives fully appreciate, even today, the importance of having an adequate personnel staff. Men who are occupied with urgent engineering and production problems simply do not have the time to acquire and exercise the necessary skills. Besides they are likely to be divided in their own minds as to the wisdom of labor policy, merely giving it lip service when a long-range labor relations program interferes with immediate output.

Third, the top executive must enforce the policies and see that the lower echelons are not afraid to stand up to pressure. Wildcat strikes and slowdowns must not be tolerated and must never serve as an excuse for compromise of an essential management function. If slowdowns, for example, are allowed to blunt the enforcement of production standards, costs are automatically out of control.

Policies must form the basis of action. There can be no true separation between policies and their administration. This means that supervisors must know that their actions, if rightfully taken in accordance with policy, will be backed up. There is no greater deterrent to effective supervision in the labor relations area than the belief that higher management does not mean what it says. If the foremen think they will not be supported, their native strength will wither; they take the easy way to avoid criticism and trouble with the union, with their men, and with their superiors. If support is forthcoming, policy will be dynamic and alive at all levels.

Fourth, top management must insist that general policies of contract administration be such as to promote flexibility and efficiency in the plant. Management must develop and assert its decisional initiative in setting work standards, assigning and scheduling workers, and employee discipline. The union and its officials must never be allowed to take over the authority of the supervisors, nor to maintain a political machine in the plant at the expense of economy and proper operating methods. Costly practices must be avoided, and if they are established, they must be weeded out. The right to improve operating methods must be preserved, even when this means discomfort or even hardship to the worker. These policies cannot be formulated without the assistance of factory management, foremen, and representatives of the personnel department. They require analysis of work situations, contract restrictions, and the skills and abilities of the employees. Top management should, however, insist that they be devised and carried into effect.

The fifth necessity is an effective system of communications, certainly between all levels of management, and possibly down to and up from the rank-and-file worker. Foremen especially must appreciate through daily contact with them the vitality and good sense of management policies. Policies which remain on paper are perhaps worse than none; they serve only to confuse.

The Ingredients of Successful Policies

The exercise of initiative obviously requires more than a purely defensive reaction to union and employee demands. The best policy is planned. It requires analysis of all areas of employee relations. Some companies audit their employee relations just as they audit their books. Questionnaires are prepared for circulation, and the results tabulated. Employee opinion polls are taken. Meetings with supervision are devoted to examining labor relations problems. Such efforts make it possible to formulate policy which is realistic and factual, and adapted to actual conditions in the plant, not someone's idea of what they ought to be. With this kind of information at hand, plant executives and labor relations men are in a position to study the management function in action, break it down into its components, and recognize and identify the factors which must be taken into account in exercising management initiative. The "why" of every management action should be clear, the reasons for each action known. This in itself will furnish protection against arbitrary action and violations of the agreement.

When the agreement is analyzed, it should be viewed not merely on the basis of what it prohibits, but what it permits. Supervisors should be trained to identify actions which are not in any sense covered by the agreement, and how to handle employee requests or complaints in such matters. For example, the wearing of gloves may be a management choice required of some employees, and prohibited to others. In these matters, employee wishes may sometimes be satisfied, but as a matter of management discretion, not of employee right. And, of course, if concessions are made, they should not be allowed to become a subject of binding "plant practice." The supervisor should know that when he grants a grievance, he should avoid making the settlement an enforceable agreement for the future.

With these precautions management may, on the other hand, do what it wishes in order to maintain a happy and effective work force. When the chips are down, the question may be one of rights under the agreement. But there is no reason why, within the framework of proper managerial responsibility, the wishes of employees should not be taken into consideration.

Where the agreement does limit management action, the supervisor should understand fully what he is obliged to do in order to reconcile the restriction with the positive action required. All areas of management action should be examined in an effort to construct reliable guides, such as in making work assignments between classifications and for overtime work, in transferring work out of the unit, and in making promotions and transfers.

It is probably under those sections of the agreement which limit management action only in general terms that most disputes occur. Disciplinary action under the "just cause" restriction accounts for 25 percent or more of arbitration cases. The promulgation and enforcement of production and quality standards is another grey area in which management is frequently checkmated. The conflict which rages over strict seniority and the consideration of ability is familiar to all. These areas, and others, will receive separate treatment in this book. Every company should endeavor to point out to the supervisor, not merely where the lines are drawn, but how he can accomplish his function without violating the agreement.

Common to all areas of employee relations are certain basic propositions which are essential to successful management action:

(A) The policy should be related to the subject in question. Excessive absenteeism may be "just cause" for discipline, and it may have a bearing on "merit," but it is not ordinarily a proper standard when the "ability" of the employee to handle a certain job is considered in connection with promotion. A physical standard may be applicable to one job or one worker, but not to another. For example, a Ford Motor Company medical policy disqualifying all employees on recall from layoff who were more than 50 pounds overweight was held to be too broad. Tests and merit rating systems, while quite properly used as a management tool, must bear a substantial relationship to the job requirements. A certain standard of dress or appearance may be required of employees who meet the public which would be wholly fanciful if applied to employees engaged in sandblasting or breaking up concrete.

(B) The policy and its administration should be objective and factual. Subjective qualities may be of value in situations which call for such qualities. Friendliness and reliability are both qualities which affect the performance of a route salesman who drives a truck and sells to customers for cash. But these must be verified by something more than mere opinion. Specific instances, for example, complaints from customers, a failure to maintain average sales or better in comparison with others, traffic violation tickets, and slipshod accounting of receipts from customers would back up the subjective opinion that the employee in question is unreliable and poorly qualified. A leader or a utility man may be selected because he has demonstrated initiative and readiness by tackling difficult jobs, remaining on all night when asked, and taking night school courses. These are facts, not opinions. Buttressed in this manner, a subjective test takes on the objectivity of the facts supporting it.

An opinion that a man does work of inferior quality is of little value unless it is supported by inspection records, scrapped jobs, and the like. Though circumstantial evidence is admitted, discipline cases must almost always be supported by provable observation. Job or machine experience, knowledge, and ability should be established by concrete records or observation. Ratings, for example, should be made by supervisors who know the job, understand how to rate performance on it, and base their ratings on personal observation of the employee with sufficient frequency, and over a long enough period, to establish the validity of their judgments.

While the feelings and "hunches" of supervisors, not supported by concrete example and observation, are of little validity, the reverse is true when such supporting data are established. The judgment of supervision, when based on facts and shown to be reasonable in its application, is given greater weight than it is in cases in which subjective qualities are not important.

(C) All standards should be applied with reasonable consistency. Consistency does not mean wooden uniformity. There may be a dozen valid reasons why one employee should be treated differently from the next, but exceptions and variations must fit into a consistent approach to application of the particular standard in individual cases. One employee may be given a certain latitude, not allowed to another, in making scrap, because of the nature of the material assigned to him, unavoidable tool problems, the tolerances required of his operation, and the like. Absenteeism on the part of an old employee who has problems at home may be tolerated while another who has not built a good record in the plant may be disciplined. As long as consistency is maintained, some variety is permissible. But arbitrary or capricious application of a standard to one and not another is not.

(D) The policy should be made known. Generally speaking, all policies and procedures should be made known and changes published, by posting or otherwise, in such a manner as to leave no excuse for failure to observe them.

A general policy which is not clearly enunciated and consistently enforced cannot be relied upon as a basis for action in particular cases. This is similar to the doctrine we have already observed in the cases dealing with plant practice. The same elements which must exist to make a practice valid must be present to make a managerial policy enforceable. If it is sporadic and fortuitous, if the area in which it applies is ill-defined, if it is not enforced with consistency when cases for its application arise, it may fall when attacked. A good illustration is contained in an arbitration case [4] in which the Prudential Insurance Company claimed that it had

---

[4] *Prudential Insurance Co.*, Barrett, 28 LA 505 (1957).

an established practice of discharging agents who failed for a three-month period, after being placed on probation, to approach the average in district sales. The arbitrator, Gerald A. Barrett, held that no policy had been proven when (1) no witness was able to testify when the claimed practice had been first established and applied, (2) there were only five applications of the claimed practice over a ten-year period among 18,000 agents, (3) both company and union officials testified they had never heard of the alleged practice, and (4) no documentary evidence of the practice was introduced.

At the same time, management must not bind itself forever to policies which might require change. In the Collins Radio case,[5] Carl Schedler held that a letter signed by the employer during contract negotiations outlining the employer's proposed system for distributing overtime was binding under the doctrine of promissory estoppel, whether or not accepted by the union, since the union acted upon the letter by abandoning its contract proposals on the subject. Appropriate reservations should be made of the right to change. Thus, if policies are temporary or depend on a certain underlying circumstance, such as the movement of shipments in and out of the plant, this fact should be stated. Such precautionary phrases as "while business conditions warrant," "until further notice," or "unless conditions change," should be considered in announcing policies.

(E) Applications of policy should be based on reasons of substance. The line between the insignificant and trivial, on one hand, and the substantial, on the other, is hard to draw and one of degree. Nevertheless, there is a difference always between major and minor, between action which verges on the arbitrary and the fanciful, and that based on compelling considerations. Management should be prepared to show, for example, in passing over an employee with many years of seniority in favor of one of little service that the job requirements are important, and that the differences between the two men are weighty. If starting and quitting times are changed without advance notice, supervision should be prepared to show that the change was necessary and that it was impossible to give notice. Case after case comes up in which men refuse overtime assigned at the end of the shift and the union

---

[5] *Collins Radio Co.*, Schedler, 36 LA 15 (1961).

demonstrates that the foreman could have assigned it the day before. Regardless of rights, management should always be able to justify its action as appropriate and required by the situation. This however is on the basis of the facts then known or ascertainable, not hindsight or second guessing by the union or the employees or an arbitrator.

Managerial Discretion

Administrative initiative necessarily must be accompanied by the use of judgment and the exercise of discretion, and management must insist upon the retention of and respect for this truth.

Mechanical application of policies in many areas is simply impossible. The supervisor is required to use his judgment in most applications of policy. As we have already said, the complex interchange of men, machines, and materials in an industrial plant requires the balancing of numerous factors when decisions must be made.

The principle that authority must accompany responsibility has been overlooked in labor relations matters to a much greater extent than is healthy from the standpoint of all parties concerned, including the unions whose representatives find themselves busy night and day prosecuting grievances which involve extensive reviews of actions taken long before as to which the facts have become obscure. Arbitrators especially should be aware of the difficulties and the injustice which frequently result from substituting their judgment for that of management long after the fact.

The principle has been stated best by Professor Neil W. Chamberlain, who says:

> I doubt that any of us disagree that the union's case is to be given an equal hearing with management's, and its facts treated as the same coin as management's facts. But there is a sense in which management must be given preferential treatment because it is the initiator, if we are to have any rationality to organizational life. The man who has not only the power but also the duty of initiating action—management, in our case—must be given the right of reasonable judgment. If, faced with some problem (a discipline case, a promotion, scheduling overtime, etc.), a member of management makes his decision and that decision is reasonable under the circumstances and under the terms of the agreement, that decision must be honored, even though the union argues that

he should have taken another course of action which might also be viewed as reasonable. That is to say, if there are two or more courses of action which are equally reasonable under the circumstances and management chooses one while the union would choose another, if that matter comes to grievance arbitration, it seems to me that management should be given preferential treatment in the sense that its right of reasonable choice is respected. Management requires initiative, and initiative requires discretion and the exercise of judgment, and if that judgment is exercised fairly, it should be upheld even though the union—equally fairly—would have it otherwise. In this case, its views are not given equal treatment with management's and I don't see how they can be if organizational sanity is to be preserved.[6]

Clauses reserving discretionary authority to management in certain areas are not uncommon. In an insurance company contract negotiation, for example, a serious issue arose as to whether or not the company would exercise the broad management rights it has reserved in the contract unfairly. To settle this objection, the company agreed to give the arbitrator power to determine its motive. The language (taken from the unpublished contract) reads as follows:

> In any case in which it is alleged that the company has exercised its rights arbitrarily or capriciously, or for the purpose of discriminating unfairly against or in favor of individual agents, the power of the arbitrator shall be limited to deciding whether or not the Company's action was in fact taken in good faith and for legitimate purposes, or was taken arbitrarily and capriciously or for the purpose of discriminating unfairly against or in favor of individual agents, . . . and the arbitrator shall have no power to substitute his judgment or discretion for that of the Company as to the reasonableness of the exercise of any such rights or of any practice, policy or rule of the Company.

Management's judgment has been upheld by prominent arbitrators without such clauses in case of choice of penalty, preference of junior employees in promotions, and merit increases, on this basis. Harry Platt has said that "there are rational limits to the competence of arbitrators" in passing on these questions.[7] This salutary observation should have wider currency.

---

[6] Neil W. Chamberlain, "Management's Reserved Rights: Discussion," *Management Rights and the Arbitration Process* (Washington: BNA Incorporated, 1956), p. 139.

[7] *McInerney Spring and Wire Co.*, Platt, 9 LA 91 (1947); *Ford Motor Company*, Opinion A-17, Shulman, unpublished; *Ford Motor Company*, Opinion A-95, Shulman, unpublished; *Stauffer Chemical Company*, Reid, 23 LA 322 (1954); *Hercules Powder Co.*, Reynolds, 10 LA 624 (1948); *Glidden Co.*, Griffin, 34 LA 265 (1960).

The exercise of discretion, however, must be solidly based. Mere thoughtless or whimsical choices cannot be upheld, and an attempt to bull through an invasion of employee rights on this basis is a fatal mistake. It has been truly said that "the arbitrary and inconsiderate use of power is a sure invitation to limitation of that power." Unions are quick to assert limitations at the bargaining table based, as they claim, "on the record."

This means that in the discretionary areas where two choices are possible, supervisory judgment must be based on the same factors which support unilateral policies in the open area left for the enforcement of the general standards clauses. A realistic appraisal of the known facts, not mere guessing, and a deliberate judgment based on all the relevant factors, are required. In other words, a discretionary judgment must be susceptible of rational explanation.

Supervision should not push naked rights in unwise and immoderate fashion. Actions which outrage an employee's sense of personal dignity or impose a new and unaccustomed burden or hardship should be undertaken with care, regardless of the "right" involved.

Also, in exercising judgment, two extremes should be avoided. One is making administrative decisions that are completely irrational because of a predetermined attitude which regards every concession as a victory for the union. Such an attitude can be justified only by a company which has set about deliberately to drive the union out of the plant and wishes to discredit and weaken it at every point; this, in many cases, means a violation of the legal obligation to bargain in good faith. The other extreme is the more familiar one of making decisions favorable to the employees simply to avoid trouble—to placate the troublemaker, the plant committee, or a rebellious rank-and-file group. Both extremes will ultimately discredit the company and destroy the authority and respect it needs to establish and enforce good policies.

Line and Staff Organization

In some plants, the line organization dominates labor relations and the personnel manager is only a figurehead. In a few, the decisions on labor relations problems are made by staff labor relations people. In some, particularly the larger companies, an effort has been made to reconcile these two functions in a system of line and staff organization which leaves the primary responsibility for decision and action to the line management, but builds strong cooperation with professional staff labor relations men in formulating policy and building administration. This reconciliation has the advantage, now emphasized almost universally, of building up the importance and competence of the first line supervisor. A really good system works on the floor of the shop, not in the personnel department.

If an enterprise is to run smoothly, a common attitude must be developed, shared not only by the various levels of line management, but by staff officials, industrial engineers, labor relations representatives, and others. A lack of understanding and cooperation between industrial engineers and foremen in the production standards area is common. A labor relations manager seeking to develop a reliable and consistent system of discipline encounters resistance from the plant manager who wishes to be liked by the men in the plant. Frequently, union officials can elicit a sympathetic response from one official who is jealous of another. Production officials may apply pressures for compromise of vital labor relations policies, thus setting bad precedents for the future. Or labor relations officials may, in their insistence upon procedures, investigations, and delay in vigorous enforcement of policy, give production management a sense of emasculation. Some labor relations officials become legalistic and negative in the eyes of the foreman or manager.

This means that production management must be educated in the importance of good labor policy, and personnel management must be trained to appreciate and further efficiency and economy in production. Just as the "bull of the woods" tendency must disappear from line management, the "human relations" expert must be checkreined in the personnel department. Only top management can provide the milieu in which this reconciliation can take place effectively. If teamwork between line and staff officials is achieved, a wholesome labor relations structure is almost inevitable. At the least, consistency and unity will result, two extremely valuable assets in management's dealing with unions. Joint management committees, foreman training, and written statements of policy can all be helpful to establish this understanding.

Analyses and labor relations audits are valuable, particularly in multi-plant operations. They bring out basic information as to such matters as: (a) the labor relations climate in the plant, (b) difference in abilities and attitudes of plant managers and personnel manager, (c) local union and plant committee policy and personalities, (d) plant practice with respect to production standards, discipline, work assignments, and similar matters, and (e) historical differences between plants, which can be particularly important when a new plant is acquired.

Two such audits are incorporated as appendices to this book. The first prepared and used by a large multi-plant manufacturing company is entitled "Labor Check List—Do You Still Have the Right to Run the Plant?" [8] This questionnaire is made up of two parts: the language of the labor agreement and plant practices. The second questionnaire [9] is used by a large rubber company with many plants and is entitled "Check List for Survey of Irregular or Unusual Plant Practices." The value of these analyses is obvious upon reading them. They enable staff experts to assist in the formulation of realistic approaches to the problems of the particular plant, thus avoiding policies which might be quite sound and workable in one plant but are not well adapted to another.

In many companies, the formulation of labor relations policies is the work of a joint committee representing production management and those staff departments which have a direct interest in the employees and their performance.

The Foreman and Labor Relations

Although the importance of the foreman in industrial management is stressed everywhere, top management has not yet fully recognized that he is the most be-deviled individual in the structure. He is assumed to be a technical expert on the materials and machinery in his department, familiar with the most intricate machine repair and tooling problems, complicated testing devices, metallurgical or chemical formulae, and what not. He is expected

---

[8] This questionnaire is reproduced as Appendix B, p. 269.
[9] Reproduced as Appendix C, p. 275.

to requisition manpower, and to select, induct, and train employees. He is expected to improve job performance and quality, and to assign, promote, and transfer employees in such a way as to utilize their services most effectively. He must have a working knowledge of safety and health standards, fire prevention, and plant security. He must counsel with his men, prevent grievances, or when filed, answer them correctly, warn and discipline, and maintain orderly conduct. He must check with production schedules, purchasing department buyers, and various kinds of engineering specialists. He must keep records and attend meetings. All these activities must be carried on within the compass of a performance and cost standard which it is his obligation to meet.

With his time spread so thinly over this diverse and divisive responsibility, the foreman is sorely tempted to gloss over areas of difficulty, especially if decisions on them are not immediately required or if they can be swept under the rug. He tends to narrow his sphere of action and authority, passing the buck to others, sometimes even to union stewards. He loses confidence in himself, in his superiors, his staff experts, and finally the company.

Any program of improving foremanship should therefore begin with the question of what the foreman is expected to do and whether these expectations are realistic. It is obvious that a foreman cannot be expected to hold scrap costs down if he is not provided with good tools. In the labor relations area, the same holds true. A good foreman will be ineffective in a plant with a bad atmosphere. A plant manager who gives in under pressure from the union can expect his foremen to avoid trouble with their stewards. A foreman who is constantly reversed in higher stages of the grievance procedure will stop making decisions in favor of the company. It will do no good to tell such foremen that they are management representatives who should protect the company's interests in disputes with the union. They know better.

Foreman training should be factual and specific. Concrete cases are far better material for training than high-flown sentiments. The case method is far superior to lectures, and the cases if possible should be built from arbitration decisions and grievance materials in the plant itself.

The ideal policy manual is one in which the company's basic and general policy is translated into concrete situations covering not only the labor agreement itself, but those areas of administration in which management has the right to act and exercise its initiative. Examples can be given collected from arbitration decisions and grievance dispositions of problems and their solutions. The foreman should know the area in which he must exercise his own independent judgment and responsibility and the area in which he must seek the advice or direction of others. Manuals prepared for foremen should be as simple and useful as possible. The following are examples of general guides given to foremen at General Motors in effecting discipline:

1. Make your instructions simple and understandable.
2. Know the rules of conduct, that is, the shop rules, and make sure your employees know them.
3. Take necessary action promptly on all violations.
4. Get all the facts.
5. Permit employees an opportunity to explain.
6. Decide what action to take. In that connection:
    a. Know the principles of 'corrective discipline' which have been developed over the years in our Umpire Decisions.
    b. Determine if the violation is a major or lesser offense, i.e., assault on supervision vs. tardiness.
    c. Determine the rule or rules that have been violated.
    d. Consider basic factors, e.g., the employee's prior conduct record, his length of service, the time elapsed since his last penalty, and the plant practice in similar cases.
    e. Decide on suspension or immediate assessment of penalty.
7. Make and keep records regarding discipline cases.[10]

One of the prime objectives of good labor relations administration is the prevention of grievances and their resolution at the foreman level. Grievances may be settled far more readily in the oral stage and the foreman should be encouraged to dispose of them then, if possible. This requires training in what not to settle. The foreman must recognize the effects of his settlements, the possibility that a course of action may result in the growth of bad practices, and that his decisions may create undesirable precedents which could have ramifications beyond his own department. He must know when to say "yes" and when to say "no." If he says "no," both he and his superiors are on the defensive.

---

[10] Morris, *Good Administration of a Labor Agreement* (Ann Arbor: University of Michigan, Bureau of Industrial Relations, 1959), p. 6.

A formal grievance is likely to be filed and carried through the procedure.

Again, we may look to General Motors for simple and effective advice to foremen:

1. *Take every employe complaint seriously.* Don't underestimate the seriousness of whatever complaint your employes may have. While it may seem trivial or even complete nonsense to you, it may be the most important thing in the world, at the moment, to an employe.

2. *Try to resolve complaints on a sound basis before they develop into serious issues.* Give any complaint your full attention and attempt to get at the source of the trouble, whether imagined or real. Experience has proved that as a case is processed through the grievance procedure, the difficulties in making a settlement are multiplied and the original complaint frequently takes on a completely new face.

3. *Call the Committeeman promptly when properly requested.* Once an employe has made a request for his Committeeman and has specified his grievances as required in the Agreement, break off your discussion and start the procedure for calling the Committeeman at once. Don't try to talk the employe out of getting his Committeeman and don't discuss his complaint further until after the Committeeman has arrived.

4. *If a grievance is written, make certain that the grievance form is completely filled out.* Names, times, and dates frequently become of critical importance. Make certain that this information is on the grievance form in the spaces provided.

5. *Deal honestly, calmly and impersonally with the Committeeman.* The best relationship you can develop with a Union Representative is one of mutual confidence and respect. This flows from a forthright approach to problems arising between you.

6. *Insist upon observance of established procedures for handling grievances.*

7. *While handling a grievance with a Committeeman, stick to the issues of the grievance.*

8. *Base your decision on facts.*

9. *Phrase your answer carefully.* Remember that the answer you finally place on a grievance, if accepted by the Union, is a binding, enforceable settlement of that grievance. For this reason, it is of the utmost importance that every Supervisor recognize the difference between single, isolated dispositions, which have no lasting effects and grievance answers which commit Management to some specific continuing obligation or course of action.

A grievance disposition, accepted by the Union, can seriously impair Management's right to operate efficiently at some future date if it contains statements such as the following: that a certain group of employes will receive all the overtime work on a particular job, or that the line speed will not be more than so many jobs per hour, or that a certain type of work falls within a higher rated classification.

10. *Record all of the facts if the grievance goes beyond your level in procedure.* The Foreman's responsibility for the grievance does not end until it is satisfactorily settled—either at the plant or by the Umpire—and in either event he supplies the basic ammunition, the facts.[11]

The important point is that the foreman must give the right answer the first time. This means an answer on which the company will back him to the end of the procedure.

Conclusion

In the chapter on management rights I stressed the importance of management function and the complexity and diversity of the decisions which must be made every day by plant management. In this chapter I have attempted to set down some principles which I believe will aid management in doing its job well. Basic to all this discussion, it must be reiterated, is the truth that policy must be based on initiative. A purely defensive reaction to union demands and problems is not productive. Analysis and study of all areas of employees' relations must be undertaken and constructive policies and procedures set up. Then the appropriate action must be taken. Policies must be more than empty slogans.

---

[11] *Id.*, at pp 8-9.

PART TWO

MANAGEMENT IN ACTION

Chapter 6

INDUSTRIAL STRUCTURES AND THEIR REVISION

An industrial operation is not static. It cannot be placed on a slide and studied under a microscope like a dead insect. It is a volatile and active human organization and its essence is change. It might be viewed as having four elements—the physical plant and equipment; the people who operate it, with their skills, their human needs, and their authority either as representatives of management or of the union; the demands of outside forces, chiefly the customers who at one time crowd the plant with orders and at another suspend buying, and also including such outsiders as the suppliers and the transporters; and the fourth and principal element, change. Equipment breaks down so the workers who operate it must be rescheduled, placed on other jobs, or perhaps laid off. At the same time, maintenance men must be taken off other repair work and assigned to repair the equipment, perhaps on an emergency basis which requires overtime work. Raw materials fail to arrive on time, a power failure occurs, or a sudden blizzard prevents workers from reaching the plant. Customers cancel orders, or double them and demand immediate shipment. Management is constantly searching for better methods, improved plant layout, faster and more economical planning and scheduling of the work flow, equipment and materials which are easier to work, more durable, or cheaper. In all such cases, some modifications of work assignments and work schedules must inevitably result and be put into effect. An industrial operation is kaleidoscopic. Change is normal.

Industrial Structures

The main structures in any industrial operation are the department and the job classification. Departments are set up for the purpose of organizing the work flow from the receiving department, through various production operations, to inspection, and finally shipping or customer delivery. A particular operation or a set of similar operations is performed under a foreman. Sometimes the department performs a service function for all or part of the plant, as is usually the case with machine and plant maintenance. Within these departments are established, formally or informally, classifications of jobs, each of which carries its own rate and each of which has its own cluster of tasks which the employees assigned to it are expected to perform. Sometimes a department and a job classification are coterminous—the plant may be large enough to have its own electrical department to which only journeymen electricians and apprentices are assigned. More frequently, there are classifications which cross departmental lines; several departments may have press operators, grinders, or lathe hands. Most departments embrace more than one classification of employees; the shipping department may include craters, packers, labelers, clerks and truck drivers in a typical plant.

The term "job classification" needs further definition. The word "job" can have several meanings. To say "I have a job at Lockheed" is not the same as to say "I have a job to do at home." We use the word "job" to mean "classification." A man is classified not on what he can do, but on the cluster of tasks which he normally and regularly performs and can be required to perform as a member of his classification.

Another point to remember is that job classifications, whether formal or informal, written or unwritten, are structures, not people working. A classification may be vacant, but it remains in the wage structure and may be filled at any time. It is quite common to find labor contracts renewed year after year with outdated classifications still listed in the section establishing rates.

The job content of a classification is determined by the employer, perhaps informally, or by written job description. In formal job evaluation plans, the union is given a description and may question its accuracy or the rating of the job. The employer's right to fix and revise its content should be reserved. In defining job content, the employer should keep in mind at least two considerations: one, the desirability of encompassing all the duties the classification may be expected to perform, and two, the identification of tasks in such a way that, if necessary, they may be split off and assigned to other classifications in or out of the bargaining unit. For example, the term "production painter" may be plain enough. But will the painter be required to do (1) fine finish painting, final touch-up, and striping, (2) mixing and matching of colors, (3) spray gun work, (4) maintenance, machine, and exterior painting, and (5) incidental tasks such as constructing and removing his own scaffolding and reinstalling objects painted? On the second aspect, the more skilled and the lesser skilled tasks within the classification, and those which partake of the nature of supervisory or clerical work, should be identified. The employer may find it necessary to reassign them. Such identification is also helpful in evaluating the employee for purposes of promotion, since it is easier to prove that the supervisor has exercised a fair judgment on the basis of the particular elements of the job which call for intelligence, skill, or other qualities which are important to promotion. Identification of key tasks makes evaluation and rate-setting easier.

It may be asked how the supervisor or the personnel department can do this in the absence of job descriptions. The answer is records of almost any kind. There is no reason why informal job descriptions should not be made up for the use of management only and kept in desk drawers. Merit rating charts, job postings, or even the foreman's pocket notebook all can be helpful in establishing job requirements, and all are better than mere memory.

Changes in Methods and Procedures

The department and the job classification are functional structures. They are established and exist solely to serve the work to be done, reflecting management's ideas of how to combine equipment and skills most effectively. When the structures must be changed, the employer is confronted with objections if the change affects the work opportunities of his employees. Because they fear a dilution of their seniority rights or their job classification rights, they attack his right to make the change.

The unions and employees view job classifications differently from employers. The worker agrees that he must do the work of the classification in order to make the rate. But he does not stop there. He lays claim to the work of the classification as his own. What the company regards as an arrangement set up to serve a set of operations in the flow of production, he regards as his "job." He asserts title to it. No one should trespass upon it, he thinks, and he should not be required to trespass upon the territory of others.

Since we are all creatures of habit, change is frequently distasteful to us and the worker is no exception. Even in cases of expansion of operations with the opportunities thereby afforded to learn new skills, to secure promotions, and to enjoy higher earnings, people find it difficult to accept new techniques. When the results of change are adverse, when security is diminished, when skills are degraded, when personal habits acquired over the years are encumbrances not aids, the resistance mounts proportionately. Understandably, workers seek to curb management's efforts to improve operations by restrictive clauses and devices.

It will be recalled, as Justice Arthur Goldberg said, that labor does not dispute the employer's right to establish manufacturing methods. But these rights, he says, cannot diminish the rights of the worker and the union: "a new method of manufacture may raise several issues of working arrangements, crews, spell periods, schedules, rates, etc." [1] Theoretically, this statement is sound. But Justice Goldberg's thesis breaks down all too often in practical application, for if the working arrangements existing under the old method of manufacture cannot be changed to conform with the new, there may be little or no gain in making it. If management finds its efforts to develop a new process or product, or to rearrange job assignments in a more efficient way, blocked by claims of contract violation, industrial progress stops.

The vice of union protective devices is that in many cases they rob management of its right to improve methods of operation. Where management seeks to be dynamic, the union tends to protect the status quo. If a worker has secured certain privileges, such as the right to choose the job on which he will work because he is the senior man in his department, management has lost the right to select the man best fitted for the job. If the job classification is sacrosanct—if those in the classification can claim all the work of the classification as their property—management is thwarted in its efforts to get work done as efficiently and economically as possible. Foremen and other non-union personnel are not allowed to touch the work of bargaining unit people, even

---

[1] Goldberg, "Management's Reserved Rights: A Labor View," *Management Rights and the Arbitration Process* (Washington: BNA Incorporated, 1956), p. 123.

if this means holding them over, or calling them in to perform minor tasks at heavy costs in overtime pay. If there is a vacancy, it must be filled, even on a temporary basis, by asking those with seniority whether they wish the work. The effect, in literally millions of cases, is stultification—glorification of the status quo at the expense of efficiency. In the end, the security and privileges which the unions protect with such diligence are lost anyway; high cost plants simply do not survive in the fierce heat of competition.

Few arbitrators deny management its right to determine the means and methods of operation. It is considered the prerogative of management to see that production programs are adjusted to meet changing demand. For example, in a case in which the company changed from a non-continuous operation to a continuous one, as a consequence requiring employees to work through their wash-up periods, Whitley McCoy put the matter this way:

> The decision as to whether or not to run a particular operation as continuous is a function of management—just as much so as the decision whether or not to replace an old machine, involving simple operations requiring ten men, with a new labor-saving and more complicated machine requiring only five men. Such changes are not the sort of changes in working conditions as require negotiation. As long as such decisions are made in good faith, in the interest of efficiency of operation, and do not involve the imposing on employees of conditions different from those already existing with respect to other employees on similar machines or operations, no injustice is done the employees. No employee has a vested right in the use of a particular old machine that would preclude the company from installing a new one nor a vested right in a particular method of operation that would preclude the company from changing that method. If the new machine, or the new method on the old results in too heavy a work load, too low pay, or any other hardship, the employee has his remedy in the grievance machinery. But he does not have the right to delay the exercise of managerial functions by insisting on prior negotiations.[2]

Industrial change comes about through a variety of causes. "Automation" has become a hobgoblin word, but the truth is that dramatic technological changes, which throw large numbers of men out of work, are relatively infrequent. Many of them are accepted by the unions, even though some hardship does result,

---

[2] Whitley P. McCoy, quoted in Elkouri and Elkouri, *How Arbitration Works* (Washington: BNA Incorporated, 1960), p. 303; this is included in an excellent discussion of changes in methods of operation which affect wages or working conditions.

because they are necessary and perhaps inevitable. The mechanization of the coal fields, accepted and even encouraged by the Mineworkers' Union, is an example. John L. Lewis fully appreciated that high productivity was required if the competition from other fuels was to be met.

The vast majority of changes are small and produce only minute effects which can in most cases be easily absorbed in the plant through seniority preferences and transfers to other departments. Many of them do not affect the operation of machinery or equipment, but are improvements in material supply, plant layout, and work scheduling. Many are improvements in methods; work simplification is studied continuously in a well-managed plant. Such changes are absolutely necessary if an employer is to keep up with his competition.

A large rubber company uses a checklist, which we have reproduced as Appendix D,[3] to remind its supervisors of the necessity of planning when instituting changes in work procedures.

As McCoy suggested, the union may be entitled to file a grievance on the results of a change on its members. The change may produce significant alteration in the degree of skill required to perform the work, and this may suggest that the work be performed by members of another classification, higher or lower in skill. The persons who performed it before may demand training so they may keep the work. It may be necessary to transfer the work from one department to another across departmental seniority lines, or other seniority problems may arise. Wage adjustments, up or down, may be indicated. The union may attempt to force the retention of the former complement of men, even though a reduction in the number of men needed should follow the change.

Revision of Classifications

We can now examine management's right to alter jobs—to eliminate them, to split off job duties and reassign them, to combine them, and to create new jobs. Closely tied in to the right to make these changes, as we shall see, is the reorganization of departmental structures. In both cases, employees may urge that their rights are vested, not subject to change without their consent,

---

[3] Appendix D, p. 279.

under the seniority or the wage classification provisions of the agreement.

In some cases, there are contract clauses which provide that classifications contained in the rate structure must remain unchanged, except with the consent of the union, for the duration of the agreement. More commonly, clauses are included which permit revision of existing classifications or the establishment of new ones. Commonly, such clauses provide that the employer may establish the new rate which is open for a period, such as thirty days, to grievance before it becomes permanent. Clauses such as this may be found in the United States Steel agreement [4] and others published in BNA's *Collective Bargaining Negotiations and Contracts* service. The Swift agreement [5] contains the important provision that if the rate is appealed to an arbitrator, he shall have "only the power to decide whether the rate is consistent with the existing rate structure." It requires the arbitrator to "consider the existing rates for jobs which require a skill comparable to that required by the new job." This eliminates the possibility of distortion of the rate structure on the basis of factors irrelevant to the worker's own skill and effort, such as improved technology.

In the motor car industry, the provisions as to the revision of jobs are sketchy, yet the right to alter jobs is clear.

In General Motors—UAW Case No. G-232,[6] Nathan Feinsinger dealt with a situation in which the company, in order to reduce lost time involved in assigning several skilled classifications, such as electricians, pipefitters, machine repairmen, and others, to the work of constructing, installing, and maintaining various kinds of plant equipment, consolidated several of the classifications into one "multiple-skill" classification. The union protested this action as not creating a new job under Section 102(a). The umpire upheld the company.

The right was said to exist, notwithstanding the union's contention that "the desired increase in efficiency can be accomplished by improved supervision and the exercise of management's right

---

[4] United States Steel agreement, Article IX, §D, BNA, *Collective Bargaining Negotiations and Contracts*, p. 22:155 (June 22, 1962).

[5] The Swift agreement is not published. See *Lukens Steel Co.*, Crawford, 37 LA 711 (1961). See Milton Rubin, "The Right of Management to Split Jobs and Assign Work to Other Jobs; Management Rights and Labor Arbitration: A Symposium," *Industrial and Labor Relations Review, op. cit.* (Ch. 2, n. 2), at 205.

[6] Unpublished.

of job assignment, such as, for example, assigning an electrician to do pipefitting work without changing his classification."

At Ford, Shulman was asked to decide a case involving the assignment of the duties of crane dispatchers (crane operators who kept track of the movement of cranes, transmitted instructions over the telephone, and performed clerical duties) to plant clerks who were part of the bargaining unit and received a lower rate. The crane dispatchers were reassigned to crane operation without a change in their rate of pay. After noting that the duties were essentially similar to those already performed by the clerks, and that no loss of employment was to be suffered by the dispatchers, Shulman, in a much-quoted paragraph, said:

> Jobs, like technological processes, cannot remain static in an industrial society. The multiple subdivision and simplification of jobs have been outstanding factors in the mass production industry. . . . Without that simplification and subdivision it is difficult to conceive of the development of this great industry. While this process may cause hardship in specific cases, its general tendency is deemed to be advantageous to both labor and capital and in the general welfare. . . . It has not stopped any more than technological improvement has stopped. Union organization and the Union contract with the employer has not frozen jobs, just as it has not frozen technical processes. The contract provides protection for the employees in a variety of circumstances. But it cannot and does not undertake to stop the continuous development of new methods in . . . continuously developing industry.[7]

The right to revise the job content of classifications is not set forth explicitly in either the General Motors or the Ford agreements. The provision in Section 102 of the General Motors agreement, "when new jobs are placed in production . . ." can be construed to cover the G-232 situation. The somewhat similar clause in the Ford agreement would hardly cover the Shulman case since no new job was created; a job was abolished. The only true basis is the management rights clause—the right to determine the "methods, means and processes" of manufacturing. In other words, the right is included in the fundamental and exclusive right to determine the product, the machine to be used, the plant organization, and the method to be employed.

In the absence of directions in the agreement itself, most arbi-

---

[7] *Ford Motor Company*, Opinion A-91, Shulman, quoted in *Reynolds Metal Company*, Prasow, 25 LA 44 at 49 (1955). See *Quaker Oats Co.*, Bothwell, 34 LA 24 at 28 (1959).

trators will uphold management's right to eliminate, combine, or split job classifications when done in good faith for legitimate operating reasons. Such reasons include the lack of sufficient work to keep members of the classification fully employed, changes in machinery and equipment, or improvements in methods of operation.

These decisions must be contrasted with certain illustrative *ad hoc* decisions, which hold in effect that the establishment of a classification and agreement on a rate for it freeze the content of the classification for the duration of the agreement, unless it is changed by mutual consent. In an Esso Standard Oil Company case, Whitley McCoy denied the right of the company to abolish the job of "burner," adding its duties to the "welder" classification, and giving those holding the burner classification the right after training to move up to the welder classification or to remain on a "red circle" basis in the burner classification. In other words, the company proposed to let the classification die by not adding any more burners. The contract said simply, "Rates of pay in the respective classifications shall be as set forth in Schedule "A" attached. . . ." McCoy's opinion reads:

> The contract does not expressly freeze the classifications, but the wealth of arbitration authority is to the effect that such contract provisions do evidence an intent to agree upon the classifications as well as the rates.[8]

A similar decision was rendered in Sperry Gyroscope case by James Healy, although he rested his decision upon the existence of written job descriptions. Under these, he states, the parties agreed on job content:

> The parties to this agreement have chosen to agree in very formal terms to the content of certain jobs, one of them being the job of Coverage Change Clerk. The bargaining of job descriptions has a meaning and implication which go beyond the mere ease of classifying people and, derivatively, of determining their rate of pay. It must be held that they understood in such bargaining that a given job would embrace the agreed-upon set of duties. If the job descriptions, i.e., the statement of the essential duties is a product of negotiations, it is not unreasonable to conclude that any substantive revision, either by addition or subtraction, in said duties, during the life of the agreement must also be the product of negotiations.[9]

---

[8] *Esso Standard Oil Co.*, McCoy, 19 LA 569 at 571 (1952).
[9] *Sperry Gyroscope Co.*, Healy, 30 LA 507 at 518 (1958).

It will be noticed that Healy intimates that a mere list of classifications and rates in the agreement would not, as McCoy holds, prevent revision of classification content. His comment on the absence of any clause which would support the employer's right to alter job content is also important. He says:

> Unlike most agreements, such as those which incorporate job evaluation principles, including job descriptions, in the agreement, there is not a single reference to the matter of what procedures are to be followed when a change in job content occurs. Most agreements contain language which at least inferentially suggests management's right to initiate changes, and the area of dispute is thereby transferred to the question of whether the changed job is evaluated and/or paid properly. Not so here.[10]

One comment may be made on Healy's decision. That is, that approval of job descriptions by the union may have meant only that the job was correctly described for the purpose of payment of the rate. This does not necessarily mean that the duties thus stated are frozen. The parties have agreed that the language properly describes work performed in the classification, but they have not jointly determined that only the occupants of the classification shall perform that work.

Without any doubt, the right to revise job classification is a major matter, especially in an enterprise of any complexity. In many industries the elimination of jobs, the reallocation of their functions to other classifications, and the splitting and combining of classifications are everyday matters, without which the continuous improvement in technology and methods could not be accomplished. Where these changes are substantial, new classifications may have to be established and new rates negotiated. Lacking the right to alter job content unilaterally, the employer can only hope to secure union agreement when the change is to be made or in negotiations for a new contract. This is no easy matter in cases of actual or potential loss to the employees affected.

It should be noted that even those arbitrators who take the view that job content is frozen permit the reassignment of minor, occasional, or fragmentary duties from one classification to another. It is only substantial changes which are said to be prohibited.

---

[10] *Ibid.*

Revision of Departments

We can now turn our attention to the other major operating structure, the department. As we have said, management establishes its departments on the basis of purely functional considerations. Unions seldom question management's right to change departments, to create new ones, or split or combine old ones as it sees fit. The problem arises when such rearrangement of a management structure means also a realignment of jobs and perhaps seniority units.

As an example of a reorganization of this kind, we can look at a decision rendered by Samuel Kates at the Fremont, Ohio plant of Hewitt-Robins, Inc.[11] The company had decided to discontinue the manufacture of certain sponge and rubber products and concentrate its efforts on foam rubber. This meant that two shipping and receiving departments and the jobs within them were eliminated, and a new warehousing department was established in which some of the duties of the eliminated classifications were performed by employees in new classifications. The union claimed that this was a violation of the wage provisions and the seniority rights of the employees. After reviewing the contract, Kates concluded that there was nothing in it which prevented the company from revising job classifications and, therefore, departments. The union's interest in the company's departmental organization, he said, "must be limited to its effects on the members of the bargaining unit under the contract."

In a case decided by Harry Platt at Wyandotte Chemicals Corporation, a payloader, manned by an employee assigned to the Yard Department, had been used for some years to move crude bicarbonate of soda in the Rotary Department. Its use had increased until the Yard employee spent practically all of his time and much overtime in the Rotary Department. The company decided to purchase a new payloader for use in the Rotary Department and thereupon established a new Payloader classification in the department, filling it by bid in the department in accordance with the contract. Platt upheld the company, saying:

> Under the facts in this case there can be no question but that the operation of the Payloader in the Rotary Department has become a full-time job, and I do not see how, in the absence of

[11] *Hewitt-Robins, Inc.*, Kates, 30 LA 81 (1958).

explicit Contract provision prohibiting, management can be denied the right to establish such as classification in that department. To be sure, this may affect the job and promotional opportunities of the employees in the Yard Department by reducing the amount of work now available to them. But this would follow only as a natural consequence of the requirement in the parties' Contract for exercising seniority on a departmental basis. No provision of the Contract guarantees that the job and promotional opportunities in every department will remain constant during its entire term. Nor does the Contract withhold from management the right to change its manufacturing processes or the right to disperse or combine its operations on a rational basis and in the interest of efficiency either among existing or newly established departments.[12]

Effect of Seniority Rights

Lastly, mention should be made of the principle that seniority is not a jurisdictional concept. James Healy makes this point in the Sperry Gyroscope case,[13] and in the Axelson Manufacturing Company case, Paul Prasow expresses the rule this way:

It seems to the Arbitrator that the difficulty in this issue revolves about the nature and scope of seniority rights as contrasted to jurisdictional rights over particular work. Although the two concepts are often related, the fact remains that "jurisdiction" is a matter distinct from that of "seniority." The two concepts are not synonymous. Seniority defines the rights and privileges to which an employee is entitled by virtue of his length of service in his current classification or department, whichever is the appropriate seniority. Jurisdiction, on the other hand, relates to the scope and content of the classification or job. It should be clearly recognized that seniority is a relationship between employees in the same seniority unit, rather than a relationship between jobs. Seniority protects and secures an employee's rights in relation to the rights of other employees in his seniority group; it does not protect him in relation to the existence of the job itself. By the use of an objective measure, length of service, the rights of one employee are balanced against other employees' rights.

The rights inherent in seniority do not themselves guarantee the continued existence of the job, or that it shall be maintained without change in content. Seniority can only stand as a bar to changes in job content if the contract so expressly provides, or if it can be shown that the changes are motivated on the part of management by a desire to evade the seniority clause. Although

---

[12] *Wyandotte Chemicals Corp.*, Platt, 17 LA 697 at 700 (1952).
[13] 30 LA 507.

to many workers seniority is synonymous with the job itself, it does not provide absolute job security, since it does not guarantee employment. Seniority provides preference for jobs only where jobs exist. If jobs are eliminated, changed or otherwise become unavailable, seniority offers little protection to the employee.

While it is certainly true that changes in job content of a classification may adversely affect the job opportunities of the employees involved by reducing the amount of work available to them, the problem is still essentially one of jurisdiction, rather than of seniority. It is a well-established principle in industrial arbitration that management has the right, if exercised in good faith, to transfer duties from one classification to another, to change, eliminate or establish new classifications, unless the Agreement specifically restricts this right.[14]

Employers should ponder the effect of exercising their right to improve operating procedures when reallocation of work as between departments and classifications is involved. What becomes of people whose seniority is by department or classification if the effect of the change is to eliminate their work entirely and they have no plantwide "bumping" right? If the skilled portions of a classification are eliminated through the introduction of new equipment, do the members of that classification continue to enjoy the old rate or should the rate be revised? If the second, do the employees formerly enjoying the higher rate stay in the new unskilled classification, taking the lower rate, or do they have the right to move to other classifications?

It will be found in examining some of the arbitration cases dealing with these problems that the arbitrators are silent as to results of a decision, holding merely that management has the right to alter plant operating structures, leaving their effect on seniority rights to settlement by the parties. It might be better for employers to face these problems squarely, reserving the right to change methods of manufacture and working arrangements with the results to the employees affected spelled out in so many words. For example, if a change in department structure leaves certain employees without a seniority "home," the agreement could provide that management should present the union with a seniority arrangement to take care of them, leaving the union to question the propriety of management's proposal through the grievance

---

[14] *Axelson Mfg. Co.*, Prasow, 30 LA 444 at 447 (1958); see *Fabricon Products*, Prasow, 35 LA 63 (1960).

procedure. Paragraph 59 of the General Motors contract[15] provides that "when changes in methods, products or policies would otherwise require the permanent laying off of employees, the seniority of the displaced employees shall become plantwide and they shall be transferred out of the group in line with their seniority to work they are capable of doing, as comparable to the work they have been doing as may be available, at the rate for the job to which they have been transferred." The Swift agreement[16] similarly provides for "gang rearrangements" when jobs are "eliminated or changed" so as to require the reassignment of employees.

In a Republic Steel Corp. case,[17] Harry Platt held that the laid-off employees of a discontinued department were covered by the seniority provisions in the agreement and entitled to recall in the order of their departmental seniority—not on the basis of a different recall plan established unilaterally by the company. Contract provisions to take care of situations of this kind are also indicated if the courts adopt the principle that seniority rights survive the expiration of the contract and are exercisable in plants or operations not covered originally by the contract.

---

15 BNA, *Collective Bargaining Negotiations and Contracts*, p. 20:314 (Sept. 29, 1961).
16 Unpublished.
17 *Republic Steel Corp.*, Platt, 27 LA 685 (1956).

CHAPTER 7

THE SENIORITY PRINCIPLE AND
THE ASSIGNMENT OF WORK

In the first chapter, we praised the seniority principle as one of the great contributions unions have made to industry and the protection of the worker. This wholesome concept, however, has been expanded and applied in a variety of situations far removed from its original purpose of protecting the older worker against discriminatory and unfair layoff. Some seniority systems can be described only as chaotic. Seniority is the controlling principle in job selection. This has meant a tremendous burden of industrial cost in lost production, in the payment of wages to inefficient workers who needed substantial training or were placed on jobs they could not learn adequately, and in scrapped materials and products.

Seniority has the practical appeal of being easy to administer. It is an automatic yardstick which confers a sense of security and privilege based on length of service to the worker with little or no ability and ambition. Unions find it easy to "sell" seniority; when workers are asked to give up or dilute their seniority rights, passionate resistance is encountered. Employers, too, have found it easier, in many cases, to forego the difficult task of setting up standards for the recognition of merit and ability, especially in view of the problems management has encountered in defending departures from the seniority rule in the grievance procedure and in arbitration. The result has been less resistance in practical bargaining to union restrictions on the right to assign work than one might expect.

Almost all Americans, including unionists, admire individual success. Most of us are willing to grant that the able man who works hard should have his due. But the exceptional individual in a "blue collar" job in an organized plant finds his progress blocked by the seniority rights of others. The only way to remove this block is to provide in the labor agreement for the recognition

127

of merit, skill, and ability as criteria at least as important as seniority. But such provisions are of little avail unless they are implemented by sound and well-administered selection and assignment procedures. It is management's failure to develop and use such procedures which is responsible for the steady growth over the years of the stultifying influence of seniority.

Layoff and Recall

The basic unit for the application of seniority is, or should be in most cases, the classification. Department and plantwide rights sometimes require a change in the character of the work and in the skill required to perform it. From the employer's standpoint, where skill and experience are not easily interchangeable, the smaller the unit, the better. This is recognized by the unions in the case of the skilled trades. But in production classifications, skill and ability are less demonstrable as criteria, hence the growth of the larger units in various combinations. When these combinations are established, the employer should seek to group jobs together on the basis of similar skills and experience, so that on layoff a minimum of break-in time is required.

This reduces the losses due to bumping, the displacement of junior men by senior employees from other classifications or departments. The losses due to bumping, in efficiency, in spoilage and scrap, can be high. In some plants, bumping has become a plague to management because of the wide variance of skills and job requirements in the seniority unit. This problem can be lessened in various ways, through contract language and good plant practice. Bumping should be permitted only into jobs which the senior employee can perform without training, or which he has formerly performed and is still qualified to perform. Some companies maintain a job register for each employee showing what jobs he can perform when reductions in force take place. Another device is to allow the senior employee to displace only the man with the least seniority in the unit, not giving him the privilege of picking work which he likes or is well paying. Temporary layoffs or grace periods during which layoffs and recalls can take place without regard to seniority are contained in some contracts, thus giving the senior man displacement rights only when the layoff will be of lengthy or indefinite duration or is permanent. In some plants, training and "move-up" privileges are extended to senior employees during periods of absence of regular people to minimize skill adjustments in layoffs. It must always be remembered, to quote Paul N. Lehoczky in a Pittsburgh Plate Glass Company case,[1] that "the first and foremost purpose (of seniority) is to give employees job security—not the right of job selection, especially for temporary openings."

Employers have failed to perceive that seniority loses value when layoffs, instead of bringing hardship to the employee, actually are found desirable. There have been a number of indications that some senior employees prefer layoff to pursue their personal interests in view of the substantial sums payable to them under supplemental unemployment benefit plans, especially when remaining at work means a reduction in rate. An employer who provides a program of layoff benefits should seek relaxation of strict seniority rules restricting his selection of the employees he needs, particularly in those bumping situations in which the senior employee is not fully qualified to do the available work. Since the purpose of seniority is job security, the provision of alternative financial security is a legitimate *quid pro quo* for the restoration, to a reasonable extent, of the employer's privilege to lay off and recall employees on the basis of ability as needed. Instead of this, however, the trend seems to be to give the older employee his choice of working or taking a layoff, without loss of seniority and with full unemployment benefits. The trend should be modified to take into consideration the need for efficient and economical procedures.

Reduction of Hours

Although in most manufacturing plants the device by which wage costs are reduced in times of low production is the layoff by seniority, it is also possible to provide for reduction of the workweek. Work sharing has its appeal only to limited groups— the photoengravers, for example. Most unions look on it as "sharing the misery," and their dislike of the short workweek has been accentuated when unemployment and supplementary unemployment benefits are on a weekly basis. There is little point in working for 32 hours a week if the same amount of money can be secured under the benefit plans. In 1961, the auto industry put

---

[1] *Pittsburgh Plate Glass Company*, Lehoczky, Chairman, 32 LA 945 at 948 (1959).

its benefits on a daily basis, retaining the right to reduce the workweek for specified periods.

Opinions on the right to reduce the workweek differ in *ad hoc* arbitration. Cases upholding the right to reduce stress the "work-sharing" principle, and usually some special condition makes the application of the layoff by seniority provisions impracticable, thus material shortages of indefinite duration, weather conditions making cancellation of the third shift desirable as a safety matter, the taking of inventory or the installation of new equipment, major repair work, and the like. In the Motch and Merryweather decision,[2] Samuel Kates reached the conclusion that a contract providing for a "basic working week" of 40 hours permits continuing reduction of the workweek only when layoffs would impair plant efficiency. On the other hand, where the condition does not make layoffs impracticable, work reduction may be held in violation.

The call-in pay provision found in most agreements would seem to indicate that management has no obligation to provide a full day's work for senior employees. This is certainly true where junior employees are kept on to finish up the work they are doing, and senior employees are sent home as their work is finished, although the obligation to transfer the seniors to the remaining work could be held to exist if they can readily be transferred without loss of efficiency. Likewise, management has no obligation to provide other work for the balance of the day, at least where there is no other work the senior employees can perform economically. Division of work between shifts has been held within management's rights. In Emerson Electric Manufacturing Company,[3] the employer, in the belief that he had material for only three hours of work, sent the day shift home early, and reserved the material for the second shift to avoid paying call-in pay for no work. The arbitrator, Joseph M. Klamon, held there was nothing in the contract to present this, the flow and control of work being, under the contract, within the discretion of the company. But reduction of the work day to six hours for an indefinite period of reduced

---

[2] *Motch and Merryweather Machinery Co.*, Kates, 32 LA 492 (1959). See also *Kennecott Copper Corporation*, Ross, Chairman, 32 LA 300 (1958); *Patent Button Co. of Tennessee*, Stouffer, 37 LA 877 (1961); *Struthers Wells Corp.*, May, 34 LA 372 (1959).

[3] *Emerson Electric Mfg. Co.*, 18 LA 554 (1952).

production was held by arbitrator Walter E. Boles, Jr., in a Cook Machinery case,[4] to violate the employees seniority rights.

The employer should reserve these rights. Short workweeks, for limited periods, keep the work force together. Just as many employers of skilled manpower prefer to work regular overtime schedules as against hiring additional men, they may find it advantageous not to lay them off, and thus perhaps lose them. A short workweek avoids the complicated and costly bumping procedure many contracts establish for layoffs. Reservation of the right to reduce the workweek should certainly be established by the employer if he has a supplementary unemployment compensation plan which makes up the greater part of the loss of income caused by reduced hours of work. Many a small employer fails to perceive, when he grants "pattern" benefits of this kind, that the large pattern-setting company has operating and cost reduction privileges which he is denied.

Promotions and Transfers

Second only to "bumping" procedures in complexity are union procedures designed to secure seniority preference in promotions and transfers. It is part of management's responsibility to utilize the skills and experience of its employees as effectively as possible. In the mind of the supervisor, anxious to get the job done, the chief consideration is the availability of men capable of doing the work without training. The avoidance of overtime wages is sometimes a factor. But unions seek to regulate intraplant movements, even of a temporary character, by application of the seniority principle: the more desirable openings are to be awarded to the senior man, the less desirable to the juniors, ability and economy being secondary factors, if indeed they are factors at all.

We should know what we mean by "promotion." Standing alone, it may include openings in more desirable jobs, those which are quieter or dust-free, or those which offer better promotional opportunities, increased incentive earning opportunities, or other advantages. Sometimes men prefer jobs merely because they are easier. This naturally creates problems of administration. Some contracts exclude these problems by defining promotions as "advancements to better-paid jobs," a completely certain standard.

---

[4] *Cook Machinery Co.,* Boles, 35 LA 845 (1960).

A second feature of importance is management's right to decide whether a particular vacancy should be filled by promotion or instead by new hire or transfer from some other department or group. Unions generally insist on clauses which provide that "whenever vacancies or new jobs exist within the bargaining unit, they shall be filled by (agreed procedure)." Such clauses are more common than those under which management is free to decide how best to fill the job. There are many cases in which supervision would prefer not to upgrade, and the choice should be preserved if possible.

The decision on the area or group from which the selection for promotion must be made is sometimes a difficult one. If the group is broad, say plant-wide, senior men who have little or no aptitude or training for the job may claim it; the rejection of their claims causes ill will and grievances. If the group is too small, good men in other sections of the plant are denied opportunity. The solution must be tailor-made and is sometimes left to local agreement or plant practice in the large corporations.

The unit for the exercise of promotional rights, if not set out in the contract, should not be allowed to expand beyond the employees whose experience in the plant is such that they can qualify for higher-rated jobs within a minimum of time, and with a minimum of training.

These matters should be studied carefully and not allowed to become the subject of haphazard and inconsistent plant practice. If intelligent policies are formulated and uniformly applied by supervisors, there is every chance that they will be sustained by arbitrators.

Promotions should be distinguished from transfers. Lateral movements of many different kinds are embraced within the term "transfer." They may be from one department to another, from one classification to another, from one shift to another, and they may embrace movements within classifications or occupational groups. David Wolff in a Chrysler case,[5] has said that "the transferring of employees is normally a function of management." Except as restricted by the agreement, thus, by a clause providing that all vacancies are to be filled with regard to seniority, manage-

---

[5] *Chrysler Corporation,* Wolff, 6 **LA** 276 (1947); see also *Diamond Portland Cement Co.,* Teple, 35 **LA** 162 at 167 (1960).

ment has the right to make transfers. This has been frequently recognized in arbitration, an example being the decision of Charles H. Livengood, Jr. in the United States Rubber Company case [6] already mentioned as upholding the company's right to make interdepartmental transfers without regard to seniority rights, applicable only within departments. Some agreements regulate transfers as well as promotions, both temporary and permanent. Commonly, these clauses provide for the changes, if any, which result from the transfers in the employee's seniority rights and the rate he is to be paid upon transfer. Where such provisions do not exist, the employer should mark out carefully those transfers not covered by the agreement and provide supervision with procedures for handling them. Employees' desires should be taken into account in making transfers if this is feasible and efficient. Granting that all employees cannot have the jobs they like, and that management must utilize their skills as effectively as possible, supervisors should make an effort to grant transfers when requested, or to honor the employees' desire not to transfer, since employees work more effectively on jobs they like.

Where contracts provide for the filling of vacancies and new jobs under "seniority and ability" clauses, the terms "vacancy" and "new job" should, as we have noted, be defined. These clauses do not require the filling of vacancies, even though they say such "shall" be filled, if the work is not required, since the company has the exclusive right to decide whether a job is needed and should be filled. Unless temporary vacancies are specifically mentioned, the employer is not required to fill them on a seniority basis, at least if the employee whose job is vacant is scheduled for return in the immediate future. Again, this is a situation in which past practice may compel the employer to do something which, if he had exercised his right to act unilaterally, he would not have been compelled by the contract to do.

Some confusion exists as to the rights of senior employees to "bump" into higher-rated classifications occupied by junior employees when reductions in force are in progress. This can happen under some agreements on the basis of occupational group seniority including more than one classification. But this is a windfall for the employee, not a promotion. No promotion is involved

---

[6] *United States Rubber Co.*, Livengood, 28 LA 704 (1957).

if, on reduction, an employee is assigned to an open job on a higher classification, nor does this give rise to a claim of improper promotion on the part of another employee. Ordinarily employees laid off bump only into lower classifications, and several decisions have been rendered to the effect that this is implied from the very existence of the promotion clause governing movements into higher classifications.

The employer should analyze the agreement in the light of movements of work and employees between classifications, seniority units, and departments (or interplant movements, if the contract covers more than one plant). Transfers not covered by the agreement should be identified and policies set up to govern their execution. The criteria controlling movements which are covered by the contract should be established. Finally, an appropriate system of recording changes which show on their face that the agreement has not been violated should be established.

Demotions

Demotions for disciplinary purposes are usually regarded by arbitrators as improper, unless it is shown that the employee's misconduct hampers the efficiency of his department or somehow justifies placing him in a lower classification. For example, if it can be shown that an employee's careless handling of dangerous equipment, such as a crane, endangers his fellow workers, he can be transferred off the job. The frequent absence of a lead man or a set-up man, upon whose regularity the work of others depends, may be a ground for demotion.

An employee may also be demoted if he is innately incapable of doing the work of his classification. In one case, a telephone lineman's demotion was upheld when the company showed that he was receiving industrial accident compensation for partial disability, based in part upon his testimony that he could not perform the work of his classification.

Demotions in connection with reductions in force and transfers to lower-rated occupations must ordinarily be accomplished on a seniority basis in accordance with the agreement.

Posting and Bidding Procedures

Many contracts require the company to post notice of openings which may be filled by promotion, and employees are given the opportunity to bid on them. Confusion and disputes can result if posting and bidding procedures are not delineated carefully. The posted notice of opening should be specific—it should state which jobs are open and how many openings there are, what the qualifications required are, how the bid is to be made and within what time, and how it is to be brought to the attention of the company. Forms should be provided for bids, which require definite statements from the employee as to his qualifications. Employees whose bids are rejected should be promptly informed of the reasons, even in the case of those rejected solely on a seniority basis. Nothing should be left to argument; careful documentation is important if a grievance is filed, especially in arbitration.

An application procedure could probably be installed unilaterally if desired. However, it might create a practice which might be held binding in applicable cases. Hence, if the right of employees to bid on new jobs and vacancies is confined by the contract's terms to higher-rated jobs, it might be better to leave lateral transfers of all kinds within the area of management rights for implementation by policy only. Employee wishes and seniority can still be considered when feasible.

Although not many contracts speak on the subject, the filling of a vacancy or a new job temporarily while selection for promotion is under way may be important. Management's right to make temporary transfers or to assign work should be adequate to permit this, just as management can fill vacancies due to absence, etc.

Ability v. Seniority

For years management's struggle to obtain recognition of ability as a criterion for promotion, and in cases of increase or decrease of the working forces, has been handicapped by the fact that seniority is a definite yardstick, automatic in its application. Thus, it not only promotes the union objective of maximizing job security for the older members, it relieves them of the necessity for examining the validity of management judgments on ability. Few unions care to participate in this decision-making under "mutual agreement" clauses because of the possibility of political reverberations in the membership. Hence, they prefer the role of protest and in practice tend to discount any preference except that based on seniority.

Clauses which, in some sense, recognize ability are to be found in various parts of agreements. Promotions almost always take ability into account; other occurrences in which ability may be a factor are demotions, transfers, the filling of vacant jobs and new jobs, layoffs and recalls, and wage increases based on merit. Some call for a comparative judgment as to "relative ability" of employees; others simply indicate that the seniority governs selection if the senior man has the ability to do the work. Some agreements require particular attributes such as experience; some provide for "break-in" periods, while others state expressly that the employee must be qualified to perform the job "without training." Some agreements reserve discretion to the company, providing that management's judgment can be reversed in arbitration only if arbitrary or discriminatory. The Ford agreement limits promotion grievances to complaints that management has not "exercised fairness" in judging the qualifications of available candidates.

Perhaps the principal characteristic of these clauses is that they leave so much unsettled, and hence tend to enhance the belief that seniority, the completely automatic standard, should be given greater weight than management's judgment of ability. For example, under Paragraph 63(a) of the General Motors agreement,[7] the umpire, not the corporation, set up the "head and shoulders" standard of clear superiority. If there is no candidate who is "head and shoulders" above the others, the selection must be made on a seniority basis among those who are approximately equal in ability. A large number of *ad hoc* arbitration decisions have been rendered on these questions, and the subject has received a great deal of discussion among members of the arbitration profession.

As these discussions and the decisions demonstrate, there is great variety of opinion as to the relative weight of evidence produced by management and by unions, and the degree to which the arbitrator will substitute his judgment for management's. But the employer's freedom of choice will be greatly enhanced if the contract reserves the right to compare candidates for openings (of any kind, on promotion or layoff, or others) on the basis of relative ability, merit and capacity, and provides that management's judgment, if not arbitrary or discriminatory, shall be final.

Whatever the right or wrong of the decisions, it is clear that management has lost ground in this area and that much of the

---

[7] BNA, *Collective Bargaining Negotiations and Contracts*, p. 20:314 (Sept. 29, 1961).

difficulty lies in its failure to develop adequate procedures and criteria for selection which, when called into question, can be relied upon to sustain its judgment as fair and factual.

Proof of Ability

There are several answers to the question of what proof is required to sustain a management selection of the junior candidate. Studies of the practical outcome of promotion decisions by arbitrators have tended to show that the senior employees have proved themselves able, despite management's preference for their juniors. These have cast doubt on the long-held assumption that management was the best judge of the merits of the available candidates.

On the other hand, a great many arbitrators have taken the position that they will not interfere with a *bona fide* management judgment which is not arbitrary or capricious. This point of view was well-expressed by the late Harry Shulman in an early Ford case:

> . . . the determination by the Umpire of the relative merit and ability of two or more employees is obviously a very difficult task, unless the promoted employee is clearly superior. It may be assumed that the Umpire can recognize outstanding superiority. But in other cases the determination of relative capacity is peculiarly a matter of judgment. Except in a case of clear error, an Umpire can hardly undertake to substitute his judgment on this issue for that of the men responsible for the efficiency of production and intimately familiar with the operations, the needs of the job, and the qualifications of the candidates.
>
> Lacking evidence of clear superiority, the Umpire must be satisfied that management's judgement was honest and reasonably exercised; that is, that management made an honest selection based on merit and ability, that its judgment was not a snap judgment without deliberation but was based on evidence with respect to merit and ability significant for the particular job, and that it made a deliberate appraisal of the significant merit and ability of the selected man in comparison with the eligible men having greater seniority.[8]

In a later case, Dr. Shulman imposed the burden of producing clear and specific proof in support of his choice upon the supervisor.[9] Although there are arbitration cases which require the

---

[8] *Ford Motor Co.*, Opinion A-17, Shulman, unpublished.
[9] *Ford Motor Co.*, Opinion A-198, Shulman, unpublished.

union to assume the burden of showing that management was arbitrary or discriminatory in its preference of the junior man, others, and this is perhaps the safer rule to follow in practice, require that management support its selection by proving the criteria used in making the evaluation and their applicability as between the candidates. This view, it is urged, has the merit of placing the responsibility on management, since it makes the initial choice, of sharpening its tools of selection, of improving its methods of evaluating employees, and showing that it has made an impartial and factual application of its criteria. Other arbitrators avoid discussion of the burden of proof required, and simply assess the evidence offered to reach what they consider an equitable solution.

Management has not, on the whole, accepted this challenge. The skill required on various jobs, the length of training required, the weight to be accorded to seniority (usually greater in unskilled jobs), and similar factors have not been given the serious and objective study they deserve. There is often much difference of opinion among various supervisors on these factors. The judgment of merit and ability is one of the important areas in which management must devise policies and procedures for the use of its initiative action. Criteria of employee selection must be objective and factual; they must relate directly to the requirements of the particular job under consideration; they must be made known and consistently applied. Otherwise, they will be attacked and may be held invalid or inapplicable in a particular case. If they meet these tests, management has every reason to insist that its judgment be upheld, not reviewed on the basis of union hindsight long after action is taken.

We can now turn to more specific criteria and their application. It is perhaps unnecessary to note that in most cases, not one but several criteria will be involved, some of which may be strong and others weak, and further that a standard valid in its own right can be misapplied in a particular case.

Experience

Some contracts require experience for "bumping" into a job on layoff, and others mention it as one criterion for promotion. If experience gained with other employers is counted, a system of recording it on employment applications and investigating it should be devised. The employee may have some experience on the job for which he has been selected, and some companies follow a policy of affording "move-ups" to temporary openings in order to permit employees to gain the necessary experience to qualify when a permanent opening occurs. On the other hand, it has been held discriminatory for an employer to favor a particular employee with job opportunities not allowed impartially to all and then promote the favored employee on the basis of the experience he gained on the job. Experience on comparable jobs may demonstrate ability to perform the open job even though the applicant has not held it before. Experience on wholly unrelated work does not usually demonstrate any special competence as against other factors, including seniority.

Production Records

Where a company keeps records of individual output, and even better, of scrap, machine care, and quality, they are strong evidence of a man's ability, at least on his own job. Hence, they are important particularly under contracts which permit consideration of efficiency and merit, ability, and capacity. Mere opinions that an employee is efficient should be avoided in favor of proof by specific recorded instances of his efficiency.

Merit

Under contracts which mention merit as well as ability, such factors as cooperativeness, close attention to work, and regularity of attendance, or, in reverse, absenteeism, tardiness, and misconduct, are properly taken into consideration. They have been held not relevant where the question is simply one of ability to perform the work; discipline, it is said, is the proper remedy in such cases, not denial of seniority rights. Most arbitrators are likely, even so, to take such factors into consideration, even if unconsciously, and proof of personal faults or merits should not be overlooked in any case.

Merit rating systems have a special importance, if soundly conceived and well administered (most are not) with a direct relationship to the job in question. They should be as simple and objective as possible. Some of the characteristics of a good rating system are as follows:

1. The ratings must be based on personal knowledge of the employee's performance.

2. The raters must understand the system and be able to explain and apply it.

3. Ratings must cover a specific period of time, and must be made at frequent and regular intervals.

4. The factors in the rating system must have a definite relationship to the factors of the job.

5. There must be standards for measuring the relative importance of each factor.

6. The ratings must not be arbitrary or discriminatory.

7. The employee should have the opportunity to see the rating and discuss it with his supervisor.

One of the best known procedures is the "Critical Incident" system devised by Dr. John C. Flanagan of the University of Pittsburgh. It calls for the recording of incidents, good and bad, in some 28 categories affecting physical and mental qualifications, temperament, work habits, and personal characteristics. Although this system is complicated and like any other is subject to the possibility that the supervisor will favor one employee as against another, it seems as objective as any yet devised. Its supporters believe that favoritism is bound to be revealed, since the employee is told about the incident at the time it happens and can see his record at any time.

The system is not used as the basis of discipline, which is separately undertaken, sometimes without reference to the incidents recorded on the employee's record. If these incidents are brought out in connection with discipline, they are separated from the merit-rating system as such. In its instructions to foremen on promotional choices, the employer should advise them to base their selections on facts—not conclusions or ratings.

Training and Education

Where educational requirements and special training, such as formal or informal apprenticeship programs, can be related directly to the job, they have value as criteria. On the other hand, arbitrators have been somewhat critical of these requirements where they deny the opportunity for advancement to senior em-

ployees who have not had the opportunity to acquire the education or training but have acquired "on-the-job" training. Where
these requirements are clearly needed for success in the work, some
steps should be taken to make them a condition of application for
open jobs, including, if necessary, a contract provision to that
effect. The apprenticeable trades, for example, should be removed
from bidding by members of the plant force. In this connection,
it might be added, promotional sequences which require attributes
such as education for the top jobs are likely to meet with criticism
from unions, and should be developed in a careful manner so that
the entire range of the sequence is defensible.

Tests

Tests which are established as standard and related to the job
under consideration are helpful as a management tool. Thus, in
one case, a standard test for truck drivers was held to be a proper
element in selection. Tests ordinarily should be regarded as only
one factor in making selections. Physical examinations and manual
demonstrations may be required, and if the results are clear and
bear a significant relationship to the employee's chance of succeeding on the new job, they can be advanced as one (but only one)
standard of choice.

Miscellaneous Criteria

A number of other considerations can play a part in the choice
of candidates for jobs. Age, physical condition, attitude, and
personal characteristics all may have a bearing. As we have suggested, intangible attributes, such as ability to get along with
people, initiative, and the ability to use good judgment can be
important, especially in promotions to leadership positions, or
those which bring the employee into contact with the public. But
even here, the proof of the existence or nonexistence of such qualities should rest on specific factual incidents which demonstrate and
support the conclusion, not unsupported opinion.

Break-in and Training Periods

Break-in periods are quite commonly allowed by arbitrators,
unless the contract clearly eliminates them, in cases in which the
employee's ability may be doubtful, but there is a reasonable

chance that he can succeed in the job, and the employer is not likely to suffer serious damage if he fails. On the other hand, the determination of ability should be made when the position is filled, and if the evidence is clear that the employee cannot qualify, he should not be given the job. Training rights will ordinarily not be implied.

Where management has been placed in the position of following seniority with little or no opportunity to select on the basis of comparative ability, the rewards from giving training might in the long run be great. The right to disqualify an employee who does not succeed in a new job is an inherent right of management, but it should be reserved in the contract if there is any question about it. The right to disqualify within a specific time can be and is used by unions as an argument that the employee should or must be given a trial for the stated disqualification period, but the two should be separated.

Assignments Within Classification

Questions sometimes arise as to the right of the employer to assign an employee to tasks admittedly within his classification, which, however, he has not regularly been performing. Contract restrictions on this right are not frequent, although they do exist. In a Sun Rubber Company case,[10] an employee was moved to another job within his classification, a job which required more physical exertion than the one he had held for 12 years, in order to make his old job available for another man who was in poor health and required easier work. The contract stated that it was "not the intent of the Company to move employees within their respective classifications except when it becomes necessary." The Arbitrator, Harry J. Dworkin, held that the assignment was not dictated by necessity and refused to approve it.

The problem in most plants arises only when an employee is allowed to assume through long practice that he has a vested right to a particular assignment. He may think he has the right as a senior man to pick the assignments he likes. Thus in one case an electrician who had enjoyed indoor work for some time filed a grievance when a younger man was brought in and he was assigned to outdoor work. Employees will sometimes assert the right to

---

[10] *Sun Rubber Co.,* Dworkin, 28 LA 362 (1957).

operate a particular machine, especially when they think its use will increase their incentive earnings or because it is easier to operate.

Even though such grievances will ordinarily not be upheld in arbitration, lessons in good supervisory practice can be drawn from these examples. An employee should be required from time to time to perform all the duties of his classification, or if exceptions are made, they should be recognized as such and appropriate reservations of the management right to assign work made. A man should not be allowed to stay on one machine because he likes it, or even because he is highly efficient on it, but should be required to perform all the operations in his classification. He should be required to use the high, as well as the low, skills of his classification. He should be rotated from the more to the less desirable tasks.

This, of course, is not always to the taste of the supervisor. He knows that some men are faster than others, that some do the more complex work well, and others do not, that some display more ingenuity than others, etc., and he assigns work on this basis. This practical approach has its merits but it also has its disadvantages, especially in times of layoff when the incompetent senior must be retained, in the assignment of overtime on an "equal" basis, and in cases of absence. The supervisor should, at least, make it clear that the right to assign all phases of the work to all members exists and can be exercised at any time. To put it the other way, he should not allow practices to grow which limit his right of assignment to particular employees.

Finally, assignments within a classification should not be employed in order to favor some and discriminate against other employees or to subvert seniority rights. A foreman who assigns the higher-skilled tasks to selected employees, and then relies upon the skill thus gained to promote them to higher classifications in his department, runs the risk of having the promotion upset by senior employees who have not been given the same training. A consistent and intelligent approach is necessary in assigning work as it is in so many other areas in which management has discretion.

Temporary Transfers and Assignments Outside Classification

Despite our distinction between the word "assignment" and "transfer," it may be questioned whether the terms connote any difference when temporary transfers are compared with assignments. Permanent transfers, of course, are different, whether they be promotions, demotions, lateral transfers between occupational groups in the same or an equal classification, or transfers between shifts or departments or transfers to some other unit. They all imply a movement which is permanent or of indefinite duration. A temporary transfer to, or assignment to the work of, another classification suggests no such permanence; the employee assigned or transferred does not change his status, though his rate may change.[11]

A temporary transfer, as we have said, is sometimes governed by a specific provision. In the absence of such a clause, the employer has the reserved right to make such transfers without affecting the employee's seniority. If such a transfer is made, however, under circumstances which indicate that it is actually a permanent transfer, the promotion clause may be held to apply. The Swift & Company agreement [12] contains the following provisions on temporary assignments:

> (h) Temporary Assignment—When an employe is temporarily required to fill a job paying a higher rate of pay, the employe shall receive the higher rate; provided, however, that if such job is a combination job (a combination job being a job in which the work is covered by two or more job classifications and is performed in the same work cycle) the employe shall be paid for the hours worked on such combination job at the authorized rate for the highest rated job in such combination; provided, further, that if such job consists of work which is covered by two or more job classifications where such job classifications are performed independently and separately of one another, as distinguished from two or more job classifications which are performed in the same work cycle, the employe shall be paid for the hours worked on that work day on such job at the authorized rate for the highest rated job classification included in such job and performed by the employe. If an employe is required to temporarily fill a job paying a lower rate, his rate shall not be changed.

The Ford agreement (Article VIII, Sec. 22 (a) and (b) [13] creates a special kind of temporary transfer, providing that when it is necessary to "loan" employees from one classification to another

---

11 Lloyd H. Bailer, "The Right to Assign Employees in One Job Classification to Jobs in Another Classification," *Management Rights and the Arbitration Process* (Washington: BNA Incorporated, 1956), p. 200.

12 The Swift agreement is only available in published form from Swift.

13 The Ford agreement is only available in published form from Ford.

within a unit or between units, the employee with the least seniority shall be loaned. Deviations from seniority are permissible upon notice to the committeeman. This is designed to meet production exigencies, not to balance normal and expected absenteeism. The employee loaned keeps his rate for three days, then is given a temporary reclassification, which does not affect, however, his loan status.

This right to "loan" employees may be exercised when employees are on layoff. Umpire Shulman has said, "The company may operate after a reduction in force in the same way it operated prior to a reduction. It may borrow employees from one classification to another in order to cover absenteeism or to meet the other exigencies of production . . . [but this is] . . . on the assumption that there has been no deliberate effort to avoid seniority rights by reshuffling of jobs." This language, from an unpublished memorandum opinion, was given practical application in a case in which it was held that the assignment of regular plant painting work to nonpainters, proper when painters were not laid off, was improper when they were. Such a ruling would not have been made, presumably, if the work had been assigned merely to meet the "exigencies of production."

In the absence of a clause restricting management's right to assign work, unions have relied upon the job classification agreement and the seniority clauses as prohibiting assignments across classification lines by implication.

Under the Ford agreement, it has been held that, in the case of production classifications, the company has the right to assign the members of one classification to another. After three days, under a special rate agreement, the employee's rate is changed to correspond. But the right to make the assignment is clear. Umpire Shulman said, in a case dealing with the assignment of a drill press operator to polishing, a higher-rated job: "Not a word or a line in the contract casts any doubt upon the company's right to make such an assignment." [14] Many agreements, such as the provision in the Swift contract already quoted, provide that if an employee is temporarily assigned to a higher-rated classification, he shall be paid the higher rate, and, conversely, if he is assigned to a lower-rated classification, he shall retain his rate. Other agree-

[14] Unpublished.

ments restrict the right to assign by providing that work which is "normal" or "peculiar" to a classification shall be assigned only to members of that classification. Such clauses are common in the oil refinery industry.[15]

Union support of rigid lines of demarcation between production classifications, as well as those having craft status, can be extremely troublesome to management. The problem asserts itself in a number of ways: (a) the employees directed to do the work of another classification refuse to perform it or perform it under protest, and file grievances asking that the company be directed to stop making such assignments; (b) employees on layoff claim that their work was performed by others and ask for back pay; and (c) employees ask for overtime pay for work performed by others (sometimes this claim is made even though the work is done during straight time hours by the protested employees on the theory that the grievants should have been called in for overtime work). If we assume that a right to grieve exists, whether in relation to skilled or unskilled classifications, the problem remains whether the line between the two affected classifications has in fact been crossed. Many classifications overlap each other, and work can be assigned properly to either. In other cases, the task required, even though superficially the work of another classification, may be properly assigned as incidental to the work of the classification.

These concepts of "overlapping" job content and "related and incidental" work have been discussed at some length in a Ford opinion by Harry Platt.[16] This case is not as satisfactory as General Motors-UAW C-165,[17] in which Umpire G. Allen Dash declared that the agreement did not "confine management in the assignment of particular duties or tasks to specific job classifications on the basis of the crafts, skills or abilities of the incumbents." Platt's opinion is well worth study, however, since intelligent management action can alleviate most of the problems arising from job assignment complaints, even under the restrictions implied by Platt, and even with respect to the skilled trades. One of the most wasteful practices in industry is the use of three or four different trades to get a single job done. There is no reason why, in the course of tearing down and repairing a machine, a machine repair-

---

15 *Shell Oil Co.*, Sutermeister, 37 LA 1089 (1961).
16 *Ford Motor Co.*, Platt, 30 LA 46 (1958).
17 Unpublished.

man should need the assistance of other skilled trades. He can remove guards, belts, and sprockets without calling a millwright; he can disconnect pipes and tubing without calling a pipefitter; and he can remove and replace tools without calling a toolmaker or a tool setter. All of these things are properly incidental to his daily work and should be performed by him without delay and without assistance, unless supervision, in the exercise of its own function, decides that the job will be handled better if additional trades are assigned.

As has been suggested, in drafting job descriptions and in setting up job content by daily work practices, every effort should be made to broaden the scope of classifications and to incorporate, at least by general references, all of the incidental work an employee may be expected to do. Of course, it is not possible to specify every detail of every duty. But employees should not be confined to particular tools and particular machines, nor to kinds of materials, even though they normally work with them. Employees, when necessary, should be required to sweep and clean, paint, use lift trucks and hoists, set their own machines, make minor repairs, do simple welding and burning, and simple carpenter work, such as boxing and scaffolding, operate elevators, get their own tools, etc. The importance of practice in these matters cannot be over-emphasized. If management, by long acquiescence, by written grievance settlements, or otherwise, narrows the area within which it makes job assignments, the restriction may become, in effect, part of the agreement.

When we turn to the question of whether the work of one classification can be assigned to another when members of the first are laid off, somewhat different considerations must be taken into account. Here the grievant asserts that he should have been called in and asks for back pay. He asserts that the work performed is his regular and normal work. Management may have had the right to assign it to the second classification, but if, in fact, it had regularly assigned it to the classification from which the grievance comes, the grievance may be upheld. A similar approach can be taken to grievances which allege that overtime work has been given to the wrong classification. The practice—even if management has the right to change it—may be controlling as to the assignment.

It follows that it is dangerous to assign work when the assignment clearly impinges on the overtime rights or the seniority rights of the aggrieved employees. But this general warning is subject to a number of possible exceptions. These may be listed:

a. The work assigned must be that exclusively assigned to the aggrieved classification. If it is work performed by both classifications, the classification assigned to it is doing its own work.

b. Casual and intermittent assignments, designed to cover absentee situations or other exigencies, should not be considered a violation. This is particularly true if the necessity for the work could not be foreseen.

c. The performance of work for short periods, even though it is clearly that of another classification, should be permitted. If employees properly called for work have spare time, the employer should have the right to keep them occupied.

d. The practical difficulties attendant on calling employees in who are laid off, or during overtime periods, should be taken into account. Under recall procedures, it may be some time before a complement of men can be obtained. In the meantime, the work must go on.

e. Management should have the right to assign any classification to emergency work at any time.

If management is to avoid wasteful and inefficient restrictions upon the use of labor, skilled and unskilled, it must develop a more affirmative approach to the assignment of work as between classifications. Where two or more classifications are, by training and experience, capable of performing the same kinds of work, it should be assigned from time to time to both, not allowed through consistent practice to become the property of one. To take an illustration from the Platt decision we have mentioned, it was held that there was no consistent practice as to the division of the work of die truck repair as between millwrights and machine repairmen. Obviously, this gives the supervisor an opportunity to get this work done by either classification when its members are available. If, as the union sought to establish, the work was exclusively that of millwrights, machine repairmen might stand idle or be laid off, while millwrights were called off other jobs clearly within their classification to repair die trucks or were kept overtime for that purpose. Similarly, the concept of "incidental and related work" should be studied and broadened. The use of other classifications, already in the plant, to do occasional work in cases where the classification normally performing the work is not available, and in the other special cases, should likewise be given attention. Of course, it is necessary to avoid consistent and protracted uses of manpower in such a way as to violate the seniority and overtime rights of the aggrieved employees. The precise point at which this occurs—that is, at which the management right to assign ends and the employee right to enjoy a particular area of work begins—can only be determined on a case-by-case basis. But much of the doubt could be removed in advance by discussion and planning of the management function.

Reclassifications

There are, generally speaking, two types of wage payment systems. There are formalized systems, including job descriptions, and the "slotting" of each classification within a labor grade on the basis of evaluation, as to each classification of various factors, such as skill (including education, experience, ingenuity, etc.), effort (both physical and mental), responsibility (for equipment and material, safety, and work of others), and job conditions (including noise, dirt, hazard, etc). This is the system used in the steel industry. The less formal systems used in the automobile industry consist simply of negotiation of a rate based on various features of the job in its relationship with other and similar jobs. Jobs are not slotted into labor grades as such.

In the formal systems when material changes occur, a new written description of the classification is developed. In the less formal systems, a new title and a new rate are established unless there are other jobs within the wage structure which cover the job as changed. In some cases, the rate is arbitrable, in others, not. In the meantime, the management proposal is put into effect.

There is, however, a second type of problem here which gives rise to much difficulty—that is the reclassification of one or more employees who claim they are performing the work of a higher-rated classification. The case may come up the other way. Management may attempt to downgrade employees on the theory that they are no longer performing the work of their original classification and should be downgraded. These are not cases in which the job content of the classification itself has been revised—it still exists, at least in wage structure theory, and the employee simply is no longer performing it.

How troublesome these problems can be is well illustrated by the report of Professor Morrison Handsaker to the members of

the National Academy of Arbitrators in an arbitrators' Workshop
on Classification Problems:

> Attention was also given to the question of the right of a company to "fraction" a job. The following instance was cited and formed the basis of considerable discussion: In a situation in which an A class machinist is required by his job description to operate all types of machine tools, a group of A class machinists are, as a matter of fact, for a period of years, for the convenience of the company, confined exclusively to the operation of the milling machine. Subsequently the company, faced with severe economic pressure by competition, attempts to reclassify these men downward to Milling Machine operator since their work is confined to the operation of that type of machine only. There was considerable sentiment in the group that this would, in the light of past practice, be an improper procedure on the part of the company. In short, the view was expressed by some that how job descriptions are interpreted and applied by the company may be more significant than the literal wording by the descriptions.
>
> The reverse of the situation just described was also considered. The question was posed in this fashion: Suppose that the company has had men classified as machinists who, in fact, are operating only milling machines. Another worker, classified as a milling machine operator and performing the same work as the men designated as machinists files a grievance asking to be similarly classified as a machinist. Some in the group, contending that the man was properly classified for the work he was doing as a milling machine operator, held that the grievance should be denied. Others, arguing that his fellow workers doing the same tasks were classified in the higher job of machinist, maintained that the grievance of the milling machine operator should be granted.[18]

It may be noted that Professor Handsaker is not correct when
he states that the cases described involve the "right to 'fraction'
a job." The company did not change the job content of either
the A machinists or the milling machine operators. Probably in
most plants, when situations such as these occur, it could be shown
that there were A machinists using all types of machine tools and
milling machine operators who were performing only the duties
of their classification, and were entitled to hold the classification.
A true instance of "fractionalization" would occur if the company
split off some of the less skilled functions of the machinists and
transferred them to the milling machine operators. Or these cases
could involve the company's right to assign the work of one classifi-

---

[18] Morrison Handsaker, "Classification Problems," *Management Rights and the Arbitration Process, op. cit.* at pp. 54, 56.

cation to another. The milling machine operator might file a grievance asking that the company be prevented from making further assignments of machinist work to him, or the machinists might file a similar grievance asking that the work be reserved for them. But the cases as presented involve only questions of reclassification of employees.

As such, they are not dissimilar to a case of transfer. If an employee is transferred to another classification, he takes the rate of the classification, i.e., he is "reclassified." But the difficulties here are not thus plain. They arise in which might be called "misclassification" situations. In negotiating classifications and rates, the parties agree that the performance of a certain task or combination of tasks will entitle an employee to a particular classification. If he has additional significant duties which he performs regularly, he may be misclassified. Likewise, he may not perform all of the tasks. This can occur in two ways: (a) an employee may be assigned some duties outside the classification when he is originally placed on the job, or (b) the functions he performs may change (abruptly or gradually) until his classification is no longer appropriate for the work. It is in this latter category that the A machinist example posed by Professor Handsaker falls.

To reach a decision as to whether an employee should be reclassified, a determination is required of the content of his own classification and the one claimed to be proper (either by the company or the union). In the absence of descriptions, the only way to determine the content of a job is by reference to past practice. But there is also the problem of comparison and evaluation. Many classifications do roughly similar work but with entirely different degrees of skill and responsibility. There are several different kinds and grades of grinders in industry. A crib attendant has a large responsibility factor; a machine operator has little. Numerous classifications use the same tools for different purposes. And here, just as in the work assignment cases, we encounter numerous instances of overlapping job content and incidental tasks, which, while they fall clearly within the job content of the classification in which it is asserted the employee should be placed, are clearly incidental to his own duties as well. To justify a reclassification, upward or downward, the employee must regularly perform significant duties of the classification sought to be applied.

There are a number of further qualifications on the right of reclassification. The fact that an employee is more (or less) proficient in the work of his classification does not justify reclassification. A change in work loads, such as the assignment of two machines instead of one, does not change the content of the employee's work. A mere change in the location of the work does not affect the classification duties. Occasional assignment to the duties of another classification, although it may justify a claim for the rate of the classification while the work is being performed, does not call for a permanent reclassification.

As the Handsaker report shows, the employer should be alert to significant changes which justify reclassification. The same may be said, of course, of the union. The passage of time with acquiescence can be a significant factor in determining whether an employee is, in truth, working out of classification. After all, if the parties wish, they may agree (through practice or expressly) that milling machine work can be called "Machinist A" and paid the machinist rate.

As is perhaps evident, the problems in this area, i.e. misclassification cases, are very similar to those in the assignment area. In the Ford case involving drill press operators doing the work of polishers,[19] the first question was the right of the company to make the assignment. This decided in favor of the company, the umpire went on to decide whether they were entitled to the polishers' rate, and held that they were not for periods of less than three days. Over that time, by agreement, they were. Had they remained in the work permanently and filed a grievance asking for reclassification, they would, it can be assumed, have received it. As we have said, our breakdown of these "within-bargaining-unit" problems is somewhat artificial. Just as it is hard to separate promotions and demotions from transfers, it is easy to confuse temporary transfers, assignments, and misclassifications. They tend to merge and overlap, and many of the tests and considerations which apply to one also apply to the others.

---

[19] Unpublished.

Chapter 8

WORK SCHEDULING AND OVERTIME

At each stage of the production process, management must make a decision not only as to who is required to perform the work and how many employees of each classification are to be used, but when they will be needed. While in practice, decisions as to who shall perform the work and decisions as to the period of time within which the individuals selected will work are made simultaneously, they must be separated in discussion because they involve different sections of the agreement and different considerations. The considerations which motivate management in making and changing work schedules relate to flexibility. Management must adjust production to customer requirements, to interdepartmental or interplant production schedules, to model or design changes, to receiving and shipping schedules, including changes by carriers, to seasonal changes, to plant maintenance and power facilities, and to balancing hours so as to distribute work as evenly as possible and to avoid (where the agreement does not prevent it) the payment of overtime. Sometimes these changes are predictable; in other cases, they are emergency changes which cannot be anticipated.

Employees, on the other hand, look at schedule changes in the light of their personal requirements. They prefer night or day work according to their family situations. They seek predictability and stability in schedules in order to plan personal and family leisure time activities; they like regular hours. On the other hand, they frequently seize opportunities to work overtime for financial reasons. In some cases changes in schedule are challenged on the ground that employees of a certain classification are entitled to do the work on overtime hours, or that the schedule has been juggled to avoid the payment of premium pay. These desires inevitably clash with the employer's interest in flexibility and economy in the use of manpower.

Altering Schedules

It is generally conceded that, in the absence of limiting language in the agreement, management has the right to alter working schedules. The general rule is discussed by Paul Prasow in a Morris P. Kirk and Sons, Inc. case [1] in connection with a change in one department from a fixed to a rotating shift basis, and by William M. Hepburn in a United States Pipe and Foundry Company case [2] in connection with changes in schedule hours. In both cases, however, it was indicated that past practice would be important in showing the intent of the agreement. If the agreement is silent, evidence that management has altered schedules in the past without union consent will be of great importance, and union testimony that such changes have not occurred except with its consent may be held to bar the right to change. On the other hand, the use of a normal schedule for years was held by Herbert Blumer in a Columbia Steel Company case [3] to be nothing more than the exercise of managerial judgment on scheduling, and not an agreement that the normal schedule would be observed.

Avoiding Premium Pay

Avoidance of unnecessary overtime costs is a permissible objective, but some contracts expressly prohibit management from laying off employees for the purpose of avoiding overtime pay. Under such a contract, Harry Platt held that delaying the starting time of employees and keeping them at work two hours after their regular quitting time was proper if there was no work for them during the first two hours of their regular shift; but that if the employer expected certain trucks to arrive for unloading in the two hours after their regular quitting time, and thus rescheduled them in order to secure their services for this period without paying overtime, he was in violation. Platt said: "Undoubtedly, an employer has the right, in the absence of a contract provision forbidding, to make sporadic changes in the regular working schedule of an employee whenever necessary to meet unexpected and unavoidable contingencies that sometimes arise in the management of his business; such contingencies, for example, as arise from failures in the power supply, breakdowns, lack of stock or

---

[1] *Morris P. Kirk & Sons, Inc.*, Prasow, 27 LA 6 (1956).
[2] *United States Pipe & Foundry Co.*, Hepburn, 28 LA 467 (1957).
[3] *Columbia Steel Co.*, Blumer, 7 LA 881 (1947).

work, etc." [4] This case, as do others, emphasizes motive—if the employer can prove that he has a valid reason for bringing the employee in early and sending him home at the end of eight hours, or bringing him in late and keeping him beyond the regular quitting time, there is no layoff to avoid payment of premium time.

The same considerations apply under similar contract provisions in cases in which employees are brought in on Saturday at straight time (under contracts providing for payment of overtime after 40 hours and not for Saturday as such) after they have been laid off one day or more during the regular workweek. If the employee was laid off on Tuesday because of lack of stock, he was not laid off for the purpose of avoiding payment of the overtime premium. In an Esso Standard Oil Company case,[5] Whitley P. McCoy held that the purpose of scheduling three men off on Thursday and Friday and bringing them in on Saturday and Sunday at straight time was to avoid laying off other employees, not to avoid the payment of overtime. The work they were called in to do on the weekend was conveyor repair work. Had the conveyor been shut down during the week, 73 employees would have had no work for two days.

Some contracts provide premium pay for Sunday work in industries which must operate on a seven-day basis. Many contracts are defective from a management standpoint in not providing for the inauguration of rotating schedules, when required, or at least in providing that certain classifications, such as boiler operators or maintenance men, can be given special workweeks including Saturday and Sunday as straight time days, with payment of premiums for the sixth and seventh day worked.

Notice Requirements

Notice of changes in schedules should be given in advance, whenever possible. Whether or not the contract provides for notice, the employees resent disruption of their personal lives and habits and, in many cases, find new schedules very inconvenient from the standpoint of transportation. Good management requires that these human desires be taken into consideration

---

[4] *Gibson Refrigerator Co.*, Platt, 17 LA 313 (1951).
[5] *Esso Standard Oil Co.*, McCoy, 16 LA 73 (1951).

when changes must be made. This is an area where inconsiderate use of management rights is likely to lead to great dissatisfaction and to demands at the bargaining table for restrictive clauses in the agreement. On the other hand, the employer should not accept a notice requirement which is impracticable.

Vacations, Lunch and Rest Periods

Unless the contract limits the right—by provision for mutual agreement or individual choice of vacation periods—management has the right to schedule vacations as operative requirements dictate, or when the plant is shut down or closed. In Aro, Inc. the arbitrator quoted from a Ford case, decided by Harry Shulman, to the effect that correlation of vacations with periods of slackness is "laudable and necessary." [6] But in an American Air Filter Company case [7], the arbitrator held that where the contract stated that "the vacation of each employee must be scheduled in advance," the employer had no right to close the plant for two weeks. Changes of vacation period not made well in advance of the time, or those made after an employee's vacation has been set for a definite time, are likely to be viewed with hostility by employees and by arbitrators.

A number of questions not easy to answer can be asked with respect to lunch periods, paid and unpaid, and the rest periods. Some contracts provide for lunch periods, and permit the company to change them. Presumably, the employer could do this in the absence of a provision, at least if his action was not arbitrary. There is considerable controversy over paid-lunch periods, and particularly over the right of employers to discontinue them when established by practice. A paid-lunch period based on a three-shift operation implies that it is impossible for the shifts to take a regular unpaid half-hour lunch period because of overlapping of operations, but where this overlapping is not a necessary consequence of three shifts, there would be no reason why the usual half-hour unpaid period could not be required. Thus, although machine operators on three shifts might be given the paid-lunch

---

[6] *Aro, Inc.*, Livengood, 30 LA 225 (1958).

[7] *American Air Filter Co.*, Drake, 30 LA 150 (1958). See also *Rockwell Standard Corp.*, Schmidt, 34 LA 693 (1960); *Vanadium Corp. of America*, Sembower, 38 LA 389 (1962). Back-pay liability is a serious consideration, *see Philip Carey Mfg. Co.*, Gill, 37 LA 134 (1961).

period, maintenance men might simply be held over to do an extra half hour of work.

Changes in lunch and rest periods should be related to some genuine exigency of production, not made arbitrarily. If so related, there would presumably be no liability for pay, unless the employee ran over into his overtime period as a result. But it is questionable whether an employee who has devoted his half-hour unpaid lunch period to work at the request of the employer should be sent home at the end of eight hours in order to avoid payment of a half-hour of overtime. It would seem also that a three-shift employee who works through a paid-lunch period would be entitled to be paid for the time, but whether he would be entitled to the lunch-period time at his overtime rate is questionable.

Overtime Work and Its Equalization

The right to require a reasonable amount of overtime work is generally conceded, although there are contracts which permit employees to refuse it, at least in cases in which the employee has a good excuse or substitutes are available. An absolute right to refuse overtime can be dangerous, since it may be used as a pressure tactic. A good example of this is described by E. E. Hilpert in his opinion in a Robertshaw-Fulton Controls Co. case.[8] What is a reasonable amount of time varies, and cases have been known in which employees insisted on working through long periods of overtime, even though the supervisor would have preferred, in the interests of safety and efficiency, to bring on a new crew. Many contracts provide that in order to compel overtime, advance notice of some period must be given. The Ford agreement (Article IV, Section 6),[9] for example, provides that except in emergencies or breakdowns, notices must be given not later than the last hour of the employee's preceding work day.

Absent express qualifications, most management people require overtime under a rule of reason which permits the employee to exercise a reasonable degree of choice; but the practice of permitting refusals should be grounded on good operating policy, not mere pleasure. The validity of the employee's excuse is also a mat-

---

[8] *Robertshaw-Fulton Controls Co.*, Hilpert, 36 LA 4 (1961).
[9] Unpublished.

ter of importance, since a bad practice may evolve if excuses are not kept within bounds.

Under most agreements, some measure must be established of the group which is to share overtime. Frequently it is rotated by classification; sometimes, by department. The General Motors agreement [10] calls for equalization among those engaged "in similar work, as far as practicable." This is left for definition in each plant, by practice or agreement, and can be so narrow as to embrace only those performing a specialized task within a classification, or so broad as to include an entire department embracing a number of classifications, even those so dissimilar as spot welders, drill press operators, and metal polishers. Seniority is not a factor; the basic rule-of-thumb is the normal assignment of the work during regular working hours. In some cases the work is normally performed by two groups, in which case it may be assigned to either during overtime periods. If it is work performed only on weekends, no group can be said to be entitled to it.

The requirement of capability must also exist, even as between members of the same classification, but the degree of capability is not a factor; if two or more are competent, the fact that one is better than the other is not significant.

In order to avoid grievances over so-called missed overtime filed on the theory that it was performed by another overtime group or classification, careful attention must be paid to the initial establishment of the overtime equalization groups, and the assignment of work between classifications and groups during the regular workweek. We have already considered the subject of assignments between classifications. The principles discussed there have great importance in the matter of overtime equalization.

Work which by its nature or by practice is properly that of supervisors or other excluded employees can be performed by them during overtime periods and does not give rise to a claim from unit employees, since it is not work they normally perform.

In assigning overtime work among members of the group to which it belongs, the supervisor should make a distinction between expected overtime work and that which cannot be foreseen. If he knows overtime work is required, he should take care to consult

---

[10] BNA, *Collective Bargaining Negotiations and Contracts*, p. 20:317, ¶71 (Sept. 29, 1961).

the list and, other things being equal, to select the low people. He has more latitude in emergency situations and in cases which arise unexpectedly during the overtime period itself. He can, in many cases, finish up a job on overtime which was started by a crew that day during regular working hours, unless it is completely practicable to assign those low on the list to it; but this rule has less application in cases of weekend overtime. The word "practicable" has been said not to include considerations of cost, in the sense that the high man on the list can be brought in at time and one-half, while the low man would be entitled (because it would be his off-day) to double time. But it does include such considerations as skill, availability of employees, scheduling difficulties, and other operating considerations.

If an employee is missed, he should be entitled only to make-up time, and the contract should so provide since many arbitration decisions award back pay. In some cases back pay is awarded if the supervisor's action in selecting employees high on the list was arbitrary or capricious, and not the exercise of an honest and deliberate selection based on considerations of what is practicable. Some agreements prescribe a "reasonable" period within which missed overtime can be made up. In others the list is a continuing one, and overtime is always somewhat out of balance, with an agreed spread or tolerance within which the company may make up overtime. The leading decisions on claims for missed overtime are cited in a case at United States Rubber Company decided by Paul M. Hebert.[11]

Many agreements provide that overtime is to be assigned as equally as practicable to employees "available" for overtime. Employees who refuse to work overtime obviously are not available and should be charged with the time. The same may hold true, depending on the agreement or the practice, in the case of employees who are absent or on sick leave, etc., and cannot be assigned to work the overtime.

---

[11] *United States Rubber Co.,* Hebert, 34 LA 643 (1960).

CHAPTER 9

THE TRANSFER OF WORK OUT OF THE BARGAINING UNIT

Transfers to Employees Excluded from the Agreement

There are in most contracts two clauses which affect the right of the employer to transfer work to employees who are not within the unit represented by the union. These are the "recognition" clause and clauses providing that supervisors and other excluded employees are not to work on the jobs of members of the contract unit, except under certain circumstances.

Practically all recognition clauses, by some form of language or another, define the categories of employees the union is entitled to represent. Some refer to NLRB certifications, others list the categories, and still others refer to "contract units" established by prior agreement at each plant or by NLRB certification.

Jurisdiction is sometimes asserted by unions over work as well as people, and such clauses are not uncommon in contracts. We have seen an example from the standard contract form of the Iron Workers Association.[1] Another example is a contract of the Hamm Brewing Company of St. Paul, which provided that the union should have jurisdiction "over the employees in the unit as certified and over their customary work in the bottling house." The employer installed new can-seam testing machines and attempted to assign their operation to machinists who were members of a different union, although the hand testing had been done by members of the production and maintenance employee unit, which excluded the machinists. It was held that the production employees had the right to the work, at least until such time as it was shown that they were incapable of operating the machines.[2]

In the absence of an express restriction of this kind (which left open the question of what constituted the "customary work" of

---

[1] Unpublished.
[2] *Hamm Brewing Co.*, Lockhart, 28 LA 46 (1956).

the employees), unions rely on the recognition clause, the classification schedules, and the seniority clauses as establishing their right, by implication, to control the work done by members of the unit as against exempt employees.[3] The New Britain Machine Co. case in which Saul Wallen upheld this point of view can be quoted as an example, although there are others upholding management's right to transfer work out of the unit in the absence of an express restriction in the contract. Dealing with the transfer of the work of watchmen to exempt guards, which resulted in permanent layoff of the watchmen, Wallen said:

> Job security is an inherent element of the labor contract, a part of its very being. If wages is the heart of the labor agreement, job security may be considered its soul. Those eligible to share in the degree of job security the contract affords are those to whom the contract applies. . . .
>
> The transfer of work customarily performed by employees in the bargaining unit to others outside the unit must therefore be regarded as an attack on the job security of the employees whom the agreement covers and therefore on one of the contract's basic purposes.
>
> . . . The management clause is designed to give management the freedom to conduct its affairs in the interest of efficient production but this right may be exercised only within the framework of the limitations imposed by the contract. That clause cannot be utilized as carte blanche to defeat one of the basic aims of the contract.
>
> If one of the purposes of the contract as a whole, and of the seniority provisions in particular, is to assure the bargaining unit employees a measure of job security, then such security would be meaningless if the Company's view in this case were to prevail. For it would mean that, without regard to prior custom or practice as to the assignment of work, the Company could continuously narrow the area of available job opportunities within which the seniority clause functions by transferring duties performed by bargaining unit employees to employees not covered by the agreement. Not only the seniority clause but the entire agreement could thus be vitiated.[4]

It will be noticed that Wallen rests his decision mainly on seniority rights. Other cases stress the negotiation of included classifications and their rates, and some decisions hold squarely that the recognition clause confers jurisdiction over work as such.

---

[3] In the discussion of implied conditions in Chapter 3, p. 59, the theory advanced by unions to support their argument is analyzed.

[4] *New Britain Machine Co.*, Wallen, 8 LA 720 at 721 (1947).

Such a decision was rendered under the General Motors contract by Umpire Feinsinger.[5] This and similar decisions represent, as I have said, the adoption of the "lump of labor" theory, disguised by a reference to the unproven and improbable supposition that the employer might destroy the entire contract.

What these restrictions, whether implied as in Wallen's decision or expressly stated in the agreement, come down to is that work of the kind regularly performed by unit employees should not be assigned to foremen or other exempt employees. The actual disputes occur usually in the "fringe" areas, in which the company claims the work properly belongs to the excluded category and the union claims the reverse. Usually, the solution must be found in past practice, and if it is plain and well established, in most cases it is controlling. If not, the character of the work itself must be examined to see whether, as a matter of comparison, it is the kind of work done by the included or the excluded group, or whether it has elements of "inherent managerial responsibility" which take it out of the class of work performed by the rank and file. For example, inspection may be carried on by engineers or foremen, not for the purpose of rejecting nonstandard production, but for the purpose of investigating and tracing to its source the reason for the defects appearing in the product, and then devising a means to correct this condition. This, as a matter of comparison and responsibility, is not the typical work of rank and file inspectors. The difference between a tool repairman and a tool engineer, in function and purpose, is obvious.

Less important, but sometimes pertinent, are such factors as the use of testing and other equipment, or tools not ordinarily used by the bargaining unit people, and the nonavailability of regular employees, especially in emergency situations.

Most grievances in this area arise when management alters the method of performing a particular operation, and as a result changes the character of the duty formerly performed by the unit employee, vesting it with the characteristics of exempt work; or the employer may transfer to exempt employees duties which though unchanged were essentially exempt from the beginning.

---

[5] *General Motors Corp.*, Feinsinger, 37 LA 192. Umpire Feinsinger states, "By this process (assignment of bargaining unit work to excluded employees), the representation rights set forth in Paragraph 3 could be nullified and the bargaining unit eroded." (p. 195). See also *DeAtley Paving & Crushing, Inc.*, Peck, 37 LA 496 (1961); *Kimberly-Clark Corp.*, Hyman, 34 LA 480 (1960).

In a Chrysler case,[6] David Wolff decided that when an employee was promoted to supervision, he could carry on the duties he had previously performed, since they were essentially supervisory in nature. The union should have objected, Wolff remarked, to his performing them when he was a member of the unit. The employer can eliminate the jobs of semi-supervisory classifications, such as leaders, reassigning the nonsupervisory work to included classifications and the supervisory elements to foremen. If work is being duplicated by two classifications, one in the unit and one excluded, the employer may eliminate the task in the included classification. Where the character of the work changes from a technical grade to professional work, it may be assigned to excluded professional employees.

Under clauses limiting the right of foremen to perform unit work, the purpose for which the work is performed assumes vital importance. Assuming that a limitation exists, the company should make every effort to broaden the foremen's permitted area to the work necessary to keep production running smoothly and efficiently, just as in the case of technical and experimental employees the lines should be drawn in such a way as to permit legitimate development of new techniques, tools, and products. Hence, if the foreman operates a machine for a purpose which is inherently supervisory in nature, he should not be criticized. Charles C. Killingsworth, in a Goodyear case, said, "The button pushing is simply a signal or instruction to the machine . . . of the same character as instructions to truckers, unit attendants and other bargaining unit employees." [7]

Instruction, a supervisory function, sometimes requires physical demonstration; this is permissible when it is not carried on past the point of instruction. In certain cases the foreman may do unit work as "incidental" to his true supervisory function, such as entering a tool crib to determine what tools should be given to his employees, doing his own clerical work without assigning it to a plant clerk, and the like. He can iron out production difficulties and do experimental and tryout work, in most cases, and he can work in an emergency, especially if regular employees are not

---

[6] *Chrysler Corporation*, Wolff, 23 **LA** 247 (1954).
[7] *Goodyear Tire & Rubber Co.*, Killingsworth, 35 **LA** 917 at 919 (1961). See also *U.S. Steel Corp.*, Garrett, 37 **LA** 302 (1961).

available. But a shortage of men is not an "emergency." If the foreman can obtain a man or call one in, he is obligated to do so.

Grievances of this kind may be denied by arbitrators as trivial if only a few minutes' work is involved. And if no one lost work through the foreman's action, back pay should be denied by the employer.

Subcontracting

Management always has before it the question of whether materials, parts, or equipment should be purchased from an outside supplier or made in the plants of the company. In extreme cases, it is possible to convert the company to nothing more than a design and sales organization, the officers relying on their technical ability, their sales efforts, and competition between suppliers to deliver a product to the customer more cheaply than it can be manufactured. In others, a manufacturer finds that by producing a component himself he can substantially improve his competitive position, so he purchases equipment, trains employees, and goes into production. In any such decision a host of factors, such as administrative, engineering, and development costs, specialized equipment, techniques, and volume must be taken into account. Similar problems attend maintenance or construction of machines and buildings, the provision of janitor service and food supply, and warehousing and trucking.

With the rise of unions, management's untrammeled freedom to decide such questions on the basis of business considerations only, without reference to their effect on employees, has been restricted as to work which has historically been performed by its union employees. All such restrictions have their origin in labor's practical adherence to the "lump of labor" theory. When men are laid off or fear they will lose work, no amount of sophisticated discussion of the long run benefits of the economical placement of work is convincing. An increasing number of contracts contain language which in one way or another restricts management's right to use outside contractors and suppliers. An interesting example is discussed by Rolf Valtin in an Alan Wood Steel Company case.[8] Clauses may require merely advance notice to the union, or they

---

[8] *Alan Wood Steel Co.*, Valtin, 34 LA 455 (1960); *Parke, Davis & Co.*, Haughton, 34 LA 554 (1960).

may list one or more conditions—such as, that no subcontracting shall take place when men are laid off, or when they will be laid off as a result of the subcontracting, or that subcontracting shall be permitted only when the company lacks the specialized machinery or equipment to do the work with its own people, or when the employees lack the necessary skills, or when the job must be completed within a time limit which the regular force could not meet.

In Chapter 3, the legal basis for the implication of restrictions on contracting work out was reviewed. There are an increasing number of decisions in *ad hoc* arbitration which hold employers in violation of the recognition and wage classification and rate clauses of the agreement, even though there is no specific restriction in the agreement, when work ordinarily performed by members of the bargaining unit is contracted out. Unfortunately, the loose reasoning on which they are based has been given the verbal blessing of Justice Brennan in his concurring opinion in Warrior and Gulf and its companion cases, although the point was not before the court for decision.[9] As L. Drew Redden said in the Volunteer Electric Cooperative case:

> The decision certainly is not authority for concluding that subcontracting is a violation of the collective bargaining agreement per se. On the contrary, it actually does nothing to disturb the rule that the one who maintains that contracting work out is a violation of a contract containing no express provision against such activity must demonstrate that the violation exists.[10]

Subcontracting cases always involve allegations of the loss of work, actual or potential. These range from direct layoff to losses to employees yet to be hired. In a Continental Can Company case,[11] John F. Sembower was dealing with a company decision to hire a janitor service firm to clean its new research building. He said that the union had sufficient "legal interest" to sustain the grievance because, although the size of the janitor force employed by the company had increased, there were 20 new jobs which might have been within the unit except for the contract with the service. On the other hand, in the Cannon Electric Company case, which is similar on its facts to the Continental case, Benjamin Aaron said: "As a legal proposition, the Union's contention (that recog-

---

9 See p. 62.
10 *Volunteer Electric Cooperative,* Redden, 36 LA 787, 795 (1961).
11 *Continental Can Co.,* Sembower, 29 LA 67 (1956).

nition includes jobs, as well as people) has validity in certain situations, but it cannot be controlling here because the Company does not have, and never has had, any janitorial 'employees' in the new building. Tó claim that the Company cannot subcontract janitorial work in that building because the Union has the right to represent all janitors 'employed' by the Company is to assume the very point in dispute." [12]

In *How Arbitration Works,* the Elkouris list a number of criteria employed by arbitrators in determining whether or not subcontracting is permissible. These are:

1. Past Practice.—Whether the company has subcontracted work in the past.

2. Justification.—Whether subcontracting is done for reasons such as economy, maintenance of secondary sources for production and manpower aid, augmenting the regular work force, plant security measures, or other sound business reasons.

3. Effect on the union.—Whether subcontracting is being used as a method of discriminating against the union and substantially prejudicing the status and integrity of the bargaining unit.

4. Effect on unit employees.—Whether members of the union are discriminated against, displaced, laid off, or deprived of jobs previously available to them, or lose regular or overtime earnings, by reason of the subcontract.

5. Type of work involved.—Whether it is work which is normally done by unit employees, or work which is frequently the subject of subcontracting in the particular industry, or work which is of a "marginal" or "incidental" nature.

6. Availability of properly qualified employees.—Whether the skills possessed by available members of the bargaining unit are sufficient to perform the work.

7. Availability of equipment and facilities.—Whether necessary equipment and facilities are presently available or can be economically purchased.

8. Regularity of subcontracting.—Whether the particular work is frequently or only intermittently subcontracted.

9. Duration of subcontracted work.—Whether the work is subcontracted for a temporary or limited period, or for a permanent or indefinite period.

10. Unusual circumstances involved.—Whether an emergency, "special" job, strike, or other unusual situation exists necessitating the action.

---

[12] *Cannon Electric Co.,* Aaron, 26 LA 870 (1956). See *Square D Co.,* Teple, 37 LA 892 (1961).

11. History of negotiations on the right to subcontract.—
Whether management's right to subcontract has been the subject
of contract negotiations.[13]

The curious thing about the use of these criteria is that they tend
to ignore the most substantial element in the "make or buy"
business decision—consideration of cost. Many of the subcontracts
which are objected to by the factory union are made with independent contractors whose employees are also organized, frequently by a craft union. It is an everyday occurrence for a maintenance contractor with craft labor to sell his service on price
to an industrial employer organized by an industrial union. Decisions which prohibit subcontracting solely for cost considerations
fall with particular hardship on the small employer, or one who
seeks to improve his competitive position. Arbitrators should not
assume to evaluate these matters. The covenant of good faith
requires a decision as to whether or not the employer was seeking,
using subcontracting as a device, to rob the union or the employees
of the fruits of their bargain. But once a legitimate business
motive is established, it is not for the arbitrator to review the
pros and cons of the decision. He should leave it to the union to
press for a restriction in the contract. These are numerous enough
to establish the fact that unions seek and obtain them when they
are seriously concerned with the problem of subcontracting. Likewise, as every experienced bargainer knows, many employers have
been equally insistent on keeping such restrictions out of
their contracts. The parties should be left to make their own
accommodation.

---

[13] Elkouri and Elkouri, *How Arbitration Works* (Washington: BNA Incorporated,
1960), p. 343. See also Donald A. Crawford, "The Arbitration of Disputes over
Subcontracting," *Challenges to Arbitration* (Washington: BNA Incorporated,
1960), p. 51.

CHAPTER 10

PRODUCTION AND QUALITY STANDARDS

Management efforts to improve employee efficiency probably produce more conflict in union-management relations than any other subject. Emotions run high; management blames labor unions for encouraging boondoggling, and unions accuse management of speed-up tactics and slave-driving.

It is certainly true that labor efficiency is a substantial element in costs, even in a plant which has the most modern equipment, since the more expensive the equipment the more efficiently it must be operated. But labor efficiency is not necessarily synonymous with individual effort; the two are related, but should be separated.

The employer's real goal is to seek a productive plant, that is, one which maximizes output and minimizes costs. The entire operation must be under scrutiny, not merely the man at machine and bench. Plant efficiency can be lowered by a number of different influences. Engineering and sales departments, and the purchasing, tooling, and supply departments affect plant productivity perhaps as much as the supervisor-worker organization in the plant. Much of the planning and scheduling of the work flow through the plant is interrupted, and sometimes stopped, by the failure of salesmen to report orders promptly, or by making changes in an irregular manner after the orders have been received. Engineers, and especially customers' engineers, have an annoying habit of thinking up improvements just after their blueprints have been sent to production departments; the time lost due to faulty blueprints and inadequate specifications can also be great. The flow of materials and parts to the job, and the prompt removal of finished products, can likewise be subject to delays and interruptions. An executive who wishes an efficient and low-cost manufacturing operation should see that unnecessary obstructions are not imposed by people who are neither responsible for nor familiar with production.

Plant management should also concern itself with overall efficiency, not merely work pace. Planning and scheduling, design
changes to improve equipment performance, job simplification
and methods improvement, and various other aspects of plant
management must be kept under constant study.

It is generally recognized that an employer has the right to
demand a "fair day's work for a fair day's pay," and that he can
determine, at least so long as the workloads are not unduly harsh
or excessive, what production schedules and inspection requirements the employees may be asked to meet. Some contracts state
expressly that the union will uphold the standard of a fair day's
work for a fair day's pay. Others state specifically the right of the
company to establish and enforce production standards on the
"basis of fairness and equity consistent with the quality of workmanship, efficiency of operations, and the reasonable working
capacities of normal operators."

These rights include the right to demand a full day's work,
so long as no unreasonable or undue hardship is placed on the
employee which could be said to be detrimental to his health or
safety. Hence, the employer should reserve his right to increase
the workload, assign an employee to other work during his idle
time, direct him to operate additional machines, decrease crew
sizes, and establish and revise production standards. In such cases
the employer is likely to encounter resistance and the charge that
he is attempting to alter established working conditions. Or a
grievance may be filed which accepts the change in workload but
seeks to establish a higher rate for increased effort.

Some arbitration cases can be compared to illustrate these
problems. In a National Container Corporation case,[1] the contract provided that working practices should remain in effect
during the life of the agreement. The company, deeming 100%
inspection of printed boxes no longer necessary, reduced a press
crew from three to two persons, and claimed that this was a change
in methods which it had the right to install, the change in working
conditions being only incidental. It also claimed that the workload had not become too heavy, and that no loss in earnings had
been sustained. A. R. Marshall upheld the company, dismissing
the union's contention that this was a prohibited change in work-

---

[1] *National Container Corp.*, Marshall, 29 LA 687 (1957).

ing conditions. In a Bethlehem Steel case,[2] the arbitrator, Rolf Valtin, was dealing with a plea for a higher rate when a milling machine operator was required to operate two machines instead of one. He held that the net effect of the change was to reduce stand-by time and refused the increase. On the other hand, in a Carlyle Tile case,[3] under a contract which clearly recognized the company's right to improve methods and technology and did not contain a working conditions clause, Harry Dworkin held that the addition of a second kiln to the duties of a fireman who had always operated one was a change in working conditions, and violation of the provision for the posting of new jobs for bid, even though the company established that, after the addition of the second kiln, the fireman was busy only about half the time. Similar decisions have been rendered when employees have been permitted to leave their work after attaining standard and this practice has continued for long periods of time.

In short, the remarks already made as to the hazards of implied restrictions based on plant practice apply in the case of efforts to increase production, eliminate unnecessary crew members, and increase workloads. The employer must be on the alert to prevent their establishment, since weeding them out takes time and effort. It can be done more easily and effectively when changes are made in machinery, equipment, and methods than it can without such changes. In some cases, management may have to resort to negotiations and economic pressure to obtain full recognition of its right to demand a fair day's work. When employers neglect to change standards to reflect improvements in tools and machinery or methods and processes, as they frequently do, the employees can hardly be blamed if they ride along on management's failure to increase the workloads to pick up the lessened effort resulting from the improvement. An arbitrator may find, as did Donald Crawford in a Worthington Corporation case,[4] that the failure to change the standard within a reasonable time after improved tools have been provided indicates acceptance by the company of the old standard as fair.

---

2 *Bethlehem Steel Co.*, Valtin, 28 LA 530 (1957).
3 *Carlyle Tile Co.*, Dworkin, 29 LA 787 (1958).
4 *Worthington Corp.*, Crawford, 34 LA 497 (1959).

Setting Standards

Whether an employee is giving a fair day's work requires a decision based, so far as possible, on objective factors. A great part of the difficulties encountered in this area comes from a lack of agreement as to objective criteria for the measurement of production. In the absence of industrial engineering studies, the best way to measure output is by comparison of the performance of a particular employee on a particular job with others. In a Weber Aircraft Corporation case,[5] George Hildebrand upheld the discharge of a jig and fixture builder on the basis of his time record for jigs which others had built in much less time under the same conditions. In this case, comparisons with quoted hours in bids from outside vendors were rejected, but there is no reason why such proof should not be used, if the work is comparable. In another case, Jonco Aircraft Corporation,[6] Maurice Merrill stated that the data produced to show substandard productivity must cover the employee's entire record without selection among tasks, and comparisons with other employees must cover all the employees in the classification and all tasks performed by them during the same period. He also said: "It is necessary, too, to take into account all factors that may have affected production, such as the adequacy or inadequacy of the information furnished for the guidance of the employee; the extent to which other departments have failed to supply essential materials, tools or services; the quality, extent and clarity of supervisory guidance and assistance, and whether this supervision was necessary and proper in the given instance."

Most larger companies have developed production standards with or without the payment of incentives for increased effort. Incentive plans are beyond the scope of this study.[7] They present many difficult administrative problems. They can easily become loose, characterized by many flaws and inequities. Many employers have now abandoned incentives in favor of daywork.

---

[5] *Weber Aircraft Corp.*, Hildebrand, 22 LA 23 (1953).

[6] *Jonco Aircraft Corp.*, Merrill, 22 LA 819 at 823 (1954).

[7] An excellent analysis of them with revealing illustrations of practical experiences in revising faulty plans is contained in: Sumner H. Slichter, James J. Healy, and E. Robert Livernash, *The Impact of Collective Bargaining on Management* (Washington: Brookings Institution, 1960). Chapter 17 includes (1) experience with wage incentives, (2) demoralized incentive plans, (3) revised incentive plans, (4) efficient incentive plans, (5) the piece-rate industries, and (6) wage incentive provisions in contracts. Chapter 18—"Measured Daywork"—is equally pertinent and valuable here.

A "fair day's work" is best set for most plants by standards, but this does not necessarily mean that these standards should be made known to the employees and enforced against the individual worker. "Ultimate" standards which merely establish management goals are used in many plants. They do not, as an individual job standard must, include specific allowances for interruptions and down time.

This system has the merit of placing the responsibility for locating and eliminating or reducing the factors which create down time; the foreman, for example, having been advised that his department is below standard, must find the causes. Other companies use known standards with the proper allowances and enforce them. This system, unlike the "ultimate" standard system, involves the standard itself, and the assumptions and data on which it is based, in the grievance procedure. Companies which do not use standards directly as a basis for discipline achieve control over effort by penalizing employees for specific offenses, such as being away from their machines, loafing, interfering with production, or failing to put forth effort.

All standards require the use of judgment to determine what is normal effort, and the task level can vary surprisingly from one plant to the next and even as between departments. Constant attention is needed to improve low performance, since direct attempts to enforce a new, higher standard will meet resistance. Such improvements are best made when improvements in technology and major changes in method take place.

Industrial Engineering

Beyond doubt, one of the most important elements in getting good production is keeping up with changes. Most standards, especially under incentive plans, become loose through failure to revise the standard as "creeping changes" occur. If the employer waits to pick up these changes all at one time, the employees resist. Hence it most important to have not merely good time study men, but good methods and work simplification engineers on the job. The foreman also should be alert to conditions which affect production, observing methods and seeing to it that the prescribed method is followed. He must also be aware of material supply difficulties, tool problems, and machine troubles.

Industrial engineering techniques can be applied, and in some cases standards and incentives have been developed for nonrepetitive work, such as repair and maintenance. Swift and Company has all plant maintenance personnel at its main plants under an incentive plan. Where jobs are not readily susceptible to time study and measurement, ratio delay or work sampling studies can be used to good effect. Robert Gunts, industrial relations manager and formerly chief industrial engineer at the Whirlpool plant in St. Joseph, Michigan, writes on the subject,

Basically, an employer can set up the following criteria for his employees.

1) He can expect them to work for the full working shift.

2) He can expect the employee to apply himself with a reasonable degree of effort.

3) He can expect them to follow a prescribed method or the best method available.

If an employee meets these three criteria, that employer will be receiving as much productivity as he could possibly expect. Any incentive system has as its foundation, these three criteria. Let us take a look at a direct piece rate incentive plan. The work is measured and evaluated to some norm which can usually be exceeded by twenty-five to thirty percent. The employer reasonably expects the employee to earn twenty-five to thirty percent bonus. This means he expects the employee to apply himself with a reasonable degree of effort. Under a piece work plan, any time a change in method occurs, the rate is revised. Usually the method on which the standard is established is the best possible method to be followed. Therefore, if the employee does not follow the prescribed method or at least the best method available, he cannot possibly meet standard. In some companies, changes in method have not been reflected in the rates. This has resulted in loose standards, the men earn unreasonable bonuses without applying effort, or may quit work early, or loiter throughout the day. In other words, an incentive system such as piece work incentive plan breaks down if any of the three criteria previously mentioned is not maintained.

Therefore, shortcutting all the mechanics of the incentive system and complicated yardsticks of measure, you can look directly at the basic criteria that employers have established for their employees and find the simplest way to control it. In examining an approach to measure large groups of employees without resorting to direct timestudy, ratio delay studies and work sampling studies seem to be the answer, particularly for small companies.

Work sampling or ratio delay requires an analyst to tour the plant or area on a random basis. By sampling performance or by sampling work vs. idle time, a composite can be developed reflecting the activities of large quantities of employees and still use little industrial engineering time.

To give you a practical example of what this means, we established an incentive system in one of our warehouses. One industrial engineer followed each employee for five consecutive days taking full eight hour studies. There were five employees, thus, five industrial engineers. After the studies were taken, the industrial engineers spent another five days subtracting and tabulating these eight hour time studies. The objective was to determine the average percent of interference and delays that would be encountered in this warehouse. This means we spent ten man days getting the information for each employee. Five employees-fifty industrial engineering man days. During the same period of time we took a ratio delay study on the same group of employees. Here, one industrial engineer toured the warehouse sampling all five employees at random times throughout the five days. His study form was so arranged that approximately one hour after the last study had been taken, the information was summarized and tabulated.

This cost the company five man days to get the information by using ratio delay study. When all the figures were in, we compared the net result for accuracy and found that the ratio delay study showed a percent of interference that was within one-half of one percent of the recorded percent of interference on the timestudies. Thus, in this case, we were able to obtain the same information with reasonable accuracy at a cost of approximately one-tenth the cost of getting the same information through eight hour timestudies.

By using this approach we were able to determine what percent of time the employees were working and what percent of time they were not working. This is a simple accurate way of determining if the employees are working for the full eight hours.

Work sampling is, in essence, the same as a ratio delay study except that every time an observation is made, you record the percent of effort that the employee is putting forth. A work sampling approach tells you whether the employee is working for the full eight hours and when he is working, exactly how hard he is working. This is a measure of two of the criteria established. A small company in several days could soon determine how much time is being wasted by the average employee and exactly how hard the employees are working when they are at the job. This is valuable information for a small company and can serve as a basis for taking corrective steps.

The remaining criterion of following the best method of a prescribed method is not quite so simple to measure or control. Usually, the method is different for each different job. There is nothing that is universally consistent about the method. Quite frequently, there are several good ways of doing the job and the best way is very hard to determine even under detailed analysis. Therefore, this criterion is one that management of any plant must shoulder. They must establish the best method. They must take the time to find the best way or else many dollars of labor will be thrown away. It is a never ending task and one that depends heavily on a well trained supervisor. Through job instruction, through careful supervision, the best method, or at least the better of several methods can be prescribed.

In the final analysis, willing cooperation on the part of the employee is the object. Willing to apply themselves and willing to work for the full eight hours is the primary objective. This is cultivated by well trained supervisors. You can determine the effectiveness of your supervisors through the work sampling technique and through accounting controls of cost to determine whether better methods are being used and adopted by the supervisors. This is the best approach that I know toward solving the problem of getting a full day's work from employees and applies not only to small companies but to large ones as well. Foster the employees to cooperate-measure the supervisor's effectiveness through work sampling and cost reducing methods adopted by the supervisor. Short of individual measurement on each job, this approach will result in the greatest productivity.[8]

While union attitudes differ, it may be said generally that they criticize industrial engineering techniques as essentially subjective and varying between one engineer and the next, and as involving assumptions which do not necessarily hold true from one case to the next. Hence they regard production standards as essentially a matter for bargaining, to be settled without reference to any specific yardstick, but on the basis of the whole complex of factors which enter into any settlement, including the expectations and experiences of the workers themselves. The function of the union time-study engineer is chiefly to provide arguments and materials to support the union's demands at the bargaining table. A quotation from an article written by one of the best known union research directors, Solomon Barkin, may emphasize how

---

[8] Robert Gunts, letter to the author. See also, Bertrand I. Hansen, *Work Sampling: For Modern Management* (New York: Prentice-Hall, 1960); and C. L. Brisley, "How You Can Put Work Sampling to Work," *Factory Management and Maintenance* (July 1952).

futile it is to expect union representatives to accept the findings
of industrial engineers as gospel, even though management and
its time-study people make every effort to be not only fair, but
liberal, in setting standards:

> The industrial engineering profession now enjoys no better
> reputation among the trade unions on this continent than it had
> in the initial decades, but the practitioners are less feared. The
> growth, in union power and bargaining ability, along with the
> changes in management attitudes, has relaxed the atmosphere.
> Management's willingness to negotiate standards, to allow workers
> to share in the benefits of higher productivity, to provide pro-
> tection for the displaced through provisions for plant seniority,
> retraining, transfers, pensions and insurance programs, and the
> great faith among workers that they will finally attain some form
> of annual wage, have made workers and unions equally ready to
> deal with the daily job problems rather than engage in disputa-
> tions on the over-all threats of unreliable techniques.

> Unfortunately, the industrial engineering techniques, as they
> affect work standards, have not been much improved in objectivity,
> validity or reliability. There is a need for fundamental re-evalua-
> tion and research on the problems of human performance and
> for exploration of the various cognate disciplines dealing with
> human performance, to build a sound scientific structure of fact.

> Unions basically represent workers and have no managerial
> responsibilities in the enterprise. They have little use for in-
> dustrial engineering techniques. Ordinarily they utilize services
> of the engineer only to strengthen their bargaining position.[9]

In some plants, however, the unions have accepted industrial
engineering techniques and appointed their own time-study representatives. Where these exist, the effectiveness of the program
depends to a large degree on whether they can operate on a professional basis without losing the support of the rank and file.

Whatever the attitude of the union, competent industrial
engineers and specialists in methods can do much to assist in maintaining good production. In small plants especially, both the
workers themselves and the foremen can be confused and uncer-
tain as to what is expected of them. Moreover, the use of engineering specialists is likely to reveal much in the way of needed machine maintenance, material flow, and other attributes of good
production which need improvement. Engineers, along with
supervisors of the right kind, can often develop a sense of coopera-

---

[9] Solomon Barkin, "New Labor Approaches to Industrial Engineering," 6 *Labor
Law Journal* 115, 122 (February 1955).

tion among the employees which automatically results in higher production.

The value of good industrial engineering as a backstop in arbitration should not be overlooked. The arbitration commission headed by Paul N. Lehoczky, Chairman of the Department of Industrial Engineering at Ohio State University, appointed after the Pittsburgh Plate Glass Company strike,[10] placed great reliance upon industrial engineering techniques in reaching its decisions, including work sampling, which the commission stated is often more accurate than continuous time study.

Grievances on Production Standards

Grievances over production standards as such are to be distinguished from grievances resulting from discipline imposed for loafing on the job, etc. Production standards grievances, under the automobile agreements, do not go to arbitration, but can be made the basis of a lawful strike after the grievance procedure has been exhausted. Other agreements permit standards grievances to be settled in arbitration.

The Swift agreement (unpublished) so provides, but the power of the arbitrator is circumscribed by the following language:

> (f) Power of Arbitrator—it is understood and agreed that in the case of grievances involving production standards the Arbitrator, under Paragraph 58, shall have only the power to decide:
>
> (1) Whether insufficient credit is being given in connection with an existing standard.
>
> (2) Whether, in the case of a changed standard, the operation has been changed so that the amount of work required to perform the job has changed.
>
> (3) Whether an approved standard has been reduced when there was no change in the job.
>
> (4) Whether a standard after being changed will permit the same opportunity for earning premium as existed under the original standard.
>
> The Arbitrator shall have no power by his award to establish, discontinue, or change any production standard. In the event the Arbitrator decides the grievance in favor of the Union, the Company will change the standard so that it will be consistent with the award of the Arbitrator.

---

[10] *Pittsburgh Plate Glass Co.*, Lehoczky, 33 LA 614 (1959).

Under the General Motors agreement [11] if there is a complaint by an employee about a standard, he must take it up with his foreman. Blanket union protests about standards are not entertained; there must be a complaint from one or more employees. If the foreman cannot settle the dispute, the union committeeman may examine the job, and the foreman or the time-study man will furnish the committeeman with "all the facts of the case," meaning the available information, such as the time study by elements, allowances, etc. The committeeman is not entitled to any special information not readily available. If not satisfied, the foreman or the time-study man will then re-examine the job with the committeeman. If not settled, the matter is then appealed through the grievance procedure. If not settled there, the union may, upon notice, authorize a strike. The umpire can determine whether the procedures in the contract have been observed, but cannot pass on the merits of the standard itself, i.e. whether it is too tight or too loose.

Discipline for Failure to Meet Standards

With or without a production standard, employees can be disciplined for wasting time, loitering, failing to follow instructions as to how a job is to be performed, leaving their work stations, spending too much time in the rest room, or other acts which affect production. It is considered better supervisory practice in many cases to impose discipline for these offenses, as against blanketing them in under a general charge that the employee has failed or refused to meet the standards of his job.

When an employee is failing to meet standard, the foreman must make a special effort to observe and record his actions to determine why he is not producing. In some cases, corrections can be made of the stock flow, the use of tools and equipment, or methods, which will produce the desired result. In other cases, the employee may, through ignorance or deliberate intent, feel that a change in the method and the standard is improper, and adhere to his old method and standard. An explanation may suffice to bring him up to standard. Sometimes the standard is wrong and should be changed without argument or insistence on its enforcement.

---

[11] General Motors Agreement, *Collective Bargaining Negotiations and Contracts*, ¶46, p. 20:315; ¶115-118, p. 332; ¶78-79, p. 322 (Sept. 29, 1961).

In some cases, the production records previously made on the job by the same or by other employees can be helpful. There are many cases in which specific instances of misconduct affecting output can be established. Even though the standard is in dispute, the employee has an obligation to put forth an honest effort while the grievance is pending.

"Slowdowns" and other deliberate failures to meet the standard are best handled by specific concrete proof. A mere charge by the foreman that a slowdown in meeting standards is taking place, without detailed proof, is hard to sustain, and can lead to irritation and irresponsible conduct. Such general charges invite criticism of the time study techniques and data, and involve management in a defense of the whole system against union charges that it is "unscientific, subjective, and management-oriented." Disciplinary action should be based on "wasting time," or "failure to follow method as instructed," or "leaving work station." Even a charge that employees are failing to put forth honest effort is better, though general, than the charge that they are not meeting standard. Obviously, comparative production records, showing indisputably a substantial drop in production, are of first importance in such cases. In all cases of discipline based solely on failure to meet standards as proof of a slowdown, accurate industrial engineering observation is practically indispensable.

Faulty Workmanship

The right of management to set its own standards of quality is unquestioned, and thus the employer's determination of what work must be scrapped and whether it can be reworked should, in the absence of proof of arbitrary or discriminatory conduct, be final. Discipline for faulty workmanship can of course be imposed.

As in cases of failure to meet standards, the employee may have many excuses for scrap or poor quality production, and again it is the responsibility of the supervisor to control the situation. Such factors as the employee's experience, the adequacy of the training given, his instructions and supervision, especially in cases of unfamiliar work, poor tools or equipment, and the lack of warnings relating to past occurrences of the same kind and other similar factors have a bearing on the right of the employer to discipline or discharge for just cause. Scrap records should be maintained so that it can be established that the employee disciplined is out of line with other employees doing similar work. It is necessary, of course, to show that the employee charged is actually responsible; if his work is mingled with that of others, it may be impossible to show that he was at fault. An excellent analysis of the problems involved in discipline for improper workmanship was made by Robert G. Howlett in his arbitration opinion in a Valley Steel Casting Company case.[12]

---

[12] *Valley Steel Casting Co.*, Howlett, 22 LA 520 (1954).

CHAPTER 11

DISCIPLINE

The word "discipline" has unpleasant associations with punishment, and in the context of industrial relations it recalls to old-timers in the labor movement the fear of peremptory discharge which the unenlightened supervisor of an earlier day used, often with senseless cruelty, as a whip to lash the workers on. But in modern factories, where addition of the "just cause" concept is a limitation on the employer's right to discipline and discharge—a development for which the unions can take lasting (and practically undivided) credit—the word has been extended to embrace a system of training and education of both the employee and his supervisor, designed to achieve orderly conduct.

As a system of orderly conduct, modern industrial discipline has many advantages for the employer and the employee alike. It enhances efficiency and reduces costs. Absenteeism and employee turnover are minimized. Cooperation between worker and supervisor replaces mere compliance, yielded perhaps with reluctance. Equipment is given better care and scrap losses decline. The employees gain a sense of security and safety. They work without fear of thoughtless and unfair penalty for misconduct which they could not reasonably be expected to avoid or prevent. Their self-respect and respect for the company is preserved. Even the employee who suffers a penalty may be enabled to understand and help himself, perhaps toward a lifetime of constructive effort.

An effective system of employee discipline is a great help to the foreman. Lacking such a system, he must resort to nagging and riding employees, since he is responsible for quality and quantity of output. This inevitably results in bad effects, both upon him and his employees.

Discipline thus becomes an integral part of good human relations. The agreement provides employees with protection against arbitrary and unreasonable management action, a frame of rights and obligations which preserves the management function effectively and, at the same time, individual dignity and freedom. To this, progressive employers, knowing the value of good morale, have added their recognition of basic human needs and personal goals and attempted to satisfy them.

Thus the two systems, one essentially legal in nature and the other reflecting the positive attributes of good group behavior derived from modern psychology, combine and enhance each other. Together they can achieve the desirable peaceful and orderly plant community in which the talents of individuals can come to fullest fruition. Paradoxically, as this hope becomes increasingly realized, as the spirit of voluntary cooperation grows, the need for discipline in the stricter sense, for rules of order and their vigilant enforcement, becomes less.

But this goal is, for the most part, in the making. Much remains to be done. Challenges to discipline imposed by management still bulk large in the grievance procedures of industry and make up more than one quarter of the work of arbitrators and umpires. The task is mainly that of management. Nothing less will do than a careful study of employee conduct and the construction and installation of intelligent and consistent programs which, once installed, must be carried out in an equally consistent and intelligent manner.

Just Cause

Although other adjectives, such as "sufficient" or "proper" are used, the most frequent expression limiting the employer's right to discipline or discharge his employees is that such actions must be taken for "just cause." This, or an equivalent phrase, is found in most labor agreements. Its meaning, though imprecise and incapable of exact delineation, is broad and has been given content chiefly by numerous arbitrators passing, in particular cases, upon union claims that the employer has violated the agreement. Harry Platt has expressed the scope of the term well, saying ". . . no standards exist to aid an arbitrator in finding a conclusive answer to such a question and, therefore, perhaps the best he can do is to decide what a reasonable man, mindful of the habits and customs of industrial life and of the standards of justice and fair dealing prevalent in the community, ought to have done under similar circumstances and, in that light, to decide whether the conduct of the discharged employee was defensible and the disciplinary penalty just." [1] In short, the offense and the penalty imposed upon the employee must be such as to satisfy the arbitrator's natural sense of justice.

But if definition is lacking, the elements of just cause are not. Of them, the keystone is the principle of "corrective" or "progressive" discipline, that is, that misconduct, except in certain serious and flagrant cases, must be handled under a system of warnings and graduated penalties which gives the employee time to reflect upon his errors and mend his ways before the final act of discharge, when efforts at correction have failed. Employers are expected to be consistent in these matters. Lax enforcement, even of the common and well-known obligations of employment, will blunt the power of effective discipline.

Discharge is not lightly regarded in arbitration, especially in view of the numerous valuable perquisites of long service. A man loses more than a job today when he loses his seniority standing with its various privileges and preferences, his insurance and pension benefits, and, in many cases, his unemployment compensation. Many employers have discovered that their decisions have been reversed; in fact, statistics show that employers win less than half of the discharge cases appealed to arbitration. In all of them, it is safe to say, the arbitrator concluded that "just cause" did not exist for discharge, though he may have placed his decision on other grounds, and may have imposed a lesser penalty which he considered suitable.

Indeed, it would hardly be saying too much to characterize the remainder of our study of discipline as an exploration of the "just cause" concept.

Discipline as a Management Function and the Role of the Union

Although in the early days of collective bargaining in industry it was not uncommon to find employers and unions attempting to settle jointly upon rules of conduct, today it is conceded by most union representatives that discipline is properly a management function in which the union does not initially take part. The union's true role here is that of protagonist in protecting its

---

[1] *Riley Stoker Corp.*, Platt, 7 LA 764 at 765 (1947). For a full review of the "common law" of discipline, see Lawrence Stessin, *Employee Discipline* (Washington: BNA Incorporated, 1960).

members against unjust and discriminatory management action. And it is also generally conceded that management's decisions, with some difference of opinion as to its judgment in assessing penalties, are subject to review through the grievance procedure by an impartial arbitrator.

The reasons for this consensus are impressive and sound, touching as they do not only upon effective direction of the work in the plant, but also upon the primary office of the union as the agent of the employees. Management has a large stake in the maintenance of orderly conduct not only in the interests of efficient work performance, but the protection of company property and equipment and the avoidance of liability for accident and injury as well. The imposition of discipline is frequently only an aspect of other managerial functions, such as work assignments and safety measures. Granted that management must act wisely and fairly; to abdicate the power to maintain order is to encourage anarchy and to give shop malcontents an opportunity to breed discontent and difficulty.

Like the employer, a sensible union wants order in the plant. It represents all of the employees, not merely those in trouble with the company. It has an interest in correcting the trouble-maker who is disturbing the peace of others, and in assisting the employee who persists in violating rules of conduct to understand that correction is imperative. In his excellent discussion of some of the thorny problems of discipline, Howard Meyers has said that in cases of obvious failure to observe reasonable standards of conduct, "the union probably does the membership more good by facing the facts of life than by passing the buck to an arbitrator"; and that "even the political case or the squeaking wheel can be informed by the union that there is less to be lost by accepting instructions and assignments than by facing charges of insubordination." [2] Some unions, indeed, consider it natural and necessary to admonish their members to maintain acceptable standards or face the consequences without union support.

But such a position almost inevitably clashes with the most vital service rendered by the union during the life of the agreement: to represent its members with diligence in the protection of their

---

[2] A. Howard Myers, "Concepts of Industrial Discipline," *Management Rights and the Arbitration Process* (Washington: BNA Incorporated, 1956), p. 70.

rights. Discipline cases, in particular, call for vigilant correction when injustice is done to an individual worker. The union should keep itself free to assert these rights without any restriction, except any clearly imposed by the agreement. It is not always easy, even for an experienced union representative, to judge the merits of a case—to dismiss it as political, perhaps, or to dismiss the complainant as a "squeaking wheel." More significantly, the union loses not merely political favor, but the force of its position as well, if it assumes or shares the management role in discipline. A rule which has been agreed upon cannot be challenged on its face as arbitrary and unreasonable, even though the union has reserved the right to challenge its application in an individual case. If the union consents to the imposition of a particular penalty in one case, it assumes to a degree the burden of proving that the next case, though similar, can and should be differentiated and the penalty modified. The union should retain its full freedom to protest disciplinary action through the grievance procedure and by ultimate recourse to arbitration.

Of course, there are situations in which employers and their union counterparts may wish to consult about these matters, not in an effort to share the decisional responsibility, but in order to improve understanding and gain acceptance from the workers. Such consultation may be important to the launching of a new program or the tightening up and enforcement of an old one which has been allowed to lapse. Policies of consultation are a matter for decision by individual employers or individual plant managers. They may or may not be advisable in a particular context of union-management relationships. But here we are talking not of such policies, but of the nature of the discipline function and its execution by management, to whom it properly belongs.

But with or without union or employee participation in the formulation and execution of disciplinary policy, employers must be realistic and reasonable. A sound program is bound to win the approbation of the overwhelming majority of employees; a bad one will meet evasion and resistance. Only a small minority with bad habits or psychological problems will resist reasonable rules. But if these few are allowed untrammeled sway, the rot will spread. In the end, both firmness and reasonableness are essential. As Charles Killingsworth has said, "acceptance of authority of the company and its agents by all employees is a basic necessity in any enterprise. . . . One in authority must meet every challenge to that authority with firmness. Any resort to debate or quibbling is likely to be interpreted as a sign of weakness or uncertainty." [3] An effective policy takes into account both the need for the acceptance of the majority—the people of good will—and the equal necessity for firm and prompt enforcement against the malefactors, especially those of the chronic kind.

Limitations on Management's Right to Discipline

The right to discipline and discharge employees is clearly one of the "terms and conditions of employment" which is within the "mandatory" area of collective bargaining under the Taft-Hartley Act, and the same is true of plant rules which govern employee conduct. Having accepted this point, it seems equally clear that if no contract exists, there can be no violation of it even in the case of discharge without cause of any kind, although discharge for union activity would be a violation of the Act. A troublesome problem of contract interpretation arises, however, when a contract is executed containing the usual provisions as to union recognition and seniority rights but omitting any mention of discharge, or giving the employer the right to discharge but omitting the proviso that the right should be exercised only for "just cause" or an equivalent limitation. This is a question which has divided the arbitral profession. Some adhere to the view that what is not expressed falls within the area of "retained" or residual rights, and others express the opinion that while the right to discharge exists perhaps as an unexpressed retained right, it would nevertheless by implication be restricted by the "just cause" concept.[4]

---

[3] *Triumph Explosives, Inc.*, Killingsworth, 2 LA 617 at 618 (1945).

[4] In *Fruehauf Trailer Co.*, 4 LA 399 (1946), Dudley E. Whiting held that where the contract had expired and the new contract had not become effective, a discharge in the interim period was a matter for exclusive determination by the employer. A statement apparently contrary to this appears in *Daily World Publishing Co.*, Rogers, 3 LA 815 (1946), but the issue was not actually present in the case since it came to arbitration under a submission giving the arbitrator the right to examine the justice of the cause for discharge. Implied limitations on the employer's right to discharge were rejected in *Okenite Co.*, Krivonos, 22 LA 756 (1954), and in *Meletron Corp.*, Warren, 24 LA 680 (1955), although in both instances the contracts provided that seniority should be lost upon "discharge for just cause." The opposite view is taken in *Coca-Cola Bottling Co.*, reprinted in Cox, *Cases on Labor Law* (New York: The Foundation Press, 1958), pp. 583, 586. See Cox, "The Legal Nature of Collective Bargaining Agreements, 57 *Michigan Law Review* 1 at 28 (Nov., 1958), reprinted by the Institute of Labor and Industrial Relations, The University of Michigan-Wayne State University, Reprint Series No. 6 (1958).

Most contracts, by appropriate language, make it clear that the employer has the right to discipline or discharge, but only for just cause. Some require written warnings to the employee with notice to the union of their issuance. Some prescribe a time limit at the expiration of which previous warnings and penalties are erased from the employee's record and can no longer be taken into account in imposing discipline on subsequent infractions. Procedural requirements designed to acquaint the union with the facts of the case and secure prompt disposition of it if the discipline imposed is improper are common. Some of these require that the employee be suspended and the asserted offense investigated and discussed before the penalty is actually imposed by management. Others permit the employee to demand a hearing with a union representative present before he is compelled to leave the plant. Still others require the prompt presentation of the employee's grievance; these are usually accompanied by a guarantee that the case, in its first stage, will be heard and answered promptly by management.

These procedural limitations, although they must be strictly observed, are not the source of many problems. Most cases find their way through the grievance procedure and to arbitration because of the "just cause" proviso, which embraces an ill-defined but enormous area of limitation.

Whether the employer's power to discipline employees is recognized in express language or is asserted as part of his retained right to direct the working forces, there still remains a problem of how far his authority extends. Three influences bear upon this problem. One is the contractual obligation of the employee. The second is the proximate relationship of the offense to the employer's business. The third appears in the enforcement of plant rules; the union may claim that the rule, though perhaps within the general scope of the employment relationship is unreasonable.

Contracts frequently specify one or more offenses which lay the basis for discipline. The most common, perhaps, is the provision in the no-strike clause that employees found guilty of taking part in a work stoppage prohibited by the agreement are subject to discipline and discharge. Other contracts specify one or more causes for discipline and discharge. The question then arises (the same problem occurs in connection with written plant rules specifying offenses which merit discipline) as to whether other offenses, not mentioned in the agreement, can be made the subject of discipline, or whether, instead, enumeration of particular offenses has excluded others from consideration under the familiar rule that to express one thing is to exclude others. Construing such a contract, one which stated several causes for discharge, Clarence Updegraff said that the list "cannot be regarded as excluding all alleged causes for discharge not therein expressly stated. As examples of just cause for discharge not included in the list may be stated arson, or other malicious destruction of employer's property, rape, or attempted rape, committed by one employee against another on the employer's premises, intentional indecent exposure, intentional fouling or sabotaging employer's products, et cetera." [5] He concludes that the parties intended to include on the list only causes concerning which there had been some dispute, or that the list was merely illustrative, not exclusive.

It must be remembered that the collective agreement is not the only source of obligation between the employer and the employee. Within its framework, and frequently controlled by it, is another significant contractual relationship, the individual contract of hire. This, under the law, gives rise to what may be called the "common obligations of employment," binding both upon the employer and the employee. The employee must report for work on time, he must work the required number of hours, he must do a fair day's work, respect orders, and conduct himself in an orderly way. Except as they are modified by the collective agreement, he is expected to perform these obligations, and violation of them fits within the definition of "just cause" for discipline, though not, of course, in all cases, for discharge.

The inquiry turns in many cases not on the source of the obligation but whether it can be related to the business of the employer, a question mainly involving charges of misconduct off the employer's premises. In these cases, to quote Harry Shulman, the

---

[5] *Kraft Foods, Inc.*, Updegraff, 9 LA 397 (1947). See, however, *Pacific Press, Inc.*, Hildebrand, 26 LA 339 (1956). Harry Shulman dealt with the construction of plant rules, which in the early days of the Ford agreement had been jointly agreed, in two cases. In the first, although the rules did not mention unexcused absence as an occasion for discipline, he held that it was, the obligation to report for work being inherent in the individual employment relationship, *Ford Motor Co.*, Opinion A-13, reprinted in Shulman and Chamberlain, *Cases on Labor Relations* (New York: The Foundation Press, 1949), p. 397. In the second, he held that the rule against gambling on company property with no mention of card playing without gambling circumscribed the area of conduct forbidden and precluded the imposition of a penalty for card playing alone, Opinion A-133, *Id.*, at p. 398.

jurisdictional line which limits the employer's power to discipline "is a functional, not a physical line." [6] The difference, he goes on to say, lies in the "proximity of the relationship between the conduct and the employment." The question of proximity is simply one of fact; for an artificial line is substituted the exercise of judgment as to the effect of the misconduct on the employment relationship. Thus a bus company might be sustained in the discharge of a driver for drinking in public, since the company's reputation for safety is a valuable element in its business, but this would not be true of most employees who have no such responsibility. A plant guard who brandishes a weapon in a private quarrel off the premises might be discharged as a poor industrial risk. Both these examples illustrate the point that the character of the employer's business and the responsibility of particular kinds of employees, as against others, may be significant factors. In one case, a rule prohibiting parking on the street in front of the company's offices was held enforceable, the chief reason for the rule being ease of access for customers and other visitors to the offices. Some outside misconduct, such as fighting, must be materially related to events occurring within the plant and shown to be an outgrowth of plant relationships. Unless there is some proximate connection between the misconduct and the employer's business interest, the matter concerns only the personal life of the employee, and perhaps the civil authority. It is outside the scope of the employer's right to discipline.

The third circumscription upon the authority of the employer is the principle of "reasonableness," which, like proximity, can be illustrated but not defined. It implies a solid foundation for the rule in question—a rule well-aimed at a specific result which is a legitimate concern of the employer, and designed to achieve that result, not so undiscriminating and scattered in its effects that it prohibits employee conduct which has no relation to evils which the rule, properly constructed, would curb or eliminate.

In his well-known "Case of the Lady in Red Slacks," [7] Dr. Shulman pointed out that there was no rule against slacks, indeed they

---

[6] *Ford Motor Co.*, Opinion A-132, *Cases on Labor Relations, op. cit.*, n. 9, p. 415. *Wolverine Shoe & Tanning Corp.*, Platt, 18 LA 809 (1952). Daykin, *Management's Right to Discharge Employees for Conduct Off the Job*, Research Series No. 15 (Iowa City: Bureau of Labor and Management, College of Commerce, State University of Iowa, reprinted, April 1958).

[7] *Ford Motor Co.*, Opinion A-117, *Cases on Labor Relations, op. cit.*, n. 9, p. 374; see *Ford Motor Co.*, Shulman, 8 LA 1015 (1947).

were required attire for females, and no rule as to color. The company objected to the slacks in question for "safety" reasons; they were said to distract the attention of male employees. Saying that "it is common knowledge that wolves, unlike bulls, may be attracted by colors other than red and by various other enticements in the art and fit of female attire," he rescinded the penalty imposed because "there was no effort to survey the field and to prescribe knowable and enforceable rules. The matter was left largely to the idiosyncracy of circumstance and of persons in authority. That is not the way to prescribe and enforce rules of conduct."

These and similar decisions are all that we have to mark out the boundary of the "reasonable rule" area.[8] Both triviality and technicality should be avoided in the formulation of policy; the employer should seek out substance and impose discipline only under rules which serve a straightforward and useful purpose. And they must accurately serve their purpose, not cut with such a wide swath that they injure employees without accomplishing the purpose.

The Characteristics of Effective Plant Rules

An indispensable attribute of a plant rule and to its enforcement is that employees are made aware of the rule and understand it. This is not merely a condition of enforcement; it is part of the educational aspect of discipline as an important element of employee morale. Consequently, while posting is desirable,[9] and inclusion of the rules in employee handbooks even more so, the employer's concern with the matter does not end at that point. He should go further and discuss the rules with the supervisors and with the employees, so that full appreciation of the scope of each rule—what it covers and does not cover, the purposes it is intended to achieve and the penalties violation may bring—is accomplished. Indeed, a rule which is not made known cannot be enforced, as many employers have learned in arbitration, and failure to post a rule, though not always fatal to its enforcement,

---

[8] Although an act which is wrong *per se*, such as theft of company property, may be the premise of discharge, this is not true of offenses not of such character unless they are made known to employees, *Norwich Pharmaceutical Co.*, Shipman, 5 LA 536 (1946).

[9] As to posting, see *Bethlehem Steel Co.*, Larkin, 6 LA 453 (1947), and *Bethlehem Steel Co.*, Killingsworth, 7 LA 334 (1946).

materially weakens the employer's case if the employee pleads ignorance of its existence. Naturally, this is all the more the case when rules are changed, or when established and well-known rules are supplemented by new ones.

Care must be taken, too, in publishing written rules, to steer a prudent course between rules which are so general that employees do not know what is expected of them and those which are so specific that they do not cover the entire area of conduct forbidden. They should be simple and, generally speaking, few in number. Rules borrowed from another company may not relate entirely to matters which are of genuine importance to the employer adopting them. It is well, in drafting them, to consult with foremen and plant protection officials, and, in some cases at least, with union employees and their representatives, in order to arrive at a set of rules which realistically reflect the needs of the plant.[10] This in turn serves the purpose of education and employee acceptance.

Flexibility in the assessment of penalties should be established. As to each offense (or all of them in a prefatory statement), the range of possible penalty should be given—for example, "Reprimand and Warning to Discharge." If it is intended to make it clear that serious offenses, such as theft or sabotage, will be punished by immediate discharge, the fact should be stated. But statements should be avoided to the effect that successive violations of each rule will be punished by an established penalty, such as "first offense—reprimand, second offense—three day suspension, third offense—six week suspension, fourth offense—discharge." Such automatic machinery for the administration of rules is deceptive; it robs management of the power to take various individual circumstances into consideration, and runs afoul of the opinion that arbitrators who are empowered under the "just cause" proviso to review the appropriateness of the penalty should also take such circumstances into consideration.[11] There are exceptions, of course—some companies find that in the case of garnishment, it is better to make discharge automatic upon a specific number of garnishments within a specified period, but

---

[10] A set of "suggested shop rules," which is distributed by a large corporation to its numerous plants, is reproduced as Appendix E, p. 280.

[11] Automatic penalties are said to be improper in several decisions, *John H. Morrell & Co.*, Gilden, 9 LA 931 (1948); *Nineteen Hundred Corp.*, Ziegler, Chairman, 6 LA 709 (1946); *Riley Stoker Co.*, Platt, 7 LA 746 (1947).

even in this case one finds occasion to wish there were possibilities of choice.

While flexibility is necessary, it is also required that rules apply throughout the plant, not in one department and not in another, unless, of course, special rules are established for departments where conditions are dangerous such as the marking off of "no-smoking" areas, or other conditions make such differentiation logical and proper. With this and kindred exceptions, rules should apply uniformly to all.[12]

A disciplinary system must be maintained and implemented with care and persistence. Systems break down if policies are lacking as to production standards, quality, absenteeism, and other employment requirements. Foremen sometimes refuse to face up to their responsibility to discipline. Discipline must progress; warnings which do not lead to more severe penalties are meaningless.

Finally, rules must not be allowed to lapse. Lax enforcement or repeated condonation of violation of a rule will break down its force, and any sudden "crack-down" will not only be resented, but will fail if grievances are prosecuted on behalf of offenders who establish that they have been lulled into the belief that the rule had become a dead letter. The proper way to enforce such a rule is to give unequivocal notice that it must be respected, and in this case it is especially important to make certain that employees who have been violating it with impunity are warned that it will be enforced in the future.

Although some employers prefer to operate without written rules of conduct, relying instead on the common understanding of proper conduct and building the structure by application of this understanding in successive instances, the value of written rules for most plants can hardly be doubted, since they confer a quality of assurance and certainty which is helpful to both the employees and to their supervisors. If nothing else, they serve an educational end.

The Administration of Discipline

In the fore of a program of discipline is the question of who shall administer it. It is universally conceded, I believe, that it

---

[12] Uniformity among departments, *Lockheed Aviation Corp.*, Aaron, 9 **LA** 353 (1947).

is properly one of the functions of line management, since they give the orders which keep the plant running and are responsible for their proper execution. It is considered best that personnel staff officials should act, in the first instance, as advisers to operating management. This means, of course, that for all practical purposes, discipline is administered by the immediate supervisor, normally a foreman. There may be certain exceptions, chiefly in cases which have no relation to the job, such as: garnishment; offenses which transcend departmental lines, such as work stoppages; and those which require a considerable amount of investigation—theft, gambling, and conduct outside the plant. A close liaison should be established between the employee's foreman and labor relations officials on all types of offenses; the foreman should be required to consult on extraordinary cases or those which require a special penalty such as transfer or demotion, and the labor relations office should keep the foreman informed of disciplinary actions affecting his employees, so that, if called upon, he can explain and defend the company's action and help the employee correct his misconduct in the future.

In the end, the success of discipline depends almost entirely on the foreman, and the extent to which he has been trained to adopt an intelligent and reasonable approach to discipline, which is at once firm and fair. A foreman who is genuinely a leader will lessen the need for discipline, since the very quality of his leadership brings voluntary and positive cooperation which makes correction unnecessary. One who is weak and indulgent, plays favorites, or is strict or stern according to his momentary mood, will meet resistance and very likely reversal in the grievance procedure. There cannot be too much foreman training in the administration of discipline.

Certain guides can be given to the foremen. The first is complete understanding of the contract, the plant rules, and the safety rules. Participation in the formulation of policies is helpful to the foreman, but, at any rate, policies should be thoroughly illustrated and made clear through the use of manuals, training meetings, and especially discussions of actual problems as they develop in the plant. The foremen should understand the basic elements of each offense and the kind of proof necessary to sustain discipline based on a particular rule. For example, an employee who is discovered sitting in a partially concealed area away from his own department with his head in his hands may be guilty of sleeping. But sleeping is difficult to prove. He may be guilty of being away from his department without permission, and, almost certainly, he is guilty of loitering or wasting time. In such a case, if he is charged with sleeping and the charge is not proved, it will be difficult to sustain the penalty.

Foremen should be certain that employees understand their instructions. In the case of instructions which are not routine, an explanation of the reason is desirable.

Clarity and explanation are not only prerequisites for disciplinary action; they mark the leader, the man who can secure cooperation from employees who are willing because they understand the necessity of doing what is required of them. And the foreman should be quick to be aware of the contribution he or some other member of management has made to the fault charged to the employee. Management's own inadequate performance of its functions has resulted in numerous cases of reversal of discipline or modification of the penalty by arbitrators. In a General Motors case, Ralph Seward said that when an employee seeks reversal of a penalty, "he places at issue not only his own conduct, but that of his employer as well. Present in every such case is the question of whether or not the employer was properly exercising his disciplinary functions under the agreement." [13] Lack of clarity is only one of many faults management may possess; equipment may be lacking or in poor repair, stock may be of poor quality, blueprints may be in error, and supervision may participate in the very offenses it punishes employees for committing.

One of the major errors of management is laxity amounting to the condonation of misconduct. The supervisor must not overlook violations, even minor or technical ones. He must move promptly to take the action he considers appropriate, even if it consists only of advising the employee that he is aware of the transgression. Inaction will not only loosen the bands of voluntary cooperation and obedience; it will result, if continued, in the rule's becoming a dead letter which cannot be enforced. Of course, in this as in other places of contact, the supervisor should attempt to educate and encourage, not merely admonish, and if it is necessary to give the employee a written reprimand, he should be conscious of the

---

[13] Seward is quoted in *U.S. Pipe and Foundry Co.*, McCoy, 10 LA 48 at 50 (1948).

reverberations which might result, not only from the employee but from the union steward and the other employees.

Obviously, the imposition of disciplinary penalties requires proof of the commission of the offense charged. Logically this is a separate problem from the determination of the kind or extent of the penalty inflicted. In practice, whether in discussions of grievances and their settlement or in arbitration, the two decisions are not so easily separated because of the human tendency to uphold a mild penalty where the proof is somewhat clouded, whereas a severe penalty, especially discharge, would lead to a more critical analysis of the certainty of proof of commission.

In discipline cases, perhaps more than any others, there is no substitute for facts. It is the duty of the foreman before he takes action to investigate the case thoroughly. He must look at the records, talk with other employees, examine and preserve any physical evidence which may be important, such as scrapped work or whiskey bottles, and, most of all, have a talk with the offending employee. Hasty action without giving the employee an opportunity to explain is highly unfair and can be fatal to the employer's case. The employee's story should be believed unless the supervisor has reason to disbelieve it, and in that case, even of the chronic liar, his statements should be thoroughly investigated. Many penalties are set aside as, in the course of the grievance procedure, new facts which could have been discovered in the beginning come to light, and many arbitration cases turn on disputed questions of fact. Disciplinary action, even oral warnings, should be made the subject of a written report or, at least, the foreman should keep his own notes. Such a memorandum should include all the facts, including the employee's own version of the affair. If no penalty was imposed for an offense which ordinarily would call for it, the reason for foregoing its imposition, such as the employee's physical or mental condition, or the validity of the excuse he offered, should be recorded, since otherwise the occurrence may be advanced in the future as an example of lax enforcement.

Some rules violations, especially those which involve concerted activity such as organized theft, gambling, or covert group drinking, may require surveillance before evidence is accumulated sufficient to support penalties. Although spying may be resented, it is sometimes necessary to post foremen and others in strategic places for observation in an attempt to catch the offenders red-handed or build a web of evidence which, even though circumstantial, is convincing. Supervision should not fall into the error, however, of setting traps. As Harold Gilden remarked, mere suspicion that gambling is going on is not entrapment, and "must be carefully differentiated from [a situation] where a carefully devised plan is formulated and bait is set or invitations extended for the express purpose of capturing persons in the commission of a wrongful act." [14] The foreman who can prevent the employee from wrongdoing should do so, not wait until the employee has acted and then descend upon him to impose a penalty. In these actions, as in all disciplinary problems, intelligence, as well as prompt and firm action, is required.

Discussions of burden of proof are likely to prove sterile. But in discipline cases, the employer, since he undertakes the responsibility for imposing the penalty, must assume the burden of proving the offense. Although this has been established, the union may have the burden, in its turn, of establishing that the offense did not merit the penalty thought by the employer to be just. The important consideration to remember here, especially for foremen, is that the collection and preservation of evidence is necessary, not only because the employer undertakes to act with "just cause," but because discipline not supported by adequate evidence can only breed suspicion among the workers that the company is unfair. Management not only has the burden of proof; it has the high responsibility of acting only with the best of motives and for reasons of weight and substance. It should always be prepared to justify its actions in discipline cases, regardless of technical considerations in the field of evidence.

This is especially true in discharge cases where the employer may be held to the standard of proof in criminal cases—"beyond a reasonable doubt." In all cases, the proof should be clear and sufficient to convince a reasonable person that the offense *was* committed. Generally, this calls for eyewitness and documentary proof. But circumstantial evidence can be used and may be sufficient without direct proof, especially in cases such as participation in commercial gambling and concerted limitations on production which are otherwise difficult to prove.

---

[14] *Borg-Warner Corp.*, Gilden, 3 LA 423 at 434 (1944).

The investigation completed, the foreman must decide whether to impose a penalty—one of the most complex and difficult decisions a foreman is required to make. In some cases, contracts require suspension and hearing as a preliminary to penalty. But even without such a provision, suspension may be wise if further investigation is needed, and yet it is advisable to get the employee out of the plant. On the other hand, the time off will be counted as part of the penalty, and if the employee is cleared, he will be entitled to back pay.

If a penalty must be imposed, it must be regarded as an aspect of the educational process, even in cases of serious offenses which call for discharge. Corrective discipline is concerned with causes and explanations, not punishment. The employee should be talked to in private, in the presence of his union representative if the contract so requires. Not infrequently a supervisor finds that there are hidden causes for the employee's failure to cooperate, such as family or other personal relationships and, in some cases, deep-seated psychiatric disorders. Employees with such problems should be referred to a counselling service, if possible. In all cases, an attempt should be made to convince the employee that disciplinary action is fair and just, and that he has not been the object of discrimination or unjust action. In these interviews the supervisor should maintain a dignified and reasonable manner, avoiding arguments and intemperate scenes so far as possible. Under no circumstances should he lay hands on the employee, even though the gesture be intended as conciliatory, and if he is himself attacked, he should avoid striking back, leaving the scene if necessary, and using no force except where absolutely required in self-defense. In a difficult case, a plant guard should be called to escort the employee out of the plant.

If the employee accepts the discipline in good spirit, the supervisor should compliment him on his attitude, and when he returns to work following a suspension, should follow up to make certain that any latent resentment is diminished. Everything possible should be done to assure that the penalty has had a constructive effect upon the employee himself and upon his fellow employees.

The appraisal and assessment of penalties is an art. It cannot be reduced to a mathematical formula but must be learned through study, observation, and experience. It is compounded of numerous factors, so diverse in their application that no case can be regarded as a precedent for another. The first thing for the supervisor to learn is that penalties consist only of written reprimands and warnings, layoffs (suspension is a better word), and discharge. Demotions and transfers are used only in exceptional circumstances. Ordinarily, an employee may not be deprived of his seniority rights for disciplinary reasons; for example, he may not be denied a promotion for which he is otherwise eligible.[15] Demotion may be appropriate when the employee lacks the innate capacity to do his work, a condition which cannot be corrected by warnings and disciplinary suspensions; but if his failure to do his work properly is due to carelessness or lack of application, discipline, not demotion, is indicated. Demotion of an inspector, taken after proper warning as a measure to improve quality and not as a disciplinary action, has been upheld.

Transfer to a different job may be proper when there is a clear relation between the employee's misconduct and the work he has been doing. For example, an employee who has been selling tickets in a numbers pool, taking advantage of his position as a stock supply man to do so, could be transferred to a job which limited his contacts with his fellow employees.

Penalties should be imposed as soon as possible, given a reasonable time for investigation. They cannot be postponed and accumulated for action in the future, and they should be certain, imposed for a fixed period without conditions.

The so-called double jeopardy concept has been applied in arbitration cases in which, after inflicting a penalty, the employer later decides, upon discovery of further circumstances affecting his judgment, to impose an additional penalty for the same offense. Generally speaking, it is true that an employee should be entitled to believe when the first penalty is imposed that his debt has been paid. But, said Shulman, this should not be carried to the point of interposing "technical, legalistic barriers . . . in the way of sensible solutions." [16] This was apropos of a discharge made after the employee had been given one week off for fighting, when it was discovered that he was actually guilty of a vicious assault on his foreman who could not be present when the employee was first disciplined, because he was receiving medical aid, and the first penalty was imposed on the basis of the employee's

---

[15] *Western Automatic Screw Machine Co.*, Lehoczky, 9 LA 606 (1948).
[16] *Ford Motor Co.*, Opinion A-31. *Cases on Labor Relations, op. cit.*, n. 9, p. 465.

own report. Nor would the "double jeopardy" doctrine apply in case of a penalty increased because following its imposition, the employee continued the misconduct or increased it. The existence of the doctrine emphasizes the necessity for thorough investigation preceding discipline.

In appraising a particular case the foreman must first decide whether the offense is so serious as to warrant discharge. Theft, instigation and leadership of a work stoppage, assault upon a member of supervision, assault on another employee with a deadly weapon, sabotage, and reckless disregard of the safety of others are typical of offenses in this group, though it can never be said with assurance that mitigating factors may not affect even such offenses.

If discharge is not justified, the supervisor must decide what lesser penalty is appropriate; here the principle of corrective discipline comes into play. Though there is no fixed and accepted system of progression, this normally means that discharge will be preceded by warnings and suspensions. In cases which do not respond to short suspensions, it is recommended that a long suspension, perhaps four to six weeks, be meted out with a clear warning that the employee is in danger of discharge. In any case, the penalties should be progressively severe. The employee should not be misled into believing his misconduct is of little consequence. Mere slaps on the wrist, not followed by more severe treatment and clear indications that the employee must reform, will not sustain discharge. Likewise, the imposition of a stiff penalty should not be followed by a series of mild ones, unless good reasons exist for such indulgence. In such a case, the reasons for not imposing more drastic sanctions should be recorded and explained to the employee, so he will not assume that all is forgiven and he is no longer in jeopardy.

Repeated and habitual misconduct is of itself cause for discharge; it is not necessary that the misconduct be serious if it can be shown that the worker has no interest in conforming to accepted standards.

No two cases of discipline are alike, and the supervisor must adapt his punishment to a number of factors as they appear in individual cases. It is probably impossible to list all such factors definitely, but many are employed and are well known in arbitration. Consultation between foremen is advisable, since one element in the assessment of penalties may be the practices of different supervisors in similar situations. It is good policy, as well as part of the weighing of "just cause," that some degree of consistency be maintained throughout the plant.

Length of service is important. An older man who, through personal or physical causes, strikes a period of poor morale and finds it difficult to perform his work properly or gives way to fits of temperament, is entitled to more consideration than a youngster who exhibits an attitude of brash indifference and persists in misconduct. Improvement and even sincere effort weigh in the employee's favor, even though he is not fully successful in eliminating his faults.

Misconduct may be more or less serious in different occupations—sleeping by a night boiler operator is dangerous, and careless workmanship by a machine repairman is costly. There are various circumstances which mitigate or augment the gravity of the offense. Excuses offered by an employee, accepted as true, may diminish the seriousness of his conduct, just as his refusal to explain or justify his action may aggravate it. Family responsibilities, transportation difficulties, and physical conditions should all be taken into account. A fist fight between two employees may justify only a short suspension of both participants; but if one, having knocked the other down, kicks and beats him brutally, he is deserving of a heavy penalty while the lesser one remains appropriate for his antagonist. What has been called the exercise of "humane discretion" must temper the supervisor's judgment as to the penalty.

If two major considerations were to be selected from the host of factors which enter into the reversal or reduction of penalties in arbitration, they would probably be: first, the degree to which management has itself failed to perform its affirmative functions; and second, the extent to which management has failed to enforce rules of conduct consistently, but instead, through a process of laxity and condonation, has allowed the employees to relax into a condition of disrespect and disinterest in proper conduct and workmanship.

Faulty or inadequate training and instruction, lack of effective supervision, tool and equipment problems, inferior raw materials,

poor methods and scheduling, and many other reasons are advanced for faulty workmanship and damage to company property
or product. To offset penalties for insubordination, employees
plead that instructions were muddled or contradictory; that they
resisted for fear of injury to themselves or others; or that the
supervisor interfered with the processing of grievances under the
agreement. Foremen are accused of hostile and provocatory conduct which induces insubordination and even retaliation. It may
be asserted that the foreman is guilty of the same offense for
which he has inflicted penalties upon his men, such as drinking
or smoking. It may be shown that penalties have not been assessed
on others who in the past have been guilty of the same or similar
offenses, that employees have not been informed of the rules, that
certain employees have been selected for punishment to serve as
examples and hence discriminated against. Management's actions
are characterized as haphazard and spasmodic. If these charges
or, strictly speaking, any one of them is established to the satisfaction of the arbitrator, he is quite likely to uphold the employee's
grievance, especially in a discharge case.

As we have said, such a variety of influences makes it imperative
that management avoid efforts to set up a system on the theory
that it will be practically automatic and self-executing. Instead,
management should teach foremen that discipline is and must be
maintained as a flexible system in which each case is given individual consideration on its own merits; foremen must be trained
to look into all the facts which go to make up a sound judgment as
to penalty. A reasonable pattern of consistency, rather than
wooden uniformity, should be employed and applied. Harry
Shulman dealt with the subject of equal penalties in these words:

> Normally, when other considerations are equal, employees
> guilty of the same offense should receive substantially the same
> treatment. . . . [But the object of industrial discipline is future]
> improvement, not retribution. The union does not generally
> contend that penalties should be imposed automatically without
> regard for circumstances peculiar to the individual employees.
> In prior determinations, I have urged upon the Company that,
> in imposing disciplinary penalties, it should exercise a humane
> and statesmanlike discretion in each case rather than strike out
> automatically; and that, in this exercise of humane and wise
> discretion, the employee's past record, a reasonable judgment as
> to his future prospect, and a reasonable estimate of the effect of

possible disciplinary action on the general situation are important factors. When such factors are taken into account—as they are also in our courts—different treatment for the same offense may very well result. Such civilized differentiation is not unjust discrimination.[17]

By now, it is abundantly clear that arbitrators insist upon a very strict standard of "just cause" for discipline, especially in discharge cases, and that penalties are likely to be rescinded or reduced for a remarkable variety of exceptions taken to management conduct in this field. Indeed, it is not too much to say that many management representatives feel arbitral review has come to amount to marked interference in the management function, and that arbitrators are, if anything, too diligent in their search for excuses for reversal of management's judgment, particularly as to penalties.

Whether this is true or not, management should remember that there are two doctrines which bear upon the scope of review. One is the limitation, by the express terms of the contract itself, of the power of the arbitrator to review penalties, assuming guilt is established to his satisfaction. Opinions differ as to the wisdom of such limitations. The United States Steel contract limits the Board of Arbitration in its jurisdiction to modify penalties, while the General Motors clause states that the "Corporation delegates to the umpire full discretion in cases of discipline. . . ."

The other doctrine we have already considered generally. In cases which require evaluation and the exercise of judgment, the discretion of management, if reasonable and not exercised in an arbitrary or discriminatory manner, should be respected by the arbitrator, even though looking at the matter originally he might have come to a different result. Dr. Shulman spoke of a "range of reasonableness," saying "the contract does not specify exact penalties for specific violations of orders under various circumstances. The initial and primary responsibility for determination of the penalty is vested in the company. Within a reasonable range of penalties, the company may exercise discretion as to the particular one to be selected."[18] In the early Stockham Pipe Fittings Company case, Whitley P. McCoy said:

> Where an employee has violated a rule or engaged in conduct meriting disciplinary action, it is primarily the function of

---

[17] *Ford Motor Co.*, Opinion A-197, *Id.*, at n. 9, p. 508.
[18] *Ford Motor Co.*, Opinion A-2. *Id.*, at n. 9, pp. 524-525.

management to decide upon the proper penalty. If management acts in good faith upon a fair investigation and fixes a penalty not inconsistent with that imposed in other like cases, an arbitrator should not disturb it. The mere fact that management has imposed a somewhat different penalty or a somewhat more severe penalty than the arbitrator would have, if he had had the decision to make originally, is no justification for changing it. The minds of equally reasonable men differ. A consideration which would weigh heavily with one man will seem of less importance to another. A circumstance which highly aggravates an offense in one man's eyes may be only slight aggravation to another. If an arbitrator could substitute his judgment and discretion for the judgment and discretion honestly exercised by management, then the functions of management would have been abdicated, and unions would take every case to arbitration. The result would be as intolerable to employees as to management. The only circumstances under which a penalty imposed by management can be rightfully set aside by an arbitrator are those where discrimination, unfairness, or capricious and arbitrary action are proved—in other words, where there has been abuse of discretion.[19]

Particular Offenses

By its nature, industrial discipline is, like the law, "a seamless web." It is impossible to break down factory conduct, good or bad, into neat little patterns into which particular actions can be fitted with precision. We have already seen that orderly conduct is an aspect of plant morale, depending upon the subtle interaction of many personal and psychological factors, chiefly resting upon good supervision. As we have indicated, there are certain serious offenses, such as assault with a deadly weapon or theft, which may justify immediate discharge, but this is not always true. In some companies minor thievery—for example, of beer from a brewery or loaves of stale bread from a bakery—is frequently overlooked. An employee discharged for assault may succeed in convincing an arbitrator that he picked up a hammer to strike his

---

[19] *Stockham Pipe Fittings Co.*, McCoy, 1 LA 160 at 162 (1945). Harry Platt discussed the problem in broader terms, concluding that the arbitrator has power to change the penalty "if it is found to be improper or too severe under all the circumstances of the situation . . . in a word, do justice and fair dealing warrant a reduction in the penalty." Platt, "The Arbitration Process in the Settlement of Labor Disputes," *Journal of the American Judicature Society* (August 1947), pp. 54, 58. In one case, even though the contract specifically reserved to management the right to exercise discretion, the arbitrator held that broad scope of the "just cause" provision made it unnecessary for him to make an express finding that management's action constituted an abuse of discretion, *Bakelite Corp.*, Lewis, Chairman, 1 LA 227 (1945).

antagonist only in self-defense. Likewise, the proof may sustain one charge but not another; the appraisal of the proper penalty in a single case requires the evaluation of all the relevant circumstances affecting the employee, and the employer's own conduct and record.

The same generality obtains when one attempts to classify offenses which may merit penalties. Offenses tend to resemble each other and to merge both in intent and in effect. Thus, faulty workmanship may be the result of carelessness or failure to obey orders or both. Or faulty workmanship may suggest a charge of malicious destruction of company property or even sabotage. Or it may indicate merely a lack of innate capacity to do the work. Similarly, failure to produce the proper quota of work may be deliberate refusal to produce up to standard; it may be the result of loitering or leaving the work station; it may be the result of an insubordinate refusal to follow the prescribed method; or it may result from the employee's lack of physical strength. In other words, the exact cause of the failure of the employee is important and must be ascertained before he is charged with a specific offense. This is why it is difficult to draft written rules with precision, in confidence that they cover all the offenses which should be mentioned and without overlapping.

Here we have attempted segregation for the purposes of discussion, but at the same time tried to indicate the linkages which exist between various offenses. This is an attempt which, if viewed definitively, is bound to fail. Employers would be wise to explain to foremen that before employees are charged with offenses and penalties are imposed upon them, the facts should be carefully reviewed to ascertain exactly what, if anything, the employee is guilty of. Obviously an employee who refuses to follow the prescribed method is a different case from one who loiters. The former probably needs instruction and persuasion more than he needs punishment, and very possibly his own view of the proper method is dictated by a belief that the other method will result in scrap or something of the kind. Intensive analysis of each case is necessary, and there is no better method of teaching foremen the proper differentiation between cases than by demonstrating the various types of cases by example.

Improper Performance of Work

We have already considered discipline for failure to meet production standards. It should perhaps be re-emphasized here that, while the employer may demand a fair day's work and production of workmanlike quality on the basis of fair standards, there are many cases in which management has failed to sustain its penalty, because the employee was successful in asserting a defense which, to some extent, made the company responsible for his faults or at least convinced the arbitrator that this was the case. In all such cases discharge probably cannot be justified until supervision has exhausted correctional measures.

In cases of making scrap and damage to company property, while the standard of care is that required of other employees doing similar work and having similar training and experience, there are, as has been indicated, many situations in which the foreman or some other management representative has contributed to the problem. There are several degrees of intent involved in these cases—in some, the damage is due to mere thoughtlessness; in others, to the lack of care which would be expected of a prudent man under like circumstances; in others, such ordinary negligence is aggravated by conduct amounting to abandon or recklessness without intent to cause loss; and, finally, there are situations in which damage is intentional or even malicious. These shades of guilt must be taken into account when the penalty is considered.

Other distinctions may be noted—reckless operation of a hi-lo truck may be careless workmanship, or it may be a violation of rules regarding the safe use of company equipment, but it is not making scrap. In these cases, as in those involving failure to produce standard, discharge may be deemed improper where mitigating factors exist, such as a long record of service without fault, condonation of similar trespasses by others in the past, failure to insist that proper methods be followed, and lack of knowledge by the employee that damage would result from his action.

Malicious destruction of company property and sabotage are serious offenses. They require a high degree of proof and a showing of motive, such as communist inspiration or other animus. Unless the employer is certain of his proof he would be better able, in most cases, to sustain a severe penalty for reckless misuse or damage to company property. On the other hand, discharge is appropriate if there is proof.

Insubordination

This is a broad category which may take many forms and relate closely to other offenses. It may consist of failure to follow instructions as to the method of performance of a job, a change in starting time, the assignment to a different job or department, a refusal to report for a medical examination, or non-compliance with orders from plant protection men. It may consist of a refusal to work overtime, although this offense is also closely related to leaving the plant without permission or to absenteeism. The employee is charged with the duty of following any reasonable order, although it has been said that such orders must be "necessary and desirable for the proper conduct of the business," and that orders must be "legitimate" and "within the bounds of propriety."

This does not mean, however, that an employee may refuse to obey an order which is in violation of the agreement, since the very purpose of the grievance procedure is to afford redress for violations of the agreement. Nor is it a defense that the supervisor who gave the order was not in authority over the employee refusing. An employee may not question the orders of other members of management, although if he is given contradictory instructions, the circumstance will probably prevent the imposition of a penalty.

There are, generally speaking, only two defenses available to an employee who refuses to follow an order, clearly stated and understood by him and reasonably necessary for the conduct of the business. These are: (1) the order which creates a hazard to health and safety, either of the worker or his fellows, and (2) an order which constitutes an interference with the proper conduct of the grievance procedure.

The employee who pleads a health or safety hazard must show that such a condition actually exists, or at least that he has good grounds for believing it exists. A hazard which is wholly fanciful will not suffice. Nor will it suffice for a union steward to allege health and safety as a reason for directing an employee not to obey an order when the employee himself does not believe any hazard exists.

Similarly, if the union function interfered with is not a proper one under the contract, it is not a defense to a charge of refusal to obey instructions. The grievance procedure is not interfered with when a union official acts outside the scope of his capacity and is ordered back to work.

Absence From the Job

This topic includes not only absenteeism and tardiness, but leaving the plant early and refusal to work overtime. This is so because all have the common element of the justification offered by the employee for his absence. Of these, the fourth, refusal to work overtime, is somewhat special since the contract may reserve the right to the employee to refuse overtime work if he likes, and it may make it mandatory. Usually, however, the employer has the right to compel overtime work unless the employee can offer a reasonable excuse. If no excuse is given, refusal to work overtime constitutes insubordination. A good excuse may prevail against attempts to discipline in all four situations.

The employer has the right to insist that employees come to work regularly though it is not customary to inquire deeply into infrequent, occasional absence. Likewise, the employer has the right to ask the employee to come to work on time and to stay for the full shift. In all these cases, and this is equally true with over-time work, irresponsibility can interfere with production and with the work of others—in some cases, to the point of causing people to be sent home for lack of work. Absence is costly.

What is a good excuse? The employee's own illness is a sufficient reason for absence and the one most frequently given. A medical certificate should be required of chronic or suspicious cases, but it must be accepted, unless the employer has good evidence that the certificate is false and was given to accommodate the employee. Forcing the chronic absentee to proof in the case of every absence is necessary, and will ultimately force him either to reform or to give up his job. In the case of a person subject to recurring illness, a medical leave of absence should be arranged if possible.

Illness in the immediate family, especially if the employee is needed, or other family emergencies, jury duty, or funerals may constitute sufficient cause for absence, tardiness, or leaving work early. Unanticipated storms may delay arrival at the plant, but ordinarily an employee must take weather and traffic conditions into account and plan his start early enough to be at work. Absence to take care of personal business or confinement in jail ordinarily are not good excuses.

The employee must decide whether he has a sufficient excuse; mere good faith is not the criterion, although it may be a factor, if established, in determining the penalty. He must also submit adequate proof, and in doubtful cases his proof should be thoroughly investigated by the personnel department or plant protection men. If his proof turns out to be false and can be proven to be, he may be discharged. But if he has a valid excuse for the day in question, he should not be disciplined merely because on frequent occasions in the past he has been absent without sufficient cause.

In tardiness cases there is no obligation to supply a man with work if it means reshuffling employees already assigned for the day. On the other hand, where there are utility men available or the employee's place has not been taken, it is wiser usually to give him his work for the balance of the day.

It must be remembered that in this category, perhaps more than any, an employee's length of service and record are important. A probationary employee who shows signs of becoming a chronic absentee should be discharged promptly, before he acquires seniority status. An older employee who has a good record must be treated with some leniency, and an effort must be made to help him maintain his good record, even when the causes of his recent lapses lie outside his employment.

Personal Misconduct

While in a sense, of course, every transgression is personal misconduct, the term is here used to cover such offenses as assault and theft, which have no relationship to the work done by the employee.

Fighting between employees is viewed somewhat differently from assault, which presumably involves no invitation or challenge to fisticuffs as a means of settling a dispute. Assault is a serious offense and should be severely punished, especially when it is aggravated by the use of weapons or by conduct showing intent to do great bodily harm, such as kicking a man who has been knocked down. Assault upon a member of supervision is viewed with even more gravity, since foremen are themselves expected to exercise a high degree of forebearance and, in most plants, are given clear instructions not to engage in physical encounters under any but the most extreme circumstances, such as when necessary for self-defense. Assault is not ordinarily excused by provocative conduct, such as the use of abusive, profane, or even threatening language. Nor can minor physical coercion, such as pushing, be advanced as an excuse for violence.

In penalizing employees for fighting, the distribution of blame must be carefully examined, since if both employees are equally guilty, neither contributing more than the other to the aggravation and seriousness of the situation, equal penalties are probably in order. In differentiating between employees, such circumstances as age, physical strength, record and seniority, provocation, the extent to which order was disrupted, and many other factors should be considered before the penalty is assessed.

While abusive language and threats do not justify resort to blows in answer, they are cause for discipline, its severity depending on the circumstances. Mere "shop talk," not actually intended to be profane or abusive under the prevailing standards of the plant, is not punishable. Nor is a serious penalty warranted if there is no real intention to carry a threat into action and that is known. But if the abuse and threatening language are accompanied by the immediate possibility of harm, the case may be quite different. Abuse and threats directed to supervisors and plant protection men are even more serious, since these persons are expected to exercise a high standard of restraint.

Horseplay ranges all the way from wholesome banter to serious misuse of tools, throwing, running, etc., which can result in violations of safety principles and endanger not only the participants but passersby. Booing of foremen and mass catcalling may also occur. Such offenses cannot be condoned unless they are truly of no consequence—they lead to disorder and provoke retaliation, sometimes of a violent nature. The penalty should be graded according to the nature of the offense and its repetition.

Gambling of all kinds is forbidden in most plants, although some employers permit card games and similar pastimes for amusement during luncheon periods. A rule against gambling is not violated by card-playing, and it is difficult to prove gambling since it can be carried on without money on the table, and employees will sometimes claim they were merely looking on. Such gambling, especially when petty in nature, such as pitching pennies, does not call for severe discipline unless it is repeated to the point where it becomes a problem.

Commercial gambling is a more serious matter, and discharge is justified for runners and pick-up men working for number pools and similar syndicates. Merely purchasing a number calls for corrective discipline. Ordinarily, solicitation for lotteries, even for church-supported affairs, is not permitted.

Drinking and intoxication include drinking on the premises, having liquor in possession on the premises, or reporting for or being at work under the influence of intoxicating liquors. Needless to remark, these are important violations, since they constitute threats not only to productive efficiency but to order and safety. Habitual intoxication is usually associated with absenteeism.

Of course, proof of these violations can be difficult. Bloodshot eyes, staggering, loud and boisterous conduct, odor, and impairment of speech all point to drunkenness. If a bottle is found, it should be kept and its contents verified as alcoholic.

Generally, an employee should be sent home, especially if he is so drunk he is unable to understand. The penalty can be imposed the following day. If he is in possession of his faculties, it is better to impose the penalty immediately.

Sleeping on the job can be a serious offense when the employee has a special responsibility, such as a power-house operator whose laxity may endanger the safety of the equipment and other employees. Ordinarily, it is a matter for corrective discipline. In some cases, an employee who shows a tendency not to be alert should be transferred. An employee who seeks a place to hide while he sleeps aggravates his offense.

Theft, a serious offense, usually calls for discharge, although this is not always true. Theft must be proved conclusively, and any evidence of a physical nature, such as the articles stolen, should be preserved as evidence. Theft should always be given the most intensive investigation, perhaps by labor relations or the plant protection department. An attempted theft, such as removal of an article to the employee's locker, is equivalent to actual theft. Sale of an article stolen aggravates the offense. If time is needed, the employee may be suspended pending completion of the full investigation.

Garnishment involves the company in bookkeeping expense and the risk of liability. This should be explained to the employee and he should be warned to get his affairs in order. Progressively severe penalties should be imposed, depending on the employee's service record, and his efforts to correct the situation, until discharge may finally be necessary.

Employees are sometimes guilty of fraud, or perhaps, better stated, falsification of records, such as their employment applications, applications for leaves of absence, production record counts, medical records, time cards, and applications for unemployment compensation. All such offenses, if established, are punishable, the penalty depending upon all the circumstances, including the lapse of time since the offense occurred, whether the company acted promptly after its discovery, and whether the misstatements, if such, are intentional and of importance or of the character which might easily be the result of vague memory, lack of understanding, or simply the belief that they are of little or no importance. Thus, an illness, long since cured, might be considered not worth the mention.

Misstatements in employment applications, if material, are ground for discharge since the company can maintain that the employee would not have been hired had his application reflected the true facts. But such errors, even if material and intentional, may not be ground for discharge if they are not discovered for a long time, and in the meantime the employee has served the company faithfully and well. Misstatements in other records are usually within the corrective discipline area and are not grounds for immediate discharge.

Work Stoppages

One of the ugliest aspects of American industrial relations is the use of the wildcat strike by militant unionists to force management to make concessions in addition to those given through collective bargaining and reflected in the contract. A weak company, forced to bow under such pressure, may find as the years go by that its very existence has become precarious as a result of these concessions. Management now realizes that it must face up to this challenge.

Writing in the *Harvard Business Review,* Garth Mangum comments:

> The true explanation of the wildcat strike phenomenon is pragmatic. If nothing is gained from the stoppages, the employees will become disillusioned with their use. Wildcat strikes exist in a continuing pattern in any firm only because they work. They work only where management is weak enough to reward them.
>
> One by one, managements were forced to face up to the problem and to begin exerting discipline to control costs and stabilize labor practices. In many cases the workers had become so accustomed to management weakness that the companies had to endure lengthy strikes to prove that the climate had changed.
>
> While the disciplinary measures now used by companies vary, they have one thing in common: the successful ones substitute costs to the participants for gains from wildcat strike action. As discipline has increased in these cases, the problem has diminished or disappeared.[20]

Employers who wish to maintain a good record in suppressing wildcat strikes should give their supervisors a guide to their actions when these activities occur. The supervisor should be alert to signs of dissatisfaction and should see that grievances in his department do not accumulate. In some cases, foremen can enter a problem and settle it before the irresponsible union leader can use it to provoke walkouts. The foreman, accordingly, must investigate all rumors or threats of strikes. This is a situation, above all others, in which an ounce of prevention is worth a pound of cure.

When a strike occurs, there is much confusion and excitement. People mill around and it is difficult to make records. Nevertheless, the supervisor should keep calm, observe and record events, and, if possible, get his men back to work. He can, in some cases, identify the leaders, i.e., those who make early preparations to leave their jobs, shut off their machines in advance of the rest, wave or call to others to join them, shut down machines or equipment other than their own, or who act as advocates or spokesmen for their fellows. Picketing is leadership. The foreman should not leave his department, but should notify his superiors of the occurrence by messenger, if necessary.

The foreman should tell his men to go back to work, saying in so many words that they are in violation of the contract and that

---

[20] Mangum, "Taming Wildcat Strikes", *Harvard Business Review* (March-April, 1960), p. 95.

they are to stay on the job. He should not indicate that they are free to choose whether they will work or go home. Employees who cannot work because the line is stopped should be told to remain at their work places, even if it is impossible for them to work. The foreman should continue to urge his men, singly and in groups, to go back to work until a decision has been made by his own superiors to abandon efforts to resume work and consider the plant on strike.

The supervisor should make every effort to force the union committeeman who represents the striking employees to undertake his responsibility to get the employees back to work. A sincere union official will join management in its efforts to persuade the employees that they are in violation of the agreement and that they should return to work. The foreman should point this out to the committeeman, if necessary, since "negative leadership"—that is, refusal on his part to discharge his responsibility affirmatively and positively—is in itself ground for discipline, even if the committeeman does nothing to encourage the employees to leave work.

As soon as possible the foreman should write his observations of the occurrence in detail, including the exact time, the names of those involved, and all the facts.

While penalties for wildcat strikes, like others, should be imposed as soon as possible after the event, in many cases the determination of penalties must await the result of investigation. This is particularly true when the stoppage affects a large number of employees and more than one department. Hence, in most cases, the foreman may not practically discharge this function.

Penalties should be imposed according to the principles of corrective discipline. Discharge on the first offense is appropriate only in clear cases of instigation and leadership. Where employees are guilty merely of passive participation, penalties may range from written warnings on the first offense, through the range of disciplinary suspensions on subsequent offenses, to discharge. The important point is to establish in the mind of every employee that strikes will not be tolerated, that they will fail, and that he will pay a penalty for participation.

The employer should avoid making distinctions based on the degree of leadership as between leaders, and also the degree of participation between participants. The fact that one union steward was obviously provocative while another did nothing more than walk the picket line should be disregarded. The same is true if one employee left promptly when the strike started, despite instructions to remain at work, and his fellow worker waited around at his machine to see what would happen, leaving in the end without permission from his supervisor. If distinctions are to be made in such cases, they should be based on other factors, such as the employee's record in previous stoppages, his seniority, and his work record. Proof of degrees of guilt, both in leadership cases and participation cases, is difficult. But penalties should be substantially more severe for leaders than participants.

Conclusion

Numerous other offenses can be mentioned, such as smoking in restricted areas, violations of safety rules, soliciting, sex offenses, the taking of photographs on company premises, molestation of records, and others. But they require no special comment beyond the obvious one, that for the most part they must be handled in accordance with the principles of corrective discipline, unless they are obviously so flagrant as to justify immediate discharge.

Although a penalty is usually based on a specific offense, the employee's record is always material; charging him at the same time with "repeated and habitual" violations adds to the strength of the case. It has been held in arbitration that a course of wrongful conduct existing over a sufficient period will sustain discharge even though the final act of misconduct alone would not justify the penalty.

At this point, having treated the complexities and difficulties inherent in employee discipline at some length, it may be well to resume the positive note with which this discussion started. The purpose of discipline is order, and, in its finer aspects, order is based not on unrestrained authority but upon consent. It preserves, so far as the common interest permits, the possibilities of free choice. Limitations upon license are understood; they serve useful ends which everyone can understand and accept. No one feels under duress because implicit in such a texture of relationships is the acceptance of leadership and that all liberty implies some restraint in the interest of others. Hence, except for the genuine malefactor or the psychopath, employees like men of good intention in all social organizations, accept discipline because it brings security and certainty. They know rules are for their own protection.

Constructive discipline is a living thing, a social principle, a means to cooperation and working together, not a system of offenses and penalties. It is not rules, categories, and evidence, but employee growth and development, which take into consideration many factors of a human nature in order to build a strong and enthusiastic work force. Discipline in a regiment or a symphony orchestra can be an inspiration. So can it be in industry.

As the numerous arbitration cases show, most industries have fallen far short of this goal. There are many reasons for this. One is the lack of interest shown by industrial leadership in human relations; a second the lack of time and opportunity for foremen, busy as they are with production problems, to counsel with their men; and a third, the relentless resistence of some union officials to supervisory authority. Men are not yet angels even when they are members of management, and supervisors are subject to the same limitations of temperament as their men. It is the rare official who does not sometimes yield to fits of temper, who is always in clear communication with his subordinates, and who does not sometimes make a hasty and ill-considered decision. Union men should understand this.

Another important reason for the failure of corrective discipline to build a more wholesome and constructive system of relationships is the complexity of the subject itself, as a whole and in its several applications. The rules of good discipline are well-known in the larger firms, especially those with umpire systems. But in thousands of smaller shops they are still uncharted problem areas seldom governed by rational and consistent principle. Even in those companies in which the rules are well-known and foreman training is advanced, the application of the system to the myriad of individual fact situations which occur is most difficult. To this confusion, the arbitrators have contributed, in a sense, by failing to recognize that when management does exercise a reasonable restraint in assessing penalties in an earnest effort to follow the principles of corrective discipline, the reduction of a not unreasonable penalty (say, from two weeks to one, or, even worse, from five days to three) is an exercise in frustration for management and an invitation to take grievances with little merit to arbitration.

But whatever its defects, the growth and proliferation of the corrective discipline system under the "just cause" concept is a great advance in American industry. For it, as I have said, the unions deserve chief credit, although enlightened management and the arbitral profession also may share. In time, it will breed a sense of responsibility and cooperation and go far to achieve creative participation by individuals in the significant work of their companies as well as to protect their contractual rights.

PART THREE

ENFORCEMENT OF THE AGREEMENT

CHAPTER 12

UNION REPRESENTATION

The labor agreement being, as we have noted, a compilation of "shop law," it is necessary to provide a means of government to enforce its provisions. Practically, this means a system of representation for the employees, whose rights are protected through the grievance procedure and arbitration. Most contracts contain some reference, however scanty, to employee representation by the union. Many contain elaborate provisions for the recognition by the employer of committeemen or stewards at all levels from the foreman to a top-ranking company executive, at which point the union is also represented by its leaders. Some unions prefer little participation by elected representatives from the rank and file and are little concerned with everyday shop gripes. Others promote rank and file interest to the point of erecting political machines in the plants at the expense of the employer. To a large extent, a smooth and well-functioning plant government depends more on union and management attitudes than it does upon the structures set up under the contract. A "fair but firm" attitude on both sides is conducive to good relations. Weakness on either side leads to imbalance, and, at the other end, if the union and the employer carry excessively hostile attitudes in their everyday handling of grievances, turmoil is almost inevitable.

Restrictions on Union Representation

The employer may fail to appreciate that the union official has several interests to pursue which have little or nothing to do with the success of the business. At their worst, unions are absorbed with petty politics which are reflected in the day-to-day affairs of shop representatives. But even the best of unions have institutional concerns which, to the employer, often result in excessive grievance activity. The union representative must keep these concerns in mind. There is, first, the obvious objective of seeing that each employee receives the full benefit of the contract. Here the committeeman or steward acts much in the manner of a shop lawyer. He must know the agreement thoroughly. He must be capable of analyzing a grievance, or action which could be asserted as a grievance, so effectively that it can be asserted successfully; or, if he finds the complaint to be unmeritorious, he must be able to explain to the employee, in such a manner as to satisfy him, that the matter should be dropped. Like the foreman, he must check the facts of each occurrence thoroughly, and he is wise to maintain records of them in case the occurrence is later cited by the company to support its position in another dispute. He should know plant precedents as they are reflected in grievance settlements and arbitration awards, especially when they establish the interpretation of some obscure or disputed provision of the agreement. He must be capable of arguing his constituents' cases effectively.

Normally, like the foreman, the committeeman does not act as a judge. It is his duty to represent the interests of the workers as the workers see them, not as he does, if there is any plausible basis for their position under the agreement. It is his duty to reject only grievances which he is convinced are truly "phony"; as to others, he should give his members the benefit of the doubt.

He also represents the union, and this means that he advances its political position with the workers and resists efforts either on the part of management or dissident groups to weaken effective representation through union channels. Unions do not easily agree to procedures which permit management to settle directly with the aggrieved worker, preferring to have all grievances pass through the hands of their officials. In this way "deals" made between the foreman and the individual employee which may affect others adversely can be avoided, undesirable precedents can be eliminated which might otherwise establish plant practice inimical to union interest, and employees cannot be misled into dropping meritorious claims which, had the shop-lawyer steward investigated them, might have been pressed to the advantage of the employee himself, or even perhaps to the advantage of others.

Union control of the grievance procedure gives the union an opportunity to settle grievances on the broad basis of the interests of all employees, rather than that of the employees immediately concerned. Not infrequently, a settlement has ramifications which are vital to the employees of another department, those on another shift, or those possessing skilled trades qualifications as against the rank-and-file production man. It is considered by the courts and other authorities on the subject that the union, not the individual employee or a minority group, controls the interpretation and administration of the agreement.

Union officials are vulnerable to the attacks of dissident groups within the union, perhaps a group seeking to install a rival union as the bargaining agent, one which covertly foments trouble (common with communist elements) in order to embarrass the union both with the workers and with the company, or simply a group of plant workers who want more drastic action against the company than the union seems to them to be taking in their interests. All such groups tend to focus on employee complaints and encourage their enhancement into sore spots in the plant relationships. The promotion of all grievances, regardless of merit or their intrinsic importance, tends to weaken the union in various ways: it breeds hostility from management, costs union officials much time, tends to increase arbitration costs, and disrupts union relationships.

Employers who find union activities in the plant an obstruction to efficient operations seek to restrict them in various ways. Although some unions do not ask for the right to handle grievance activities on company time, most do. In such cases, the employer seeks first to restrict union representatives to handling grievances, and nothing else. Some contracts are so broad in language as to permit the carrying on of "union business" or "union activity" in the plant, which is taken by the union to include, not merely grievances, but union political and organizational matters. Some employers reserve the right to enforce such a limitation by a demand that the union committeeman disclose what the grievance is which takes him away from his work, and he must obtain the permission of his foreman before leaving to handle the grievance. It is common also to require that if a representative enters a department other than his own, he must seek out the foreman of that department and disclose his business to him before proceeding.

Many contracts restrict the number of union representatives on a per employee basis, the number ranging from one to every 25 employees in some small shops to one to every 250 employees in larger plants. Some restrict the number of hours which can be spent in a week upon grievance activity; others place the restriction in the wages paid by providing a lesser rate for grievance work. Some restrict the number of persons who will be paid. Meetings are limited, and nothing is paid for meetings not with management, that is, meetings of the union representatives only. Provision is sometimes made that meetings must be held outside working hours. All these and other devices are employed to reduce the cost of the union's representatives in the plant, which if not curtailed can be substantial.

Authority of Union Representatives

Although formality in grievance handling is not a desirable attribute in itself, the employer must take some care to be certain that the assurances given by union representatives and their agreements are valid and binding. It is well to remember, for example, that the contract is not made with the plant committee or the employees, but with the union. In a New York Times case,[1] for example, it was held that the union could demand arbitration of a dispute, notwithstanding the vote of the membership not to take the matter to arbitration. In another case, it was held that an oral agreement made honestly and in good faith to protect junior employees from layoff at the expense of the plant-wide seniority rights of older employees was invalid.[2] On the other hand, where the contract provides for certain communications to the employees themselves, such as notice of impending layoff, it is not sufficient to communicate with the union.[3] In short, the contract must be literally observed, and assurances that its provisions need not be met are likely to be ineffective, as are attempts to modify it without the observance of the same formalities as attended its ratification and execution by the union.[4]

On the other hand, the usual principles of agency apply. The actions of union officials acting within the scope of their apparent authority, the company being unaware of their lack of true authority, are binding.[5]

---

[1] *New York Times Company* v. *Newspaper Guild of New York,* 26 LA 607 (N.Y. App. Div., 1956).
[2] *American Suppliers, Inc.,* Warns, 28 LA 424 (1957).
[3] *Curtis Screw Co.,* Thompson, 23 LA 89 (1954).
[4] *Valley Metal Products,* Ryder, 25 LA 83 (1955).
[5] *Lockheed Aircraft Corp.,* Marshall, 23 LA 815 (1955); see also *Midwest Mfg. Co.,* Anrod, 29 LA 848 (1957).

Responsibility of Union Representatives

Just as it is the responsibility of the company and its supervisors to accord a union representative the right to provide adequate representation to the employees within his domain, it is the responsibility of the representative to respect the company's rights and the supervisors who exercise them. In the first place, they are employees as well as union officials and the latter office does not confer any immunity upon them for derelictions in their duties as employees.[6] In handling grievances, they must follow the agreement; thus if the contract gives them the right to be present when the employee is called into the foreman's office for the purpose of imposing discipline upon the employee, the union representative does not have the right to be present when no discipline is imposed or intended. When the agreement permits expressly or by implication a reasonable time for the handling of grievances, they must not abuse the privilege by taking excessive time, as in one Ford case, where the committeeman lined up the complaining employees, and then, taking each at a time, wrote a single grievance, had the employee sign it, and then took it to the foreman while the rest waited. However, except in cases such as these which show outright dishonesty or pretense, there must be clear proof that the time taken is excessive. An arbitrator is not likely to uphold discipline in a case in which there is an honest difference of opinion as to the time required.[7] Records, such as grievance time cards, are helpful in such cases.

It is not the committeeman's function to take the place of the foreman in giving orders. If he objects, or the employee objects, to the instructions given, the representative has no right to direct that the order be disobeyed. He must tell the employee to follow the directions given him and, if desired, file a grievance. If an employee asks him for directions as to the conduct of his work, the representative should tell the employee to get his instructions from his supervisor. These observations apply to cases in which a violation of the agreement seems clear to the representative, as in a case in which an employee is improperly required to work overtime or directed to work at a pace over standard. If an element of danger or serious physical detriment is present, this would not apply.

---

[6] *Symington-Gould Corp.*, Whiting, Payne, Wright, 9 LA 819 (1948).
[7] *North American Aviation*, Komaroff, 21 LA 67 (1953).

Special Rights and Privileges of Union Representatives

Unions commonly insist that they have representatives present in the plant whenever any of their members are working. This leads to the assertion of contract demands which, if agreed upon, give them special seniority and overtime privileges. Superseniority rights apply only to periods of layoff; they do not usually entitle the union representative to any preference when promotions or transfers are under consideration. On the other hand, it may be a violation of the agreement for the employer to transfer a committeeman into an area or job which will frustrate the effective discharge of his duty as an elected or appointed representative.

From the employer's point of view, the chief difficulty with these provisions, including those which require the presence of the committeeman when overtime is being worked by the men he represents, is that the representative is not capable, or fully capable, of doing the work. Appropriate reservations of the right to require that the representative be qualified, or that he can be assigned to any work management desires, should be made in the agreement. Provision should likewise be made that no other employees can complain that the union representative, by working in a task designated by the employer during periods when the complaining employees were laid off, or when they might have been called upon for overtime, deprived them of work for which they should be paid, possibly at overtime rates. In short, the need of the union to secure adequate representation should not cause the employer to pay twice to get his work done.

It is common to give union representatives leaves of absence for periods when they hold union (and under some contracts, public) offices, and for the purpose of attending union conventions. While it is common to permit the accumulation of seniority during such periods, they should not be eligible to accumulate pension or other credits, which for the rest of the employees are based on length of service. It should also be provided that they may be used in any job available, which in the opinion of the company they are qualified to perform, especially if they return after years of absence.

The right of union officials to leave their work, either to handle grievances outside their departments or attend union meetings, especially those outside the plant during working hours, can cause serious interruptions to production if the representative is not easily replaced. While liberality in such matters may be indicated, the foreman of the department should have enough control over the union official's departure to see that no serious consequences flow from his absence. In all cases, the foreman should be notified, as far in advance as possible.

Union representatives enter some plants freely, not even asking permission. In others, their right to enter is conditioned on the consent of the company, which is usually given after explanation of the occasion for the visit, and the persons and departments they wish to visit.

Management Policy Toward Union Representatives

The aim of every employer must be to secure a proper functioning of the union government in his plant, which means on the one hand that he must not deny to the union its right to represent the employees effectively, and on the other hand that he does not allow its representatives to dilute or overcome the exercise of supervisory authority.

The wise employer, realizing this, will attempt to deal with union officials and the grievances they present on their merits. He will avoid deals and compromises which may have undesirable aftereffects. He will, above all, remain aloof from union politics, even if he thinks he sees clearly which are the responsible elements and which the trouble-makers.

Above all, the employer will not yield to pressure or threats, nor permit union representatives to overawe supervisors. They should not be allowed special privileges not given to the men they represent. Whatever the broad political or institutional problems of the union may be, the employer must remember they are not his problems. The time accorded union representatives is designed to enable them to represent the employees under the contract in an adequate manner, no more. If the employer enforces this policy firmly and reasonably, he will in the long run achieve a stable system of grievance adjustment.

CHAPTER 13

THE GRIEVANCE PROCEDURE AND ARBITRATION

As pointed out in Chapter 5, the labor agreement, viewed procedurally, contemplates the exercise by management of its right to act—the right of administrative initiative—the employee's reaction being, except in extraordinary cases, through use of the grievance procedure. From the standpoint of dynamics, the grievance procedure is probably the most important single aspect of the agreement, and, indeed, of the entire labor-management relationship. One might almost say a well-administered grievance procedure is equal to good labor relations. For a good grievance procedure is more than a means of resolving disputes. Used as a means of communication, it can produce understanding of the workers' views and needs for management, and the workers in turn can be educated in the fundamentals of good management. Used as an analytical tool, it can promote good administrative and supervisory techniques and enhance employee acceptance of them. A perceptive management may be able to discover under the surface hidden sources of hostility to good administration—perhaps an overly militant union clique, an abusive supervisor who rules by threat or a weak one who permits himself to be intimidated by fear of grievances, or a latent insecurity which leads to poor production.

Of course, the grievance procedure operates in a context of basic relationships which may affect it. Slichter, Healy, and Livernash say: "The most striking finding from a review of the grievance rates in many plants is that the satisfaction of individual workmen has relatively little to do with the grievance rate. The chief determinants appear to be organizational and institutional conditions." [1] Among these are union policies and union politics, which may have a relationship to management's own attitude and policies

---

[1] *The Impact of Collective Bargaining on Management* (Washington: Brookings Institution, 1960), pp. 701-702.

toward the union, or may not. Changes in methods of operation, cost reduction programs, and extensive layoffs often lead to increases in grievances. Of these influences, management policy toward the settlement of grievances is of great significance. And fundamental to good administration is a good procedure.

The Elements of a Good Grievance Procedure

At the threshold of any inquiry into the administration of grievances is the question of what can be considered in the procedure— what is a "grievance"? Employers are usually loathe to include in the procedure complaints which cannot be traced to a violation of the agreement. The broadest approach is to submit all disputes over wages, hours, and working conditions not only to settlement in the steps between the parties themselves, but to final disposition by arbitration. A compromise is to permit all complaints to be heard at all stages of the procedure but confine the arbitrator to grievances involving a violation of the agreement. Closely allied is the question of whether the union representative must be consulted by the employee, or whether the employee is free to take up a complaint with his foreman. Again, a compromise appears in some contracts which permits the employee to choose for himself whether he wishes the union representative present. Such contracts provide that if the employee requests, the committeeman must be sent for without further discussion of the grievance by the foreman.

The union, of course, prefers to have the procedure open to all complaints, whether bottomed in the agreement or merely on a condition which the employee thinks should be remedied, and, on the second point, to have the representative present at all discussions. This not only enhances the power and prestige of the union and its officials, but prevents the foreman from dealing with his men on an individual basis. Most employers seek to narrow the area of intervention by the union in order to preserve a relationship of confidence between the foreman and his men. Added to this is the belief in the minds of many management people that union representatives make political hay by stirring up grievances.

Although with the growth of "industrial jurisprudence" grievance adjustment has become more formal, it is probably wise to foster settlement in oral discussion at the first stage. A company which does not repose confidence in its line supervision sufficiently to permit this would do well to re-examine its position. If foremen are expected to give orders, they should have the authority to handle grievances, just as they should have the primary responsibility for discipline in their departments. Nor should they be required to be legalistic, at least until the grievance goes to the second stage. An atmosphere of trust and respect between foreman and employee and foreman and steward has its own value. A dramatic example of this policy occurred at International Harvester Company.[2] In 1960, the company and the Auto Workers, desperate because of the accumulation of a tremendous number of unresolved grievances, instituted a new approach to grievance handling. They concentrated on talking them through to a settlement when they arose in the shops. The flood of grievances receded promptly. Since then, both company and union officials have held firmly to the view that whenever grievances are written out and passed on to a higher authority they show a failure on the part of the individuals responsible for "talking things out" in the initial step of the grievance procedure. If necessary, higher management officials and specialists are brought in at the "talk out" stage. The approach is regarded as highly successful at Harvester.

This approach, or some modification of it, has a number of advantages. It maintains the position of the foreman. It keeps grievances from changing their character and becoming legalistic as they move away from their operating context to the higher stages. Most importantly, it assures real understanding and thorough agreement where it counts.

One large public utility company has an understanding with the union that settlements in the first and second steps of the procedure cannot be cited as precedents. This is helpful, since in most cases settlements are very good evidence not only of plant practice but of contract interpretation by the parties. In the absence of such an understanding, undesirable settlements, or even those which are in themselves desirable, may create unfortunate precedents. Such risks can be minimized by good supervisory training. Ordinarily, when the grievance goes to the level above the foreman, the union should be required to put it in writing. The more definite and specific this written claim is, the better.

---

[2] The International Harvester grievance program is described in *Grievance Handling—A Case Study of a New Approach*, IRM No. 139 (New York: Industrial Relations Counselors, 1961).

The employees affected should be identified and perhaps be required to sign the grievance, especially if back pay is claimed.

Higher stages of the grievance procedure vary between companies and unions. Some prefer to keep them as simple as possible, sometimes referring them to arbitration after the first meeting. Others have complicated five- and six-step procedures, although such procedures commonly have provisions for the initiation of grievances at higher levels, as in the case of "policy" grievances which necessitate broad decisions affecting the entire work force. Sometimes the more complicated procedures require final statements of position on each side with the aim of screening out cases which one side or the other thinks unworthy of presentation to the arbitrator.

At the last stage before arbitration it is common to insist that the issues be frozen and that all relevent facts then within the knowledge of the parties be disclosed. Disclosure of the facts tends to make full explanation and justification of the opposing views necessary, whereas the conscious withholding of information tends to clog the grievance procedure and lead the arbitrator to go into the issues anew, deciding not whether the parties acted rightly on the facts known to them, but whether they were actually right on the basis of the facts brought out at the hearing. Management should also avoid changing position as the grievance goes into the appellate stages. If the employer contradicts an earlier reply, or adds inconsistent arguments, he stands convicted of ineptitude.

Although offers of settlement are not accepted in evidence in arbitration as admissions, arbitrators are quick to sense the point at which management would have been willing to compromise. It is not good practice, therefore, to make offers of settlement, especially those which are compromises of basic management rights or important principles of contract interpretation, and then withdraw the offer and resume one's original position. If such offers are made, the employer should make it clear that they are not to be construed as admissions or precedents affecting other grievances, but are made solely in order to settle the grievance under consideration, with the right reserved to adopt a different position in the future. It is possible to insert in the answer or the agreement of settlement appropriate language of reservation, such as the statement: "This settlement shall apply solely to the grievance of X, and shall be not construed as a waiver of the Company's position that it has the right to (insert a statement of the management position)." The usual legal expression for reservations of this kind is simply "without prejudice," which means without prejudice to one's own rights or claims.

Time Limits

Grievance procedures commonly contain some provision to bar the assertion of stale claims, and to encourage promptness in filing and appealing grievances. It is usual to provide that a grievance must be filed within a certain number of days after the occurrence giving rise to the grievance, and that "a written decision at any step of the grievance procedure shall be considered final unless the grievance is taken to the next step" within a given number of days. Sometimes the limitation is merely that a grievance must be filed within a reasonable time and appealed within a reasonable time to the next step. Provisions for extension of the time limits by mutual agreement in writing are also frequently included.

These provisions are part of the agreement and will be recognized and enforced in arbitration. Arbitrators are in accord with the healthy principle that dispatch is essential to the success of the grievance procedure. Stalling and clogging the procedure naturally deprives it of much of its usefulness. But the employer will do wisely to administer the time limit provisions with a sense of fairness and justice. Reasonable diligence is all that should be required. The fact that the company itself is not misled or prejudiced is important. Has the employee actual knowledge of the condition, or can it be fairly imputed to him? If not, should he be penalized for his failure to file a grievance? Has the foreman or some other management representative given him to understand that the matter is under investigation, thus in effect waiving the strict requirement of time to file a grievance? Failure to observe the time limitation may be due to good cause, such as ignorance of essential facts, absence of a key employee or union official, misunderstanding of the company's answer, or assurance by a supervisor that the matter would be corrected. In such cases, the time limit should be waived, but the waiver should be accompanied by a statement that it is not a precedent for future cases of untimely filing or appeal. If this reservation is not made, and time limits are waived in a haphazard and inconsistent manner, they are likely to lose their effectiveness. Arbitrators will then hold that the company's failure to insist on prompt filing and appeal has lulled the union into the belief that the time limits can be violated without loss. Similarly, if the failure to observe the time limit is not raised at each step, it cannot be raised in arbitration. Discussion of a grievance on the merits is always desirable, but the discussion should be accompanied by the statement at each stage that the time limit bars the grievance regardless of its merits.

Time limits do not usually apply to continuing grievances. Thus, in a steel case the continued refusal of a company to abide by an established working condition of assigning a helper to each boiler maker was held open for grievance, despite expiration of the time limit after the initial repudiation by the company of the working condition. The continued layoff of an employee not according to seniority may be a continuing grievance even though the initial violation was outside the time limitation. A continuing failure to pay the proper incentive rate is the same. In such cases, however, arbitrators will award back pay only from the date the written grievance is filed, except in cases in which the delay in filing is excusable or is the fault of the company.

Back Pay

Some contracts limit the time within which back pay may be claimed, and provide for offset against any pay due of sums earned in other employment and unemployment compensation received and not repaid. The General Motors contract contains such provisions.

Employers have not been as diligent as they might be in this regard. Employees should receive awards of back pay only in cases of actual loss. Settlements should be confined to reimbursement of wages which would otherwise have been earned by the employee. Back-pay settlements should be limited to individual signed grievances. Back pay should never be allowed on "policy grievances," which should be confined to declarations of rights. Payments of missed overtime work should be avoided in favor of later equalization. Work assigned to the wrong classification should not be the basis of a back-pay award unless the employee whose work was performed by others actually lost time. If the employer falls into the habit of paying one or two hours for such violations to the senior man or the persons who happen to file the grievance, naturally such grievances multiply. They are used as a means of political favor in some plants.

Likewise, the usual principles of mitigation of damages should be applied. An employee who has been improperly discharged, especially if he has been off work some time, should be required upon reinstatement to show he used reasonable diligence in seeking other employment while he was off. The dischargee in NLRB cases is required to present such proof under present day court decisions. Certainly he should be charged with any loss due to his wilful failure to accept other employment, and, since under ordinary rules the employer cannot deduct the amount of unemployment compensation he has received, the contract should provide for its return to the state, or it should be deducted.

In Philip Carey Mfg. Co.,[3] Lewis M. Gill set forth the usual rule that "punitive" damages, or damages for mere inconvenience, will not be awarded in arbitration. In the same case, he held that employees who were deprived of unemployment compensation because of the employer's breach of contract were entitled to be reimbursed for it.

The Individual Employee and the Grievance Procedure

Section 9 of the National Labor Relations Act provides that individual employees "shall have the right at any time to present grievances to their employer and to have such grievances adjusted, without the intervention of the bargaining representative as long as the adjustment is not inconsistent with the terms of a collective bargaining contract or agreement then in effect. . . ." Does this permit the employee to handle his own grievance to the exclusion of the union? Is he bound by a settlement made by the union without his approval? The same problem exists with respect to the right of the individual to participate in his arbitration case. In the Elgin Railway case,[4] arising under the Railway Labor Act, the Supreme Court held that the union could not make a binding settlement of the employee's grievance without his consent. Most authorities think the institutional requirements of collective bar-

---

[3] *Philip Carey Mfg. Co.*, Gill, 37 LA 134 (1961).

[4] *Elgin, Joliet & Eastern Ry. Co.* v. *Burley*, 325 U.S. 711 (1945), 65 S. Ct. 1282, 16 LRRM 749. See discussion in Elkouri and Elkouri, *How Arbitration Works* (Washington: BNA Incorporated, 1960), p. 96. In *Kister Lumber Co.*, 37 LA 356 (1961), Marlin M. Valz held that under Section 9 (a), a grievance directly affecting individual rights could not be settled or compromised without the grievant's consent.

gaining, the group interests it must serve, warrant the exclusion of the individual from the grievance process. Opponents of this view place individual rights to the fore. Many contracts contain provisions that the union shall have exclusive authority to process grievances beyond the first step, and that the individual employee is bound to any settlement made by the union.

Analysis of Grievances

A "What, Where, When and Why" approach to grievance analysis has been recommended. The first three are largely objective and capable of statistical tabulation. "What" divides grievances by sections of the agreement, showing that in one plant or department the problem may be division of overtime, in another, seniority preferences, and in a third, discipline. "Where" shows that certain plants and departments are more (or less) affected. A search may reveal that the reason department "A" has no grievances is that the foreman lets the steward run his department, deciding on work assignments, standards, and employee conduct, while in Department "B" the exact opposite holds true: the supervisor has his men, and the steward also, thoroughly under his thumb, afraid to lift their voices. "When" shows that grievances are likely to mushroom upon the occurrence of certain events, such as the approach of negotiations, the introduction of improved methods and standards, or the prevalence of layoffs.

"Why" is, of course, not objective. It involves analysis frequently of underlying causes and motivations which can be detected only by persons of experience and judgment who are familiar with the social and psychological factors which may cause unrest in any group situation.

Analysis of the "why" of grievances, or the lack of them, is important also for the reason that statistics can be deceptive. It is difficult to include grievances which have been settled orally, and a small number of written grievances is no indication that they are not present at the oral stage, nor that they are being settled, if they exist, promptly and properly. Likewise, the filing of a large number of written grievances may be an indication that adjustments at the oral stage are faulty, or it may only be an indication that the union officials or the foremen want to get their positions on record in a commendable effort to introduce certainty into their procedures. Some unions make an effort to screen out grievances with little merit at the oral stage; others as a matter of policy prefer to "pass the buck" for settlement at a stage more remote from the man on the floor. In some plants, numerous individual grievances are filed on matters which could be handled as well or better through a single "policy" grievance.

Management Policy on the Settlement of Grievances

The range of possibility in an employer's attitude toward grievances is wide. Some companies rely largely on personality and good will to dispose of problems, even to the extent of allowing the procedure set up in the agreement to fall into disuse. Some unions favor the approach which simply calls the business agent in when the employees complain to him, whereupon he settles the problem with a management official at a high level, not infrequently disregarding the terms of the contract in the process. Others go to the other extreme—they regard every grievance as an exercise in legal logic, and dismiss it curtly if the union steward fails to show a violation of the agreement. Not infrequently, such employers insist on the word "grievance" being defined in the first instance as a claim of violation.

The middle approach, and probably that most frequently used, is sometimes labeled the "fair but firm" policy. This excludes settlements based on force or threats of force, and also those which dilute management rights to establish efficiency and order in the plants. Compromises are not frowned upon if the grievance has merit, but they should be compromises which do not establish precedents for future complaints of similar sort.

The middle approach does not exclude from the procedure mere gripes, or complaints not based on the agreement. A wise management is willing to listen to its employees—and learn from them, even though prior to the arbitration step it gives a final "No" as its answer.

Under the governmental theory of the labor agreement, which characterizes the agreement as the constitution of the shop, to be filled in by the industrial common law, the settlement of grievances has the greatest importance. The employer who thinks of his actions in the grievance procedure as merely defensive is overlooking his opportunity to build the law of the shop in accordance with sound principles. Unions have been alert to broaden the protections afforded by the agreement, even to the point in some cases of securing rights by implication which were not contemplated by the employer when he executed the agreement. Employers have not been equally alert to use the area of management initiative and to insist, in the settlement of grievances, upon the recognition of good administrative practices, including the all-important principle of the exercise of managerial discretion as to matters not clearly set out in the agreement.

Arbitration

Scores of articles and a number of books have been written on labor arbitration [5] and I have no desire to add to the torrent of

---

[5] Two recent books on labor arbitration are Elkouri and Elkouri, *How Arbitration Works, op. cit.,* and Updegraff, *Arbitration of Labor Disputes by Updegraff and McCoy,* Second Edition (Washington: BNA Incorporated, 1961). A more elementary study is Beatty, *Labor-Management Arbitration Manual* (New York: E. E. Eppler & Son, 1960). The practical aspects of arbitration are discussed in *The Impact of Collective Bargaining on Management, op. cit.,* Chapter 26. The Annual Proceedings of the National Academy of Arbitrators are published under various titles by BNA. The American Arbitration Association publishes the *Arbitration Journal,* a quarterly review of arbitration, including digests of court decisions. Three commercial labor arbitration loose-leaf services are sold, and the AAA also circulates digests of opinions.
Leading references on important aspects of arbitration are:
    a. Legal problems: Russell A. Smith, "The Question of 'Arbitrability'—The Roles of the Arbitrator, the Court, and the Parties," Address delivered at the 8th Annual Institute on Labor Law, Southwestern Legal Foundation, November 4, 1961, *Southwestern Law Journal* (Vol. XVI: No. 1, 1962), p. 1., reprinted by the Institute of Labor and Industrial Relations, The University of Michigan-Wayne State University, Reprint Series No. 22 (1962). Cox, "Reflections upon Labor Arbitration", 72 *Harvard Law Review* 1482 (1959); Kagel, "Recent Supreme Court Decisions and the Arbitration Process", *Arbitration and Public Policy* (Washington: BNA Incorporated, 1961), p. 1.
    b. Arbitration clauses: BNA, *Collective Bargaining Negotiations and Contracts,* p. 51:261 (May 25, 1962). Clauses are included on such subjects as the arbitrator's right to decide what is arbitrable (International Harvester) and the submission of this question to court (General Electric) and exclusion of specific subjects from arbitration, procedures for the selection of an arbitrator and advance specification of issues, filing of prehearing briefs, etc.
    c. Rights of the individual employee: Fleming, "Due Process and Fair Procedure in Arbitration", *Arbitration and Public Policy, op. cit.,* p. 69. Clyde W. Summers, "Individual Rights in Collective Agreements—A Preliminary Analysis", *Twelfth Annual Conference on Labor,* New York University (Albany: Matthew Bender & Co., 1959), p. 63. Cox, "Individual Enforcement of Collective Labor Agreements", 8 *Labor Law Journal* 850 (1957). See also *Clark* v. *Hein-Werner Corp.,* 8 Wis. 2d 264, 99 N.W. 2d 132, 45 LRRM 2137 (1959).
    d. Procedural problems: The American Arbitration Association publishes the *Lawyers' Arbitration Letter,* which reviews court decisions and other legal authority on such matters as notice of hearing, examination before hearing, and ex parte arbitration. For discussion of evidence and the rules of evidence in ar-

words on the subject. Pre-eminent among these discussions today is the effect of the Supreme Court decisions, particularly the Warrior and Gulf case, and its companion decisions, which we have already discussed in connection with management rights. Sam Kagel, speaking at the Fourteenth Annual Meeting of the National Academy of Arbitrators, has given most sensible advice to everyone concerned with these decisions. Quoting Harry Shulman's statement that the arbitrator serves at the pleasure of the parties "to administer the rule of law established by their collective agreement," Kagel concludes:

> *To the Arbitrators:* Act within the authority that the parties give you—no more, no less.
>
> In grievance arbitration, "interpret and apply" the agreement in accordance with its terms. Unless the parties specify otherwise, use the industrial "common law" only as one of the available aids to resolve ambiguities.
>
> Write your opinions as suggested by Dean Shulman.
>
> Above all, remember that you represent only one of the techniques used in the collective bargaining process, and that the collective bargaining agreement itself represents the outer limits or objectives of the process. It is the parties who have the right to determine within what orbit they want arbitration to operate— a wide or a narrow one. It is your responsibility to remain within the orbit delineated by the parties.[6]

Criticisms of arbitration have come from unions or professors who think the process has become too formal and lengthy, with a consequent rise in expense to the parties.

Informality, they say, has always been characteristic of labor arbitration proceedings, and to the extent that it is hampered by excessive resort to legal procedures, especially those of the technical sort little appreciated by laymen, stultification of the arbitral process has resulted. At one extreme is what Secretary of Labor Willard Wirtz has described as ". . . shirt sleeves, seat-of-the-pants, look, no hands . . ." arbitration. At the other is the case

bitration, see Elkouri and Elkouri, *How Arbitration Works, op. cit.*, Chapter 8, and Siegel, *Proving Your Arbitration Case* (Washington: BNA Incorporated, 1961).

e. Hearings and Preparation of Cases: McCoy, "Some Pitfalls in Arbitration", 11 *Labor Law Journal* 23 (Jan., 1960). Sam Kagel, *Anatomy of a Labor Arbitration* (Washington: BNA Incorporated, 1961).

f. Arbitration and the NLRB: Beatty, "Arbitration of Labor Disputes", 14 *Arbitration Journal* 180 (1959), see n. 14 for other articles of interest.

[6] "Recent Supreme Court Decisions and the Arbitration Process", *Arbitration and Public Policy, op. cit.*, p. 10.

in which the parties rely on voluminous briefs and exhaustive references to decisions of courts and other arbitrators on the same or similar questions. Such a case frequently ends in a lengthy and complex opinion which only the professionals who prepared the briefs understand. George Brooks, Research Director of the Pulp, Sulphite and Paper Mill Workers, has given strong expression to the view that a system of "emerging common law" of arbitration has its weaknesses from the practical union man's standpoint.[7] It tends to increase the costs of arbitration and to remove it from the hands and the comprehension of rank-and-file workers. Because it is too complex, he says, the process tends to become the property of a priesthood, or elite corps, of lawyers and economists who tend to glorify each other, not the people whom they are hired to serve.

Dr. Julius Manson, in the same vein, has written:

> The original attractions of arbitration were speed, simplicity, and inexpensiveness. Judged by these standards, modern arbitration isn't what it used to be. Now sluggish, complicated and costly, the process has nurtured some peculiar techniques for dubious ends. Once hailed as a gentle substitute for violence, it is now often deployed as a weapon in a cold war. Jaded disputants engaged in the pursuit of specific ends are not burdened with visions of the once high purpose of voluntary arbitration.[8]

Employers, for their part, resent the use of arbitration as a political device to demonstrate to the rank and file the diligent protection the union officials in the plant give them. Their elected representatives like arbitration, despite its cost to the union and the employer, because it gives them (and they demand) the opportunity to take the most minor complaints to hearing and decision. If they lose, they simply blame the arbitrator and the company. If they win, they can pass out a company check for back pay, perhaps for one or two hours, or a day, of unworked time at overtime rates, or perhaps for two or three days' back pay when a penalty is modified. These inconsequential grievances, I suspect, form a large part of the business of the professional arbitrator today. The really significant gains made by the unions in limiting

---

[7] Brooks, "Union Criticisms of Arbitration", speech delivered at a conference at Massachusetts Institute of Technology (1957), 41 LRR 28.

[8] Julius J. Manson, "Is Arbitration Expendable", *Twelfth Annual Conference on Labor*, New York University (Albany: Matthew Bender & Co., 1959), p. 1. Dr. Manson cites numerous studies by arbitrators and union spokesmen critical of the present trends in arbitration.

arbitrary employer conduct are largely history; what is left is a residue of chicken feed complaints against a hapless foreman who, in the haste and pressure of getting his work out, has innocently assigned the wrong man to the job, or called in the worker on overtime whom he knew he could depend on to do a good job on a rush order, or in some other minor way failed to foresee and guard against complaint.

In these cases, the arbitrator does not dismiss the grievance as unworthy of his expensive attention, by no means. He writes a grave exposition at length of the arguments of both sides, and gives his decision with an air of apology as though resolution of the problem required the wisdom of Solomon. It would be wonderfully instructive to these learned gentlemen if they could spend a few weeks running a production or maintenance department and making on-the-spot decisions as supervisors must do every day. One is tempted to wonder if the protection of civil rights in industry through a system of shop law is not being carried to the point of the ridiculous in many cases.

The arbitration process and the system of industrial jurisprudence it has developed has also, many employers think, done much to stultify supervisory initiative. Foremen must know not only what is in the contract, but what the arbitrator might say. In the larger companies, they are required to study and keep in mind scores of arbitration decisions on discipline, work assignments and work scheduling, seniority rights, vacation and holiday pay benefits, and many others. Moreover, if they settle a grievance, it may be cited against them in arbitration as a binding precedent. Confused and squeezed on both sides, both by their own superiors who want the work out, and the union's vigilance in detecting minor violations, they tend to withdraw from difficult decisions and maintain the status quo. In the end, this hurts everyone concerned.

A sensible evaluation of the arbitration process stems from the admitted fact that arbitration is what the parties choose to make it. The best remedy the employer or the union has against abuses is to control the arbitrator and the arbitration process. This may call for a redefinition of the arbitrator's powers, but such a dramatic stand would seem unnecessary in most cases. The careful selection of the arbitrator will produce good decisions. The "pro" in the arbitration field is entirely conscious of the fact that his notion of what may heighten morale or increase productivity is not what the parties bargained for; they want a decision on a specific issue under the contract.

Similarly, the parties can, if they choose, keep arbitration a simple and inexpensive process by weeding out political cases, delineating the issues carefully in advance, and presenting their cases on stipulated facts where possible, eliminating elaborate briefs and citations of authority, and controlling the arbitrator's fee. Elaborate opinions which prove only that the arbitrator is thorough and conscientious should be avoided. If the parties are not certain that the arbitrator possesses these qualities, they should not have appointed him in the first place. Justice Holmes once said, "It is judgment the world pays for." Honest judgment is all we need from arbitration.

It would seem highly undesirable to arbitrate grievances for damage to the employer from breach of the no-strike clause. Such disputes are not in the realm of shop law and practice which call for the arbitrator's friendly interest in the continuing relationship. They are bitter terminal conflicts resulting in a money award, if the employer is successful. The average arbitrator would find the performance of his duty here painful and difficult, especially if he were confronted by passionate union testimony that the employer had no one but himself to blame for the strike—that the supervisors were arbitrary, that the company sought to frustrate the grievance procedure, and that similar strikes in the past had gone unpunished to the point of inviting the one under discussion as the accepted solution to explosive shop dissatisfaction. The arbitrator may be asked to rule that the employer's own conduct was such as to constitute a material breach of the covenant of good faith (i.e. an effort to destroy the union or the entire contractual relationship), thus excusing the union from performance of its covenant not to strike. These are problems for the stern atmosphere of the federal courts, not the informal arbitration table.

This is a subject which the employer can control by appropriate language in the agreement. It should be made clear that grievances do not extend to breaches of the no-strike clause.

In the two Supreme Court decisions on the subject, *Atkinson* v. *Sinclair Refining Co.* and *Drake Bakeries, Inc.* v. *Local 50, Ameri-*

can Bakery and Confectionery Workers, the language of two contracts was considered.[9] In the Sinclair case the Court said:

> There is not a word in the grievance and arbitration article pro-
> viding for the submission of grievances by the company. Instead,
> there is the express, flat limitation that arbitration boards should
> consider only employee grievances. Furthermore, the article ex-
> pressly provides that arbitration may be invoked only at the
> option of the union. At no place in the contract does the union
> agree to arbitrate at the behest of the company. The company is
> to take its claims elsewhere, which it has now done.

In the Drake case, the language was much broader and the Court
ruled that the employer's claim for damages was arbitrable.

Employers who have studied the problem agree that management should rely upon its own right of administrative initiative,
taking action directly which it believed to be within its rights and
leaving claims of violation to be made by the union. An appeal by
management, via the grievance procedure, to establish its rights
is an anomalous procedure which contradicts the basic theory of
management's reserved rights. It also involves, if management
may invoke arbitration, an appeal to a third party to establish
management's right to run the business. This is more than
anomalous—the business would grind to a stop. If management
feels that its rights have been blunted by the agreement, the place
to secure acknowledgment of these rights is at the bargaining table.

---

[9] *Atkinson* v. *Sinclair Refining Co.,* 370 U.S. 238 (1962), 50 LRRM 2433. *Drake
Bakeries, Inc.* v. *Local 50, American Bakery and Confectionery Workers,* 370 U.S.
254 (1962), 50 LRRM 2440. These cases were decided concurrently with *Sinclair
Refining Co.* v. *Atkinson,* 370 U.S. 195 (1962), 50 LRRM 2420, in which the Supreme
Court held that Section 301 of LMRA did not impliedly repeal section 4 of the
Norris-LaGuardia Act so as to remove its prohibition of injunctions against strikes,
even though the strike in question was a breach of the collective bargaining contract. It is to be hoped that Congress will correct this unfortunate (even though
technically correct) decision. A suit for damages which may drag on for years is
no substitute for the quick and efficacious injunction. The employer is usually
reluctant to sue because the suit results in strained relations for years and may bring
reprisals if he refuses to withdraw it. Discipline and discharge of his employees
for participation may have the same results. We have already seen that the employer who condones wildcat strikes is inviting customer pressure and other economic weaknesses cannot afford to fight the union and the employees with the
bitterly hated weapon of lawsuits and strict and stern discipline. Such employers
would be immeasurably benefited if they could take the problem to the federal
court. Even unions, or their top officers (who recognize that rank and file rebellion
can follow in the wake of succcessful wildcat strikes), might find the injunction the
best answer to the problem of controlling wildcat strikes. See Clyde W. Summers,
"Analysis of 1961-1962 Supreme Court Decisions", 50 LRRM 368 (1962).

CHAPTER 14

THE FUTURE OF COLLECTIVE BARGAINING

In Chapter 1, we looked briefly at the power struggle between unions and management, stressing the important differences between management with its diverse responsibilities and labor unions with their more limited aim of securing "more and more and more." One is tempted to wonder, despite our years of experience, why these two basic institutions in our society have not achieved a better accommodation and adjustment to each other's needs.

Collective bargaining, as we know it today, has been protected by federal law for more than twenty-five years, a period of unprecedented growth in the strength and power of unions. Viewed against the backdrop of the great depression of the early 'thirties, with its grim record of wage cuts, unemployment, and bitter hostility on the part of employers to unions, the achievements of organized labor have especially been impressive. Labor has prospered in relation to other social and economic groups. A long list of benefits, protection through insurance and pension plans, supplemental unemployment compensation, vacations and paid holidays, have been provided in many industries. The system of contractually-established government within industry described at length in this book is the most impressive gain of all.

But all is not well in the House of Labor. It is under a barrage of criticism, not only from employers and large sections of the public, but from its erstwhile friends. Robert Bendiner, in *The Reporter*, sums up a commonly-shared view, when he says:

> Yet at this moment, when at least the business agents of the meek seem to have inherited the earth, the American trade-union movement is on the downgrade, its spirits low, its operations static, its horizons narrow, its public image dismal, and its forces engaged in precisely the kind of family feuding that preceded the splitting of the old AFL in the days of William Green.[1]

---

[1] Robert Bendiner, "What's Wrong in the House of Labor," *The Reporter* (October 12, 1961), p. 41. See also: William Gomberg, "The Future of Collective

Barring the chance of a renascence such as it experienced in the 'thirties, the American labor movement seems to have lost its vigor. The number of organized workers has decreased, especially as a proportion of the total work force. Its spokesmen and friends admit that it has declined in power and influence. Sol Barkin, ablest and most articulate of the intellectuals still left in the labor movement, asks "What is sapping the vitality of this essential institution of our democratic society?" Even as employers resist labor's demands more stoutly, he notes, "a certain lassitude has overtaken the trade union movement itself." Most discomforting to the leadership, he adds, is "the lack of response among employees of the newer occupational groups like the white collar personnel, professionals and technicians; the newer ethnic groups such as the Negroes, Mexicans and Puerto Ricans; the rising generation of workers in the South; the expanding army of government employees; the vast numbers of working women; and the production workers in the newer manufacturing industries." Perhaps most significantly, he charges that "the image of unions as the social conscience of the community has been considerably dimmed." [2]

What's Wrong With Unions?

There is what has been called "the sullied image" of unions in the public mind. Labor leaders have become complacent—the crusading spirit hardly fits their prosperous look as the masters of the marble and glass palaces in Washington. Even those who are above reproach have been linked by unthinking minds to the corruption uncovered by the McClellan Committee. The public is not yet persuaded that the AFL-CIO has cleaned house. The really forceful leader in the movement today is Jimmy Hoffa.

A new labor aristocracy composed of the well-paid high seniority members of the great unions has come into being. They have become essentially middle-class citizens with homes in the suburbs, cars, and savings accounts. Their "social conscience" has diminished to the vanishing point. Their leaders give out broad platitudes about advanced social reforms, but their energies are devoted

Bargaining", *The Nation* (January 20, 1962), p. 56; and A. H. Raskin, "The Squeeze on the Unions", *The Atlantic* (April 1961), p. 55. For a union rebuttal to criticisms of organized labor, see Stanley Ruttenberg, "The Future of Labor", *Union Review* (Vol. 1: No. 1, 1962), p. 46.

[2] Solomon Barkin, *The Decline of the Labor Movement*, Report to the Center for the Study of Democratic Institutions (Santa Barbara, California), pp. 7, 21, 23.

to the pragmatic aim of getting more for the special interests they represent. The slogan "more and more and more" has lost its appeal, especially to the public, now that labor's position in the community is assured. The sympathy of the "liberal" is largely reserved for the migrant farm worker, the slum dweller, and the unemployed.

Strikes and violence continue meanwhile. The wrangling over jurisdiction, which frequently shuts down important defense installation construction, goes on ceaselessly. Outmoded work rules, at times deserving the epithet "featherbedding," cannot be uprooted without the most intense opposition from organized labor.

It is little wonder, then, that the giant unions have failed to keep pace with the growth in the work force. They offer little to the new order of people who work in the service industries, technicians who install and maintain the complicated new automatic equipment now being developed, and "white collar" employees.

Wages and Profits

Employers, facing the threat of new and tough competition from our friends in Western Europe, are strongly critical of union power, claiming it is largely responsible for the wage-price spiral. They point out that wages in other countries are a small fraction of ours, and that our early advantage in technology is being rapidly dissipated by the modern plants built since World War II in the industrial nations which were devastated by the war but are now fully recovered. Adding to the argument, employers point out that profits have diminished to the point of discouraging investment. Thus, they say, growth, the real remedy for unemployment, is stunted. Taxes are too high, and labor costs are still rising. As Fortune Magazine puts it:

> What is happening is that labor is getting a very high proportion of the benefits of rising productivity. The so-called "guideposts" drawn up by the President's Council of Economic Advisers, which specify that wage advances generally should not exceed productivity advances, have not reversed this trend. Indeed, evidence is accumulating that the net effect of the guideposts has actually been to drive up labor costs faster than they would have risen if the guideposts had not been published. Indirectly, the

council, by publishing with its guideposts a table of past productivity increases, gave the impression that a 3 per cent annual productivity increase should be taken as a norm. Labor is now interpreting the guideposts to mean that everybody is entitled to a 3 per cent wage increase. "Unions that might have settled for a 2 per cent increase" says William E. Simkin, director of the Federal Mediation and Conciliation Service, "have recently held out for 3 per cent." Company after company is finding that it cannot raise wages by 3 per cent without endangering its profit margins.

Some would throw guideposts out the window, urge business to take up arms against unwarranted wage increases, and oblige labor to heed the law of supply and demand even as business has. They point to the fallacy in labor's beloved purchasing-power theory of prosperity, which holds that higher wage rates always mean higher incomes and therefore higher demand. The truth is that even when everybody employable is employed, raising money wages faster than productivity creates inflation, which of course means no gain in real wages. Today, everybody employable is not employed, and in addition a million or more new jobs must be created annually for those entering the labor force. Labor pressure for a steady 3 per cent annual increase will tend to perpetuate unemployment and slow down the expansion of the economy by decreasing the business earnings that might otherwise be invested to create additional jobs.

*   *   *   *

The important thing to remember is that, as Keynes said, "there is no possible means of curing unemployment except by restoring to employers a proper margin of profit." [3]

Government Intervention

The New Frontiersmen have their own set of remedies to apply. The famous "guideposts" are apparently only part of a vast campaign to make collective bargaining "responsive to the public, or common, interest." By this is meant increased government participation, strengthening of "preventive mediation," commissions and panels to help the parties make up their minds, with or without fact-finding or recommendations as needed, and, if necessary, the use of the Presidential edict in strikes affecting "major or critical" industries.

---

[3] Gilbert Burck, "U. S. Business in Suspense," *Fortune* (August, 1962), pp. 72, 204. See *Economic Implications of Union Power* (New York: National Association of Manufacturers, June, 1962), for an extended analysis.

This activist philosophy, employed most notably by President Kennedy against the steel industry price increase, has met with a storm of criticism.

Charles A. Reich, Associate Professor of Law at Yale University, writing in *The New Republic,* notes that the propriety of the President's methods is not the only serious issue raised by his victory, for there is also this question: "How far can a President go in demanding, without the authority of legislation, that private business conform to Administration policy?" Professor Reich concedes that the President has his own constitutional responsibility to set policy and to seek to have it followed. But,

> . . . the President has no right to *force* his economic policies on an unwilling industry *without legislation.* Unless Congress acts, the fact is that in a free society there can be no unitary public interest, no single, authoritatively fixed idea of "the public good." Freedom has little meaning if it only allows action that "responsibly" conforms to the President's idea of the national interest. He can set national goals and urge others to follow, and in areas of his constitutional authority like foreign policy, he can command obedience. But in the area of economics, private business and the public have the right to act according to their notion of the public good, until the people's elected representatives decide otherwise.[4]

In any event, Professor Reich says, the President's victory is disquieting because it demonstrates how much power government has today. "Such power, no matter how wisely exercised, is hardly any less frightening because the victim forced to surrender was a group of corporate giants and not a small business or a private citizen."

The warning is echoed by Stanley Ruttenberg, former Research Director of the AFL-CIO, in his criticism of the use of a formula based on productivity for controlling wages. This, he says, would "necessitate a controlled economy or at the very least an economy in which free collective bargaining does not exist."[5] This is precisely the view of management officials.

To some experienced and impartial observers of the labor-management scene, the "third party" at the bargaining table may become a menace, not only in the "key" industry wage-price de-

---

[4] Charles A. Reich, "Another Such Victory . . .", *The New Republic* (Vol. IV: No. 14, April 30, 1962), p. 5.
[5] Ruttenberg, "The Future of Labor", *op. cit.*

cisions, but in the thousands of less vital negotiations which, taken together, perhaps do more to influence our economic health and free decision-making than the large, spotlighted settlements. Stanley H. Brams, astute and informed publisher of *Labor Trends,* says:

> The idea of intervention, sometimes soft, sometimes hard, had already been shaped in Washington and expressed during Mr. Kennedy's administration . . . and in past administrations since the first term of Franklin Roosevelt. The Republicans helped dictate the size of the steel settlement of 1956, and their political aspirations had a good deal to do with the one of early 1960.
>
> And intervention of a new kind, intended to be directly representative of the public interest, has gradually been developing shape in the past few years. I refer to the use of hired mediators, brought in from the outside, their responsibility to help guide disputing parties to a settlement of their differences which, among other things, will be constructive to the public interest.
>
> The most noteworthy program of this sort in the past few years has been the third party procedure created by Kaiser and the Steel Workers in early 1961. A group of three public members on a nine-man panel have the contract authority to enter a bargaining dispute and recommend settlement—publicly if they so desire—in case of a deadlock. Allis-Chalmers and the Auto Workers pioneered a somewhat similar procedure as far back as 1955. Right now in Detroit one of the newspaper unions and both papers have agreed they will submit to arbitration any unsettled contract issues. The arbitrator, that is, will have the authority to write any part of the contract the parties are unable to agree on.
>
> Somewhere on this field of intervention, it would appear, the historic, traditional right of bargainers to settle their own problems disappears, given up voluntarily or involuntarily to an outsider—maybe the government, maybe the general public, or maybe a representative of either who in the final analysis may well be the representative only of what he, and he alone, thinks is fitting and proper.
>
> There is the rub. The interest of the public is often vague, maybe impossible to define. The interest of the government may well be—and very often is—grounded in the practical foundations of politics. The decision of the third party, whether umpire or representative, is not necessarily the best decision from the standpoint of either side, or even of the third force which he stands for.
>
> Nevertheless, this kind of decision hangs heavily over the tables of collective bargainers today—everywhere, important or minor, big or small. For the time being at least, and maybe from here

on, the complexion of collective bargaining has been sharply modified. The shadow of an outsider hangs over negotiating tables, and we can see that shadow getting bigger and developing more substance almost by the week.

This poses a basic question. The question is how far the processes of democracy can be stretched in the area of labor relations. One aspect of democracy is the ability of individuals—and of managements and labor unions—to arrive at their own decisions within the framework of the common good. Once someone moves in to guide that decision, or impose pressure toward it, or finally to insist on it, democracy has lost what its citizens have always regarded as a fundamental right and a fundamental characteristic. The destruction of the power to bargain collectively was a hallmark of Fascism and Nazism in Europe, and it is characteristic of Communism today. And I might add that the formal taking over of the price-making function by government is state socialism, state control, or call it what you will, pure and simple; and there may be little meaningful difference between legalized takeover of the price-making function and takeover by bombast and threat and the public relations pressure of a White House position . . .[6]

Except for a few self-designated government guardians of the "public, or common, interest," Americans on both sides of the table seem to agree that retention of what economists call "pluralistic, decentralized decision-making" is desirable. It may be better policy to let the Goliaths of labor and industry fight it out, even at the cost of some inconvenience to the public.

Perhaps in their eagerness to serve, the Washington planners have exaggerated the seriousness of this inconvenience. It is not easy to demonstrate that the 1959 steel strike actually imperiled the national health or safety. It has been asserted that by the end of 1960 the slackness of market demand had caused a loss of tonnage in the steel industry almost equal to that engendered by the 116-day strike. Federal regulation of strikes, except in the vital transportation industries and those affecting the national defense effort, is a high price to pay for the loss of the right to strike, in key industries as well as others.

---

[6] Stanley Brams, Speech delivered to the Associated Industries of Cleveland, June 21, 1962, *Labor Trends* (Detroit, Michigan). For an extended defense of tri-partite collective bargaining, see Neil W. Chamberlain, "Neutral Consultants in Collective Bargaining", *Collective Bargaining and the Arbitrator's Role* (Washington: BNA Incorporated, 1962), p. 83, and the discussions by David L. Cole and George W. Taylor, at pp. 96, 105. In a speech delivered on February 1, 1963, at the National Academy of Arbitrators, Secretary of Labor Willard Wirtz discusses the alternatives to free collective bargaining as we know it today. This speech is reprinted in *Labor Arbitration and Industrial Change* (Washington: BNA Incorporated, 1963).

Many observers believe that no federal wage-price formula is necessary because the battle against inflation had been won even before the 1959 steel strike. The pressures of the 1958 recession, and their effect on the high costs of doing business, the increasingly stiff competition among domestic producers, and the growth of foreign industry, were obvious before the Kennedy administration took office. The advance in costs in the 1959 settlement was, compared to prior years, modest enough; the strike was prolonged because of the fight over work rules.

Although both labor and business have posted "Washington-Keep Out" signs, labor is favored by intervention, even though the price is obeisance, since the politically easy choice is to give something at the expense of the employer-customer-public interest. Confronted with "hardened" management attitudes, labor may choose the government alliance as the best way to maintain its "policeman" function, keeping its gains of the past, including the plush and power of the Babbitts in the international offices, and pushing ahead of less powerful special interest groups in dividing future economic improvements. All labor leaders are familiar with the techniques of moving into the neutral mediation area with "fat" in their demands to be sliced off in the presence of the neutrals at the table with loud protests of sacrifice.

Labor's Power

Meantime, the conflict over labor's power rages with unconcealed bitterness. The issue was brought most forceably to the attention of the public when Henry Ford II and Joseph L. Block, President of Inland Steel, criticized the Report of the President's Advisory Committee on Labor-Management Policy entitled "Free and Collective Bargaining and Industrial Peace." The Ford addendum states that the excess of union power gives rise to the problem of avoiding critical strikes and states that the remedy "most consistent with economic freedom and health" is not more government intervention but "to constrain the market power of labor unions through effective legal limitation and judicial review." [7] In the view of most employers, and the view of Messrs. Ford and Block is generally shared, union power based on weapons not

---

[7] Henry Ford II, Addendum to "Free and Collective Bargaining and Industrial Peace", Report of the President's Advisory Committee on Labor-Management Policy, 50 LRR 25 (1962); see also: *Economic Implications of Union Power, op. cit.*

generally available to other elements of society: the strike, the boycott, the pressures of picketing, and other forms of compulsion—used against whole industries—is the cause of national emergency situations.

Proposals to curb the power of unions take various forms. Without indicating that he favors any one "reform," Senator Goldwater, in a speech to the American Bar Association, listed 15 union rights and privileges to give his listeners "an idea of the preferred position held by today's unions in the economic scheme of things." Goldwater's list follows:

1. Almost total immunity under the anti-trust laws.

2. Immunity from taxation.

3. Immunity from injunctions by federal courts.

4. Authority to use union funds for purposes not related to collective bargaining even where union membership is compulsory.

5. Power to compel workers to join the union as a condition of continued employment.

6. The right of a union selected by a majority of the workers to bargain for all employees. This includes the right to bargain for those who were compelled to join the union as well as those who can be arbitrarily denied membership.

7. Power to compel the employer to bargain exclusively with the majority union.

8. Absolute authority to deny union membership to workers employed in the bargaining unit, on any grounds or for no reason at all.

9. The right, in some situations, to invade the privacy of workers, even against their wishes. This deprives them of a legal right enjoyed by all other members of society.

10. The right, in some situations, to compel employers to make available for the union use the private property of the employer.

11. The right to compel the employer to provide protection against any physical violence on the part of workers who resist invasion of their privacy.

12. Unions are immune from the payment of damages for personal and property injuries inflicted on employers or others by union members engaged in activities, such as strikes or picketing. And this stands even in situations where such activities have been officially authorized and directed by the union.

13. The right to strike for objectives wholly unrelated to any proper subject of collective bargaining. This is in contrast to the severely limited right of an employer to engage in a lock-out.

14. The right, in some situations, to examine an employer's books and records—including those containing such confidential data as costs, profits and prices.

15. And finally, the almost complete immunity of unions from any liability, penalty or restriction under state law under the doctrine of federal preemption.[8]

Changes in some of these immunities would no doubt weaken the labor movement, or as its friends would put it, "further weaken" it. Barkin claims that the Taft-Hartley Act and the decisions of the Eisenhower NLRB have given a new freedom to anti-union activities, and that state right-to-work laws have drastically curtailed the ability of labor to organize new plants in the states which have them.[9] The Kennedy Board is striving to undo what it thinks of as the pro-employer bias of its predecessor.[10]

Free Decisions and Competition

In this welter of claim and counterclaim on the values of American society, one beacon exists which can guide us without the sacrifice of historic freedoms in an expanding and highly competitive world economy. This is decision-making. The vitality of the American system of enterprise lies in its variety, its flexibility, its ability to shift rapidly, through thousands of individual decisions, from one product to another, from one process to another and to experiment and improve, and thus insure the best use of the country's resources. Except during periods of war, when private impulse must be suppressed, the preservation of individual decision-making should be a paramount objective.

Closely allied to the principle of individual decision-making is the free market, i.e. the competitive market, and the forces which motivate it, profits and losses. Except for the government restraints on the free market, such as tariffs, subsidies, taxes, minimum wage

---

[8] Senator Barry Goldwater, Speech to the American Bar Association (August, 1962), 50 LRR 320, 321.

[9] Barkin, *op. cit.*

[10] Theophil C. Kammholz, Chicago attorney and former General Counsel of the NLRB, attacked the so-called Kennedy Labor Board in a speech delivered in February 1963 to the American Management Association, 52 LRR 169. Kammholz charged that the NLRB has changed the law governing employer-union relations in nearly one hundred distinct areas.

The Bureau of National Affairs, Inc. has published a special supplement to *Labor Relations Reporter*, Vol. 52: No. 26, April 1, 1963, tabulating the major principles established by the NLRB in both unfair labor practice cases and representation cases since April 13, 1961. The Supplement also contains a tabulation of disputes in which the federal government intervened in the years 1961-1963.

laws, and the like, the hope of profits and the fear of losses are the only economic regulators we have.

American businessmen are not afraid of competition in a free world. They welcome it. But expansion and new jobs can only be financed if there is a reasonable hope of profit. The future of collective bargaining depends on the health of the American economy. If the dynamism of free enterprise is dulled by labor and government, free collective bargaining will perish with its host.

Labor, too, is in competition, whether it likes it or not. It is all very well to mouth fine phrases about human values—"the labor of a human being is not a commodity in commerce"—and to pretend that the market does not exist. It does exist, and though a human being is not a commodity, the cost of labor is over seventy-five percent of the cost of goods and services in the United States.

Collective bargaining on an industry-wide basis hampers the ability of the individual company to make its own decisions in the light of its own economic situation. The effectiveness of the free economy is proportionate to the degree to which each individual competitive unit, consisting both of the employer and his employees, can be made effective. A way must be found to make collective bargaining fully compatible with this principle, otherwise it cuts across and confounds the vitality of competition.

Unions for many years have given the profit motive only lip service, attempting to foster the illusion that our rising standard of living results from union power and pressure rather than investment and economic creativity. The result has been instead a higher base of costs, both relatively and absolutely, against which employers must struggle. They deny the principle of individual competition by insisting upon industry-wide, multi-company patterns of wages, clinging to the outmoded theory that there is a working class opposed to the employer class. They separate the employees of a particular employer from any identification with the success of the enterprise upon which they depend. They foster the notion that the employer is their enemy who must be beaten down. An employer who stands up to this militancy in the belief that he has a duty to protect the enterprise against excessive costs is labeled a union-buster.

Under these circumstances, how can Solomon Barkin justify

his complaint that employers refuse to integrate the collective bargaining process "with the organizational scheme of the company"? Rather wistfully, he says, "Unions are not considered as a part of the business." What does organized labor expect when it has preached the "hate management" theme year in and year out to American workers, making it impossible for them to be loyal to the union and their fellows and at the same time interested in the welfare of the business?

No one asks that labor roll over and die. The right of workmen to associate for their mutual benefit, if they think it necessary, is everywhere granted. Collective bargaining has had its due praise from all segments of society for its achievements. The question is merely whether labor unions can discipline themselves to cooperate in a society of free men, or whether they will press on and become, not an essential element in the community, but the enemy of the rest of society.

As Barkin and others point out, there is much for labor to do. Many harsh features of our social scene require amelioration. The integration of the Negro as an equal in the work force should be a major union objective. There are thousands of agricultural workers at the subsistence level who need help. To help these people, to build schools and abolish slums, we must keep our economy free and expanding.

As things stand today, however, labor unions, and many educators and public officials, are busily engaged in promoting an economic and social philosophy which is not only outmoded but strikes at the heart of the free market and the profit-and-loss system of enterprise. They might be more honest if they admitted openly that while they live and thrive under this system, the best yet devised in the history of mankind for the efficient distribution of goods and services, they are engaged in sabotaging it by preaching collectivism under the aegis of the all-powerful state.

For many years, we have accepted the idea of the welfare state. Many businessmen will agree that there is still much to be done in aid to education, public housing, and the extension of social security and minimum wage standards to underpaid and underprivileged workers in certain areas, such as agriculture. But the campaign to take over basic economic decision-making is not welfare. It is simple collectivism.

Educators, especially, should give thought to their role. Some economists, and others who write and speak on public policy in our economy, are still dazzled by the myth that the only healthy economy is one promoted and controlled by directives and decisions from Washington. They should make it clear that union successes at the bargaining table do not create new wealth, they only divide and distribute it. They should point out that employee benefits can only be paid out of expanding markets for products of quality produced at a cost attractive to the consumer. They should encourage understanding on the part of workers that the opportunity for profit is what motivates growth. They should make it plain that increased productivity is the result of many factors, such as investment, technological improvement, and managerial ingenuity, and that the consumer, not the worker, has the primary claim to the fruits of increased productivity, a claim which the consumer can enforce by simply shopping around in the diverse markets of the world. They should help the worker achieve an understanding that capital is mobile, and that our economy is not expanding as rapidly as those of the Common Market countries and Japan. They should tell the worker that foreign capital has at least two great advantages, a post World War II industrial plant, and low labor rates.

Most of all, we should tackle the unemployment problem at the roots. The only way to provide more jobs is to provide more factories, more products, more service establishments, more exports.

In maintaining restrictions on the efficient and economical use of labor, in advocating a reduction of working hours with no reduction in labor costs, and in blaming automation for the illness of unemployment, unions are taking a short-sighted view, which can lead only to fewer jobs for labor union members. This is not to say that in particular cases some help should not be given to those who are out of work. Where private industry cannot do the job, federal or state programs should be provided to retrain and to accomplish the objective of putting a man who is able and willing to work on a job.

But these aids, important though they be, are not enough. The important objective is to increase the number of jobs, and that means accelerated expansion of our entire economy. It calls for modernization of our plants and equipment. It means the full use of our vast technical and engineering know-how to develop and market new and improved products. It requires tax reform to make new investment attractive. And it needs labor's cooperation in cost reduction by the elimination of unnecessary restrictions of the efficient use of labor. If we do these things, not only will we meet foreign competition, not only will we relieve serious unemployment, we will continue our famous tradition of spreading the benefits of these innovations throughout our own people and to those in other countries.

Appendix A

MODEL ARBITRATION CLAUSES TO PROTECT MANAGEMENT RIGHTS *

CONTENTS

**Special Sub-Committee on Arbitration
of the Labor Relations Committee
of the Chamber of Commerce of the United States**

CHAIRMAN
MALCOLM L. DENISE,
 Vice President
Labor Relations
Ford Motor Company
Dearborn, Michigan

H. B. DEVINNEY, *Vice President*
Industrial and Public Relations
Davison Chemical Company
Baltimore, Maryland

THEODORE R. ISERMAN, *Attorney*
Kelley, Drye, Newhall & Maginnes
New York, New York

HAROLD E. LANE, *Vice President*
Labor Relations and Personnel
Sheraton Corporation of America
Boston, Massachusetts

PHILIP D. MOORE, *Manager*
Union Relations Service
General Electric Company
New York, New York

* Published by Labor Relations & Legal Department, Chamber of Commerce of the United States, Washington, D.C.

INTRODUCTION

In June 1960, the Supreme Court handed down three highly important decisions dealing with the arbitration of disputes under collectively bargained agreements.

These decisions have had a significant impact on management rights and on the entire collective bargaining process. Establishing important new ground rules affecting the arbitration of disputes, these rulings are now causing employers to take a more careful look at the arbitration language in their labor contracts.

This publication is intended to help employers protect those management functions so vitally necessary to the efficient operation of a profitable business enterprise. It contains a series of specimen arbitration clauses designed to preserve management's inherent rights in the light of these decisions.

The sample clauses set forth herein are intended to serve as guidelines; they do not purport to be authoritatively final, nor are they offered as a substitute for legal counsel.

Credit for the work involved in drafting these sample clauses should go to the Chamber's Special Sub-committee on Arbitration.

It is hoped that the reader will find in this compilation a useful and practical reference source for future contract work.

> *Robert G. Kelley, Chairman*
> *Labor Relations Committee*
> *Chamber of Commerce of the*
> *United States*

September, 1961

SUPREME COURT ARBITRATION DECISIONS

The rapid growth of arbitration as a means of settling labor disputes has been one of the most important recent developments in the field of industrial relations. Today, more than 90 per cent of all collectively bargained agreements provide for binding arbitration as the ultimate step under labor-management grievance procedures.

Traditionally, where voluntarily resorted to, arbitration has been used by management and unions as an orderly means of settling disputes arising under collectively bargained agreements. In preserving its inherent proprietary rights, however, management has maintained steadfastly that its responsibilities to set policies, to establish work rules and to direct the work force should not be encroached upon by the arbitrator. Management has adhered rigidly to the position that only those precise issues specifically defined as arbitrable under the express terms of the contract should be subject to review by arbitration.

In recent years, however, as unions have come into more monopoly powers, there has been a progressive penetration by labor into once unchallenged areas of exclusive management control. Increasingly, arbitration has been used as a device by which unions have broadened their authority within the business enterprise.

Judicial decisions concerning the interpretation and application of arbitration provisions in collective bargaining agreements have raised serious new questions regarding employer-employee rights in many vital areas. These decisions, especially in three important Supreme Court cases, have prescribed significant new ground rules affecting long-standing concepts of industrial relations jurisprudence. In effect, these decisions have thrown a new light on the role of the arbitrator which has caused employers to take a more careful look at the arbitration language in their labor contracts.

The Supreme Court's rulings and rationale in the three arbitration decisions are set forth in the following sections.

Steelworkers v. Warrior & Gulf Navigation Company

In the first case, *United Steelworkers of America v. Warrior & Gulf Navigation Company,* 363 U.S. 574 (1960), the union sought to compel arbitration of a dispute involving the company's right to contract-out major repair work. Under the collective agreement in force, matters considered strictly functions of management were not deemed subject to arbitration.

The District Court and the Court of Appeals ruled in favor of the company holding that the agreement did not give an arbitrator the right to review the employer's business judgment in contracting-out work. This ruling held further that the contracting-out of repair and maintenance work, as well as construction work, is strictly a function of management not limited in any respect by the labor agreement involved here.

Reversing in favor of the union, the Supreme Court held the dispute arbitrable in the absence of an express contractual provision defining contracting out work as a function of management.

Speaking for the majority of the Court, Justice Douglas said:

> In the absence of any express provision excluding the particular grievance from arbitration, we think only the most forceful evidence of a purpose to exclude the claim from arbitration can prevail, particularly where, as here, the exclusion clause is vague and the arbitration clause quite broad.

In a dissenting opinion terming the majority rationale a "new and strong doctrine," Justice Whittaker said:

> . . . the intention of the parties to submit their contractual disputes to a final determination outside the court should be made manifest by plain language . . . such intent is not to be implied.

Steelworkers v. American Manufacturing Company

In the second case, *United Steelworkers of America v. American Manufacturing Company,* 363 U.S. 564 (1960), the union sued to compel arbitration of a dispute involving a member's seniority rights.

The union claimed that the company violated the collectively bargained contract's seniority provisions by refusing to reinstate an employee who had left his job because of injuries and who had settled a workman's compensation claim against the company for his permanent partial disability.

The employer refused to arbitrate on the ground that the dispute was not arbitrable under the collective agreement.

The lower court and the Court of Appeals held that the union member was prevented from claiming any seniority or employment rights and called the grievance a frivolous, patently baseless one, not subject to arbitration under the collective bargaining agreement.

In reversing, the Supreme Court referred to the relevant arbitration provision in the agreement which points out that any disputes arising between the parties as to the "meaning, interpretation and application of the contract" may be submitted to arbitration. In its decision, the Court gave great weight to law review articles by former Harvard professor and present Solicitor General of the United States, Archibald Cox, who said:

> . . . it seems proper to read the typical arbitration clause as a promise to arbitrate every claim, meritorious or frivolous, which the complainant bases upon the contract.

Steelworkers v. Enterprise Wheel & Car Corporation

The third case, *United Steelworkers of America v. Enterprise Wheel and Car Corporation*, 363 U.S. 593 (1960), involves the merits of an arbitrator's award directing the employer to reinstate certain discharged employees and to pay them back wages for periods both before and after expiration of the collective agreement. When the company refused to comply, the union petitioned for enforcement of the award.

The trial court sustained the arbitrator but the Court of Appeals reversed, holding that the order for reinstatement of the discharged employees was unenforceable because the contract had expired. The Supreme Court reversed the Appeals Court and ordered full enforcement. In upholding the arbitrator's award, Justice Douglas declared in the majority opinion:

> Interpretation of the collective bargaining agreement is a question for the arbitrator. It is the arbitrator's construction which was bargained for; and so far as the arbitrator's decision concerns construction of the contract, the courts have no business overruling him because their interpretation of the contract is different from his.

Practical Effect of Decisions

The principles enunciated in these decisions constitute a radical departure from long-established rules governing the jurisdiction and role of the courts in labor arbitration cases and markedly increase the importance of arbitration and the role of the arbitrator. Some management spokesmen feel the Court has completely reversed the traditional doctrine that management retains all of the rights not surrendered in the collectively bargained contract.

Other labor law specialists feel unions undoubtedly will be encouraged by these decisions and will now seek to employ arbitration as a vehicle for gaining ends previously achieved only through negotiations. Moreover, arbitrators will consider that they may now roam more freely without fear of having their decisions upset in the courts. Hence, irrespective of prior relationships and experiences, the rulings portend possible consequences for all companies whose contracts provide for arbitration.

Succinctly stated, the consequences of these decisions may be summarized as follows:

1. Where employers formerly were considered to have *retained* all inherent and common law managerial rights except those expressly modified or conferred upon the union by the contract or by statute, management now can only be certain of retaining those rights which it *specifically* spells out in the contract.

2. All grievances are now arbitrable, no matter how minuscule, unless the contract *clearly* and *specifically* excludes them from arbitration.

3. In ruling upon a dispute, an arbitrator (unless expressly limited) need no longer restrict his attention to what the contract says. He may now take into consideration the industry and company practices, plant morale, the easing of tensions and other seemingly unrelated factors, in molding "the common law of the plant."

4. The courts have no right to weigh the merits of a grievance although they believe it is patently frivolous or baseless or that the award is unsound, impractical or unsupported by the evidence. Even if the arbitrator exceeded his authority, the award is binding unless the strong presumption favoring its enforceability is overcome by express contract language.

The Need for Action

To ameliorate the effects of these decisions, concrete action must be taken with respect to arbitration language in future union contracts.

Parties desiring to withhold disputes of certain matters from arbitration must now so provide by the most precise and unambiguous wording.

Clear-cut statements which declare that the employer retains all the proprietary rights of management except as restricted by the terms of the collective agreement should be negotiated into future contracts.

The use of "wide open" arbitration clauses under which the arbitrator is given authority to decide questions raised by the union concerning any matter, whether within or without the scope of the collective bargaining agreement, should be carefully avoided. Contract ambiguities due to vague and inept terminology should be replaced by clear language so as to preclude arbitrators from substituting their judgment for that of the parties.

The specimen arbitration clauses drafted by the Chamber's Special Sub-Committee on Arbitration in the light of these decisions are set forth in the following section. Dealing broadly with various aspects of the arbitration process, the sample clauses illustrated herein are related directly to management rights, arbitration jurisdiction, and no-strike and lockout sections of the labor contract.

The management rights clauses are intended to preserve inherent rights of the employer to operate his business. The arbitration jurisdiction clauses are designed to specify the scope of the arbitrator's power and to define the procedures governing submission of disputes to arbitration. The no-strike and lockout clauses relate no-strike pledges by the union and no-lockout pledges by the employer to the arbitration process.

The language set out in the sample clauses varies broadly in form, content, and scope and should be adapted to the particular collective bargaining or contract situation.

MANAGEMENT RIGHTS CLAUSES

Sample Clause No. 1

Except as herein clearly and explicitly limited in the express terms of this Agreement, the right of the Corporation in all respects to manage its business, operations and affairs; to establish wages, hours and other terms and conditions of employment; and to change, combine, establish or discontinue jobs or operations, shall be unimpaired. The Corporation's not exercising any right hereby reserved to it, or its exercising any right in a particular way, shall not be deemed a waiver of any such right or preclude the Corporation from exercising the same in some other way not in conflict with the express terms of this Agreement.

Sample Clause No. 2

Subject only to any limitations stated in this Agreement, or in any other agreement between the Company and the Union or a Local, the Union and the Locals recognize that the Company retains the exclusive right to manage its business, including (but not limited to) the right to determine the methods and means by which its operations are to be carried on, to direct the work force and to conduct its operations in a safe and effective manner.

Sample Clause No. 3

The Company retains the sole right to manage its business and direct the working force, including the rights to decide the number and location of plants, the machine and tool equipment, the products to be manufactured, the method of manufacturing, the schedule of production, the processes of manufacturing or assembling, together with all designing, engineering, and the control of raw materials, semi-manufactured and finished parts which may be incorporated into the products manufactured; to determine whether and to what extent the work required in its business shall be performed by employees covered by this Agreement; to maintain order and efficiency in its plants and operations; to hire, layoff, assign, transfer, promote and determine the qualifications of employees; and to determine the starting and quitting time and the number of hours to be worked, subject only to such regulations governing the exercise of these rights as are expressly provided in this Agreement.

The Company retains the sole right to discipline, suspend, and discharge employees for cause, including violation of any of the terms of this Agreement.

The above rights of Management are not all-inclusive, but indicate the type of matters or rights which belong to and are inherent to Management. Any of the rights, powers, and authority the Company had prior to entering this collective bargaining are retained by the Company, except as expressly and specifically abridged, delegated, granted, or modified by this Agreement.

Sample Clause No. 4

Except as explicitly limited by a specific provision of this Agreement, the Company shall continue to have the exclusive right to take any action it deems appropriate in the mangement of the Plant and direction of the work force in accordance with its judgment. All inherent and common law management functions and prerogatives which the Company has not expressly modified or restricted by a specific provision of this Agreement are retained and vested exclusively in the Company and are not subject to arbitration under this Agreement.

The Company specifically reserves the exclusive right in accordance with its judgment to reprimand, suspend, discharge or otherwise discipline employees for cause; hire, promote, retire, demote, transfer, layoff and recall employees to work; determine the starting and quitting time and the number of hours and shifts to be worked; maintain the efficiency of employees; close down the Plant or any part thereof or expand, reduce, alter, combine, transfer, assign or cease any job, department, operation or service; control and regulate the use of machinery, equipment and other property of the Company; determine the number, location and operation of plants and divisions and departments thereof, the products to be manufactured, the schedules of production, the assignment of work and the size and composition of the work force, make or change rules, policies and practices not in conflict with the provisions of this Agreement; introduce new or improved research, development, production, maintenance, services and distribution methods, materials, machinery and equipment, and otherwise generally manage the Plant, direct the work force, and establish terms and conditions of employment, *except* as expressly modified or restricted by a specific provision of this Agreement.

The Company's not exercising any function hereby reserved to it, or its exercising any such function in a particular way, shall not be deemed a waiver of its right to exercise such function or preclude the

Company from exercising the same in some other way not in conflict with the express provisions of this Agreement.

Sample Clause No. 5

In order to conduct its business efficiently, management shall have the following rights:

- to determine the number, location and types of plants;
- to decide on the products to be manufactured, the methods of manufacture, the materials to be used, and the discontinuance of any product, material, or method of production;
- to introduce new equipment, machinery, or processes, and to change or eliminate existing equipment, machinery, or processes;
- to discontinue, temporarily or permanently, in whole or part, conduct of its business or operations;
- to decide on the nature of materials, supplies, equipment, or machinery to be used, and the price to be paid;
- to decide on the sales methods and sales price of all products;
- to subcontract any or all of the processes of manufacture, facility maintenance, or location service work;
- to select the working forces in accordance with the requirements determined by management;
- to transfer, promote or demote employees;
- to lay off, terminate, discharge, discipline, or otherwise relieve employees from duty for lack of work or other causes;
- to direct and control the work force;
- to establish rules governing employment and working conditions;
- to determine the size of the work force, including the number of employees assigned to any particular operation;
- to determine the work pace and work performance levels;
- to establish, change, combine, or abolish job classifications and the job content of any classification;
- to determine the length of the work week, and when overtime shall be worked, and to require reasonable overtime.

All other rights of management are also expressly reserved, even though not enumerated above, unless they are limited by the clear and explicit language of some other provision of this agreement.

The rights of management enumerated above, and all other rights of management not limited by the clear and explicit language of a clause of this agreement, are not subject to the arbitration procedures of this agreement.

The parties agree that this contract incorporates their full and complete understanding and that any prior oral agreements or practices are superseded by the terms of this agreement. The parties further agree that no such oral understandings or practices will be recognized in the future unless committed to writing and signed by the parties as a supplement to this agreement.

The parties agree that the power and jurisdiction of any arbitrator chosen under the terms of this agreement shall be limited to deciding whether there has been a violation of a provision of this agreement. The arbitrator shall not be empowered, and shall have no jurisdiction, to base his award on any alleged practice or oral understandings which are not incorporated in writing in the manner indicated above.

Where either party seeks arbitration and the other claims the matter is not subject to the arbitration provisions of this agreement, then the matter of arbitrability shall first be decided by a court of law.

ARBITRATION JURISDICTION CLAUSES

Sample Clause No. 1

The arbitrator shall be empowered, except as his powers are limited below, to make a decision in cases of alleged violation of rights expressly accorded by this Agreement or written local agreements supplementary thereto.

The limitations on the powers of the arbitrator are as follows:

(1) He shall have no power to add to, or subtract from, or modify any of the terms of any agreement.

(2) He shall have no power to establish wage scales or change any wage.

(3) He shall have no power to substitute his discretion for the Company's discretion in cases where the Company has retained discretion or is given discretion by this Agreement or by any supplementary agreement, except that where he finds a disciplinary layoff or discharge results from a manifestly arbitrary exercise of the Company's managerial judgment in fixing the extent of the penalty, he may make appropriate modifications of the penalty subject to [provisions concerning strike discipline].

(4) He shall have no power to [here can be recited specific matters, if any, upon which the arbitrator may not rule] decide any question which, under this Agreement, is within the right of Management to decide. In rendering decisions, the arbitrator shall have due regard for the rights and responsibilities of Management and shall so construe the Agreement that there will be no interference with the exercise of such rights and responsibilities, except as those rights may be expressly conditioned by the Agreement.

(5) The Company shall not be required to pay back wages prior to the date a written grievance is filed with the Company.

(6) All awards of back wages shall be limited to the amount of wages the employee would otherwise have earned from his employment with the Company during the periods as above defined, less any

unemployment or other compensation for personal services that he may have received from any source during the period.

If the grievance is based upon a claim of violation of rights expressly accorded by this Agreement and if the dispute is one which, under this Agreement, is within the arbitrator's power to decide, the Regional Director or other representatives of the International Union, by notifying the Central Industrial Relations Office of the Company in writing within . . . . working days after disposition made pursuant to Section [the provision governing the voluntary stage next preceding arbitration] of this Article of its intention to do so, may appeal the grievance to an impartial arbitrator, in accordance with and subject to the provisions of this Section.

The Notice of Appeal shall specify the issue raised by the grievance and shall include a statement of the nature of the grievance, together with the award requested.

Sample Clause No. 2

If any complaint or grievance that involves the interpretations or application of the explicit terms of this Agreement is not satisfactorily disposed of [in the . . . . Step of the foregoing grievance procedure], the Union may within ten (10) working days after receipt of the answer in writing, give to the Corporation by registered mail or by delivery in person a written notice of its desire to submit the matter to arbitration.

Unless otherwise mutually agreed, the submission to the arbitrator shall be based on the original written grievance submitted in the grievance procedure.

The power and authority of the arbitrator shall be strictly limited to determining the meaning and interpretation of the explicit terms of this Agreement as herein expressly set forth. He shall not have authority to add to or subtract from or modify any of said terms, or to limit or impair any right that Section . . . reserves to Management, or to establish or change any wage or rate of pay, except that he may determine the correctness of the classification of employees according to the work to which they are assigned.

The arbitrator's award shall be in accordance with the laws of the State of . . . and shall be final and binding on matters properly before him.

Should the Corporation deny the existence of an agreement to arbitrate or to arbitrate a particular issue, or the existence of a *bona fide* dispute involving the issue as to which the other party demands arbitration, or the arbitrability of such issue, the arbitrator may not decide whether he has power and authority to hear and determine the issue, which matter may be determined only by a court of competent jurisdiction in proceedings to compel or stay arbitration or in other appropriate proceedings in accordance with the substantive law of the State of . . ., and all proceedings by and before the arbitrator shall be stayed pending such judicial determination; provided, however, that the parties may, by mutual agreement in writing, submit to arbitration any question concerning the arbitrator's power and authority, in which event the Corporation shall have the right to contest the arbitrator's power and authority in proceedings to set aside the award or in other appropriate proceedings in any State or Federal court having jurisdiction of the parties.

In reducing a grievance to writing, the following information shall be stated with reasonable clearness: The exact nature of the grievance, the act or acts complained of and when they occurred, the identity of the employee or employees who claim to be aggrieved, the provisions, if any, of this Agreement that the employee or employees claim the Corporation has violated, and the remedy they seek.

No decision of an arbitrator or of the Management in one case shall create a basis for retroactive adjustment in any other case.

The Union may not withdraw any notice of its desire to arbitrate a case or otherwise discontinue arbitration proceedings except with the consent of the Corporation.

Sample Clause No. 3

The jurisdiction and authority of the arbitrator of the grievance and his opinion and award shall be confined exclusively to the interpretation of the explicit provision or provisions of this Agreement at issue between the Union and the Company.

He shall have no authority to add to, detract from, alter, amend, or modify any provision of this Agreement or impose on any party hereto a limitation or obligation not explicitly provided for in this Agreement; to establish or alter any wage rate or wage structure; to interpret any federal or state statute or local ordinance when the compliance or non-compliance therewith shall be involved in the consideration of the grievance; or to consider any understanding, practice, term or condition of employment or any other matter not explicitly set forth in an express provision of this Agreement.

The participation by the Company and/or the Union in an arbitration proceeding under this Agreement and culminating in a ruling that the grievance is arbitrable and/or an opinion and award on the merits of the grievance shall not be deemed a waiver of or prejudicial to the right of either party to contest the arbitrability of the grievance or the jurisdiction and authority of the arbitrator in proceedings for a declaratory judgment to set aside the award or other appropriate proceedings in any State or Federal Court of competent jurisdiction.

The award in writing of the arbitrator on the merits of any grievance adjudicated within his jurisdiction and authority as provided in this Agreement shall be final and binding on the aggrieved employee or employees, the Union and the Company.

Sample Clause No. 4

1. Any grievance which remains unsettled after having been fully processed pursuant to the provisions of Article . . ., and which involves either,

    (a) the interpretation or application of a provision of this Agreement, or

    (b) a disciplinary penalty (including discharge) imposed on or after the effective date of this Agreement, which is alleged to have been imposed without just cause,

shall be submitted to arbitration upon written request of either the Union or the Company, provided such request is made within 30 days after the final decision of the Company has been given to the Union pursuant to Article . . ., Section. . . . For the purpose of proceedings within the scope of (b) above, the standard to be applied by an arbitrator to cases involving disciplinary penalties (including discharge) is that such penalties shall be imposed only for just cause.

2. (a) Within 10 days following a written request for arbitration of a grievance, the Company or the Union may request the American Arbitration Association to submit a panel of names from which an arbitrator may be chosen. In the selection of an arbitrator and the conduct of any arbitration, the Voluntary Labor Arbitration Rules of the American Arbitration Association shall control, except that: (i) notwithstanding any provision of such Rules, the Association shall have no authority to appoint an arbitrator in any matter who has not been approved by both parties until and unless the parties have had submitted to them at least three panels of arbitrators and have been unable to select a mutually satisfactory arbitrator therefrom; and (ii) either party may, if it desires, be represented by Counsel.

    (b) It is further expressly understood and agreed that the American Arbitration Association shall have no authority to process a request for arbitration or appoint an arbitrator if either party shall advise the Association that such request arises under Section 1 (a) of this Article, but that the grievance desired to be arbitrated does not, in its opinion, raise an arbitrable issue. In such event, the Association shall have the authority to process the request for arbitration and appoint an arbitrator in accordance with its rules only after a final judgment of a Court has determined that the grievance upon which arbitration has been requested raises arbitrable issues and has directed arbitration of such issues. The foregoing part of this subsection (b) shall not be applicable if by its terms the request for arbitration requests only relief from a disciplinary penalty or discharge alleged to have been imposed without just cause.

3. (a) The award of an arbitrator so selected upon any grievance subject to arbitration as herein provided shall be final and binding upon all parties to this Agreement, provided that no arbitrator shall have any authority to add to, detract from, or in any way alter the provisions of this Agreement.

(b) It is specifically agreed that no arbitrator shall have the authority to establish or modify any wage, salary or piece rate, or job classification, or authority to decide the appropriate classification of any employee. Subject to the foregoing limitations on the authority of an arbitrator, nothing in this subsection (b) shall prevent arbitration of a grievance involving a violation of this Agreement.

(c) In addition, notwithstanding any contrary provision of this Article, (i) no provision of this Agreement or other agreements between the parties shall be subject to arbitration pertaining in any way to the establishment, administration, interpretation or application of Insurance or Pension Plans in which employees covered by this Agreement are eligible to participate; (ii) no arbitrator shall have the authority to review, revoke, modify, or enter any award with respect to, any discipline or discharge imposed on employees having less than six months of continuous service with the Company provided that if by local understanding a period of less than six months has been agreed upon as the probationary period for new employees, and such local understanding is applicable to the particular employee involved, such agreed upon shorter period of time shall be substituted for "six months" in the foregoing; and provided further that nothing in this subsection shall limit the authority of an arbitrator with respect to disciplinary penalties or discharges imposed in violation of Section . . . of Article . . .; and (iii) no matter of controversy concerning the provisions of Articles . . . hereof or the interpretation or application thereof, shall be subject to arbitration.

4. This Agreement and its interpretation and application shall in all respects be governed by the law of the State....................

NO-STRIKE AND LOCKOUT CLAUSES

Sample Clause No. 1

During the period of this Agreement, there shall be no strikes, stoppages, slow downs, picketing or other interference with the operations of the Corporation (all of which are hereinafter referred to as "strikes").

No officer or representative of the Union shall authorize, instigate, aid or condone any strikes, and no employee shall participate in any strike.

There shall be no lockouts during the term of this Agreement.

The Corporation shall be under no obligation to bargain with the Union concerning employees who are on strike or concerning the subject of any strike so long as the strike continues.

The Corporation may discipline or discharge any employees who engage in a strike, and such action shall not be subject to review upon any ground other than that the employee did not take part in the strike.

The foregoing provisions shall not constitute grounds on which either party hereto may demand arbitration of any dispute not covered by the explicit terms of this Agreement.

Sample Clause No. 2

For the duration of the Agreement the Union, its officers, representatives, and members shall not authorize, instigate, cause, aid, encourage, ratify, or condone, nor shall any employee take part in any strike, slow down or stoppage of work, boycott, picketing or other interruption of work at the Plant. Failure or refusal on the part of any employee to comply with any provision of this Article shall be cause for whatever disciplinary action, including suspension or discharge, deemed necessary by the Company.

In consideration of this no-strike pledge by the Union and employees, the Company shall not lockout employees for the duration of this Agreement.

Neither the violation of any provision of this Agreement nor the commission of any act constituting an unfair labor practice or otherwise made unlawful by any federal, state or local law shall excuse employees, the Union, or the Company from their obligations under the provisions of this Article.

The provisions of this Article shall not be appealable to arbitration either for the purpose of assessing damages or securing specific performance, such matters of law being determinable and enforceable in the Courts.

Sample Clause No. 3

There shall be no strike, sitdown, slowdown, employee demonstration or any other organized or concerted interference with work of any kind in connection with any matter subject to the grievance procedure, and no such interference with work shall be directly or indirectly authorized or sanctioned by a Local or the Union, or their respective officers or stewards, unless and until all of the respective provisions of the successive steps of the grievance procedure set forth in Article . . . shall have been complied with by the Local and the Union, or if the matter is submitted to arbitration as provided in Article. . . .

The Company will not lock out any employee or transfer any job under dispute from the local works, nor will the local Management take similar action while a disputed job is under discussion at any of the steps of the grievance procedure set forth in Article . . ., or if the matter is submitted to arbitration as provided in Article. . . .

Appendix B

LABOR CHECKLIST: DO YOU STILL HAVE THE RIGHT TO RUN THE PLANT?

This checklist is made up of two parts:

1. The language of the labor agreement.
2. Present plant practices.

Part 1

THE LANGUAGE OF THE LABOR AGREEMENT

Does your labor agreement give you the right to:

	Yes	No	Question-able
1. Sub-contract work, without being subject to a Union Veto?	——	——	——
A. Products you produce?	——	——	——
B. Component parts of your product?	——	——	——
C. Maintenance and repairs?	——	——	——
D. Construction of new facilities?	——	——	——
E. Plant or office services?	——	——	——
2. Increase or reduce the size of your work force, freely, as conditions require?	——	——	——
A. Can the Union force a reduction in the work week in place of layoffs?	——	——	——
B. Or can the Union insist a full work schedule be maintained with a layoff of Union employees?	——	——	——
C. Is recall from layoffs on a strict seniority basis?	——	——	——
D. That no overtime be scheduled as long as any employees are on layoff?	——	——	——
3. Adjust a job rate when the job itself is simplified?	——	——	——
A. Can the Union participate in setting a new rate?	——	——	——

269

	Yes	No	Question-able
B. Can the Union veto a new rate?	——	——	——
C. Is rate setting subject to arbitration?	——	——	——
4. Transfer work from the bargaining unit?	——	——	——
A. To management employees, technicians or others?	——	——	——
5. Set efficient work schedules?	——	——	——
A. Daily hours of work?	——	——	——
B. Weekly hours of work?	——	——	——
C. Starting times?	——	——	——
D. Schedule overtime hours?	——	——	——
E. Lunch and rest periods?	——	——	——
F. Changes in shifts?	——	——	——
G. Vacations?	——	——	——
6. Introduce new, improved or automated methods of manufacturing?	——	——	——
A. Can the Union veto new methods or machines?	——	——	——
B. Must displaced personnel be retained on the payroll?	——	——	——
C. Are methods new or old subject to arbitration?	——	——	——
7. Promote the best qualified man?	——	——	——
A. Is seniority the major factor?	——	——	——
B. Must the senior man first be given a trial period?	——	——	——
8. Require an employee to perform work outside his assigned job classification?	——	——	——
A. Only when there is no work available in his regular classification?	——	——	——
9. Change the products to be manufactured, when desirable?	——	——	——
A. Reduction of line of manufactured products?	——	——	——
B. Change in the quality of the products?	——	——	——
10. Adjust the number of employees assigned to a particular job?	——	——	——
A. Can the Union demand "full crews"?	——	——	——

	Yes	No	Question-able
B. Can the number be reduced when job is automated or simplified?	—	—	—
C. Do any employees have a *"vested interest"* in working on a particular job or machine?	—	—	—
11. Require overtime work of employees?	—	—	—
A. Can employees refuse to work overtime without penalty?	—	—	—
B. Are there complex and/or inefficient rules for distribution of overtime?	—	—	—
C. Is there superseniority for local Union officers on overtime work?	—	—	—
12. Does your labor contract exclude questions on management rights from arbitration?	—	—	—
A. Is the right to determine methods, processes and materials specifically excluded?	—	—	—
B. Is the right to sub-contract or discontinue processes or operations specifically excluded?	—	—	—
C. Is the right to determine hours per day or per week or to select and determine the number and type of employees required, specifically excluded?	—	—	—
13. Does your labor contract distinguish grievances which are arbitrable from those which are not?	—	—	—
A. Must the grievance genuinely involve the interpretation of a *specific* provision of the contract?	—	—	—
B. Are matters outside the scope of the contract excluded from the grievance procedure?	—	—	—
14. Place definite limits on the powers of an arbitrator?	—	—	—
A. Is there a provision to prevent an arbitrator's amending, altering or ignoring the provisions of the contract?	—	—	—

	Yes	No	Question-able
15. Make it clear that the contract is the sole source of arbitration claims?	——	——	——
16. Spell out that the contract embodies the sole agreement between the parties?	——	——	——
A. Is further bargaining on issues specifically barred for the duration of the contract term?	——	——	——
17. Empower management to combine or consolidate jobs?	——	——	——
A. Subject to Union veto?	——	——	——
B. Subject to joint study?	——	——	——
C. Subject to arbitration?	——	——	——
18. Give management the right to prescribe job duties and job content?	——	——	——
A. Subject to Union veto?	——	——	——
B. Subject to arbitration?	——	——	——
C. Only on *new* jobs?	——	——	——
19. Empower management to demote supervisory employees back to bargaining unit?	——	——	——
20. Does your labor contract provide that management may establish and/or change an incentive system?	——	——	——
A. Change an incentive rate where there has been a change in work content of the job?	——	——	——
B. Are incentive rates subject to arbitration?	——	——	——

PART 2

PRESENT PLANT PRACTICES

Are you certain that in your plant:

	Yes	No	Question-able
1. The foremen know the exact extent of their authority?	——	——	——
A. Are they encouraged to exercise it?	——	——	——
B. Does the foreman realize it may be lost or weakened by inaction?	——	——	——

	Yes	No	Question-able
2. The foremen understand the requirements of the labor contract?	——	——	——
A. Are they able to explain the contract in answering the questions from their employees?	——	——	——
3. The foremen have been trained to avoid the making of concessions to the Union Steward in settling day-to-day disputes?	——	——	——
A. Oral concessions?	——	——	——
B. Concessions through lax enforcement of the contract?	——	——	——
4. Employees can be assigned to other work, due to absenteeism, emergency, or they have finished a job ahead of time?	——	——	——
5. Management has the authority to keep discipline? Do you have a problem to control?	——	——	——
A. Tardiness?	——	——	——
B. Unauthorized "breaks"?	——	——	——
C. Horseplay?	——	——	——
D. Wash up?	——	——	——
6. Union activities on Company property and time are limited?	——	——	——
7. Foremen are kept abreast with changes in Company policy?	——	——	——
A. Changes are discussed with the foreman?	——	——	——
8. The foreman has the opportunity to hire or effectively recommend, also to discipline and discharge?	——	——	——
9. Are the *"upward"* and *"downward"* communications from and to foreman functioning properly?	——	——	——

APPENDIX C

CHECKLIST FOR SURVEY OF
IRREGULAR OR UNUSUAL PLANT PRACTICES

1. UNION RELATIONS—GENERAL

a. Payment for grievance or negotiating time beyond that specified in Company-Union Agreement.

b. Joint Company-Union committees not specified in Company-Union Agreement.

c. Joint Company-Union participation in or sponsorship of any activities—social, community, or other.

d. Company contribution to any union activity—social or other.

e. Furnishing any written information to union on a regular basis other than that specified in Company-Union Agreement.

f. Obtaining union approval of any management action.

g. By-passing any step in the grievance procedure except as specified in Company-Union Agreement.

2. BARGAINING UNIT

a. Jobs included in bargaining unit which are not consistent with the description of bargaining unit jobs in the recognition clause of the Company-Union Agreement, i.e.—office, clerical, timekeepers, supervisory, etc.

b. Work normally considered non-bargaining unit work which is performed as incidental duties of bargaining unit employees.

c. Work normally considered bargaining unit work which is performed by non-bargaining unit employees.

d. Use of bargaining unit employees as temporary or part-time foremen except as specified in Company-Union Agreement.

3. OUTSIDE CONTRACTS

a. Practice or understanding that union will not be notified when certain types of outside contracts are let.

b. Written notification to union of outside contracts.

c. Obtaining union approval or agreement before outside contract is let.

d. Obtaining written acknowledgment from union that explanation has been made before outside contract is let.

e. Rules or formulas for determining when outside contracts may be let because of cost or time factor other than those specifically approved by Corporate Union Relations Department.

f. Work normally considered bargaining unit work which is contracted out on a regular basis.

g. Agreements or understandings that certain types of work will or will not be contracted out.

4. UNION SECURITY

a. Requiring union membership on any basis other than specified in the Company-Union Agreement or state law.

b. Deducting anything from employees' pay for the union, other than regular monthly membership dues or first month's dues, i.e.—union fines or assessments, union-operated insurance plans, etc.

5. HOURS OF WORK

a. Any restrictions on management's right to determine when additions or reductions are to be made in job classifications, departments or plant except as specified in Company-Union Agreement.

b. Any restrictions in "equalization of hours" rules other than those specified in Company-Union Agreement.

c. Equalization of hours rules which make it necessary to have certain work done at time and one-half payment which could otherwise be done at straight time.

d. Allowing employees to enter the plant more than 20 minutes before scheduled starting time.

e. Scheduled break periods.

f. Allowing employees to leave work area during working hours.

g. Allowing employees to leave work area before actual shift change time.

h. Paid wash-up time.

6. LUNCH PERIODS

a. Permitting use of cafeteria by employees except at authorized lunch time.

b. Lunch periods of more than 20 minutes except as required by law.

c. Pay for more than 20-minute period on regular shift.

d. Extra lunch period during overtime assignment.

e. Permitting use of cafeteria by employees before or after their work shift.

7. SPECIAL RATE PAYMENT

a. Use of any special rate guarantees other than those specified in Uniform or Supplemental Agreements.

b. Authorizing special rate payment to incentive employees without requiring employees to put forth the additional effort for which incentive payment is designed to compensate.

c. Authorizing off-standard payment for non-standard conditions or extra work without specific evaluation of condition or extra work requirement and advance approval by foreman (i.e., allowing employees to pad time by claims for off-standard payment).

d. Temporary assignment of incentive employees to non-essential work to avoid payment of waiting time.

e. Payment of average paid unit hour for "experimental" work except where employees meet all of the conditions for such payment outlined in the Company-Union Agreement.

f. Use of any allowance schedules not specified in 1959 Amendatory Memorandum of Agreement (URW-represented plants).

g. Change allowance (allowance or guarantee for changing from one machine, size or product to another on same regular job).

8. ESTABLISHMENT OF STANDARDS

a. Establishment of incentive standards by any method other than that specified in Uniform Agreement.

b. Use of negotiated units.

c. Special agreements regarding use of temporary or supplemental standards.

d. Agreement or practice limiting management's right to revise standards to reflect changes in method, product, tools, material, design, or other production condition.

9. PREMIUM PAY FOR OVERTIME

a. Considering any hours paid for at time and one-half on a daily basis as hours worked in calculating hours worked in excess of 40 hours per week.

b. Premium pay for Saturday as such.

10. SENIORITY

a. Use of seniority in any instances not specified in Company-Union Agreement.

b. Failure to give consideration to qualifications in filling of vacancies to the extent permitted in Company-Union Agreement.

c. Any other side agreements or practices in the application of seniority that are more restrictive than specified in Company-Union Agreement.

11. VACATIONS

a. Permitting vacations to be taken for periods of less than a full week.

b. Commitment to permit any particular number or percentage of employees to be on vacation at any one time regardless of production requirements.

c. Any agreement with union on a special plan for vacation scheduling.

12. MISCELLANEOUS

a. Any agreement or practice limiting management's right to determine methods, equipment, job content, crew sizes, etc.

b. Any agreement or practice limiting management's right to direct the working forces of the plant except as specified in the Company-Union Agreement.

c. Any unusual practices with respect to discipline, smoking, protective clothing, tools, special hand cleaner, sale of materials to employees, package passes, plant security, lunch box inspection, use of time clocks, dispensary, special medical services, or any other plant rules or services.

CHECKLIST OF QUESTIONS WHEN INSTITUTING A CHANGE IN WORK PROCEDURE

I. PLANNING

Proper planning should assure that the viewpoints of all who are concerned with the change will be considered.

To check, ask yourself:

(1) Who will be affected?
Employees.
Union representatives.
Supervisory personnel.
Other staff groups.

(2) How will they be affected?
What new work skills will be required?
What new routines must be accepted?
Will any employees be displaced?
By what means will displaced employees be absorbed?
Is this a change which will cause employees to raise questions of their union representative?
Is this a change which requires discussion with the Union?
Is this a change of which the Union should be advised?
Does the change require instructions to or action by supervision?

II. TIMING

Determine the best (optimum) time for making the change.

To check, ask yourself:

(1) How soon should the change be initiated?
(2) How long will be required to complete the change?
(3) Are there any current problems which might encourage opposition to the change?
(4) Is there a particular shift on which the change might be better accepted?
(5) Should the change be introduced gradually?
(6) Will the change be made more difficult to accept by further delay in starting it?

III. PARTICIPATION

Participation is one of the best means of securing acceptance of change.

To check, ask yourself:
  (1) Can an opportunity for employee participation in planning the change be afforded?
  (2) Should group meetings be used:
      To discuss the change and to get employee ideas and feelings on how the change can be made smoothly?
      To explain what the change involves and why it is to be made?
      To discuss any alternative solutions?
      To give employees a chance to talk about their problems in adjusting to the change?
      To encourage suggestions for implementing the change?
      To answer any questions employees may have?
  (3) If group meetings are impractical, by what alternative means can employee cooperation be solicited?
  (4) Is there a particular employee or group of employees to whom the change must first be sold?

IV. NOTIFICATION

Notification should be given in advance to all who will be affected by the change.

To check, ask yourself:
  (1) Has the change been discussed in advance with supervision?
  (2) Has the change been discussed in advance with union representatives, or is there a compelling reason why this should not be done?
  (3) Has each employee been notified through discussion with his supervisor, by group meetings, bulletin board announcements, or letters?
  (4) Does each employee understand how he or his group will be affected?

V. FOLLOW-THROUGH

Few changes are completed in a single action. Follow-through is essential.

To check, ask yourself:
  (1) What contacts should be maintained to determine how the change is working out?
  (2) Will the reports I receive tell whether any problems are encountered in making the change?
  (3) What has been learned from this change that will be useful in making future changes?

SUGGESTED SHOP RULES

The purpose of these rules and regulations is not to restrict the rights of anyone, but to define them and protect the rights of all and insure cooperation.

Committing any of the following violations will be sufficient grounds for disciplinary action ranging from reprimand to immediate discharge, depending upon the seriousness of the offense in the judgment of management.

1. Falisfication of personnel or other records.
    (one week to discharge)
2. Ringing the clock card of another.
    (reprimand to discharge)
3. Repeated failure to ring own clock card at start and end of shift; also "out" and "in" at rest and lunch period, if leaving the plant.
    (reprimand to four weeks)
4. Absence without reasonable cause.
    (reprimand to discharge)
5. Reporting late for work.
    (reprimand to discharge)
6. Absence of five consecutive working days without notification to Management.
    (voluntary quit)
7. Leaving own department without permission or leaving plant during working hours without permission and a pass.
    (reprimand to four weeks)
8. Refusal to obey orders of foremen or other supervision.
    (one day or more to discharge)
9. Refusal or failure to do job assignment.
    (Employee must follow instructions and do work assigned. Any complaint may be taken up later through regular procedure.)
10. Making scrap unnecessarily or careless workmanship.
    (reprimand to discharge)
11. Horseplay, scuffling, running or throwing things.
    (reprimand to discharge)
12. Wasting time or loitering in toilets or on any Company property during working hours.
    (reprimand to four weeks)
13. Smoking in prohibited areas.
    (reprimand to discharge)

14. Abuse, misuse or deliberate destruction of Company property, tools, equipment or the property of employees in any manner.
(reprimand to discharge)

15. Theft or misappropriation of property of employees or of the Company.
(discharge)

16. Sabotage.
(discharge)

17. Fighting on the premises at any time.
(one week to discharge)

18. Possession of, or drinking of, alcoholic beverages on Company property. Reporting for work under influence of alcohol when suffering from alcoholic hangover or in an unsafe condition.
(two days to discharge)

19. Disregard of safety rules or common safety practices.
(reprimand to discharge)

20. Stopping work or making preparations to leave work (such as washing up or changing clothes) before proper time at rest period, lunch period, or end of shift; also failure to start work at proper time.
(reprimand to four weeks)

21. Distracting the attention of others or causing confusion by unnecessary shouting, catcalls, or demonstration in the plant.
(reprimand to discharge)

22. Creating or contributing to unsanitary conditions.
(reprimand to discharge)

23. Possession of weapons on Company premises at any time.
(two weeks to discharge)

24. Unauthorized operation of machines, tools or equipment.
(reprimand to four weeks)

25. Threatening, intimidating, coercing or interfering with employees or supervision at any time.
(reprimand to discharge)

26. Abusive language to any employee or supervision.
(reprimand to discharge)

27. Unauthorized soliciting or collecting contributions for any purpose whatsoever on Company premises.
(reprimand to four weeks)

28. Unauthorized distribution of literature, written or printed matter of any description on Company premises.
(reprimand to four weeks)

29. Posting or removal of notices, signs, or writing in any form on Company bulletin boards, or property at any time without specific approval of management.
(reprimand to four weeks)

30. Misuse or removal from the premises without proper authorization of employee lists, blue prints, Company records, or confidential information of any nature.
(discharge)

31. Gambling, lottery or any other game of chance on Company premises at any time.

(reprimand to discharge)

32. The making or publishing of false, vicious or malicious statements concerning any employee, supervisor, the Company or its products.

(reprimand to discharge)

33. Restricting output.

(reprimand to discharge)

34. Immoral conduct or indecency.

(one week to discharge)

35. Sleeping on duty.

(reprimand to discharge)

36. Repeated violations of shop or safety rules.

(discharge)

INDEX

A

Aaron, Benjamin 165
Ability
  break-in and training periods 141
  educational requirements 140
  experience as factor 138
  production records as evidence of 139
  proof of 137 et seq.
  seniority v. 135
  tests, use of 141
  training 140
Absence from job, discipline 207
Abusive language, discipline 209
AFL-CIO 242
Alan Wood Steel Co. 164
American Air Filter Co. 156
American Mfg. Co. 21, 45, 257
American National Insurance Co. 33, 49
American Oil Co. 12
Arbitration 235 et seq.
  as "quid pro quo" for no-strike clause 48 et seq.
  criticisms of 236
  damages for no-strike clause violation, arbitration of 239
  employer grievances, arbitration of 240
  individual employee, role of 232
  model arbitration clauses to protect management rights 46, 255, 263
  Supreme Court decisions 21, 45 et seq., 52, 62, 80, 236, 239, 256
Arbitrators
  disciplinary penalties, scope of review 202
  implied contract conditions, authority to impose 61
  production standards grievances, limitations on arbitrator's power 177, 178
Aro, Inc. 156
Assault, discipline for 208
Assignment of work (see Work assignments)
Automation 117, 253
Automobile industry
  arbitration agreements 50, 51
  production standards grievances, contract provisions 177, 178
  wage payment system 149

Automobile Workers 7, 12, 16, 228
Available employee, definition 86
Axelson Mfg. Co. 124

B

Back pay 231
Bailer, Lloyd H. 144
Bakke, E. W. 19
Bargaining (see Collective bargaining)
Barkin, Solomon 175, 242, 250, 251, 252
Barrett, Gerald A. 101
Bendiner, Robert 241
Bethlehem Steel Co. 7, 68, 170
Bidding for job openings 134
Block, Joseph L. 248
Blumer, Herbert 154
Boles, Walter E., Jr. 131
Borg-Warner Corp. 29, 30
Brams, Stanley H. 246
Break-in periods
  use to determine ability 141
Bridge, Structural and Ornamental Iron Workers Assn. recognition clause 65
Brooks, George 237
Bumping
  break-in and training periods 141
  definition 85
  experience as factor 138
  into higher-rated classification 133
  losses due to, reduction in 128
Burden of proof, discipline cases 196

C

Cannon Electric Co. 165
Carlyle Tile Co. 170
Carpenters Union 29
Chamber of Commerce of U.S. 14
  model arbitration clauses to protect management rights, pamphlet 46, 255
Chamberlain, Neil W. 102
Charles Bruning Co., Inc. 56
Chrysler Corp. 132, 163
Classifications (see Job classifications)
Collective bargaining
  as creative conflict 18
  "Boulwareism" approach 32